Action in Israel
& THE PALESTINIAN AUTHORITY

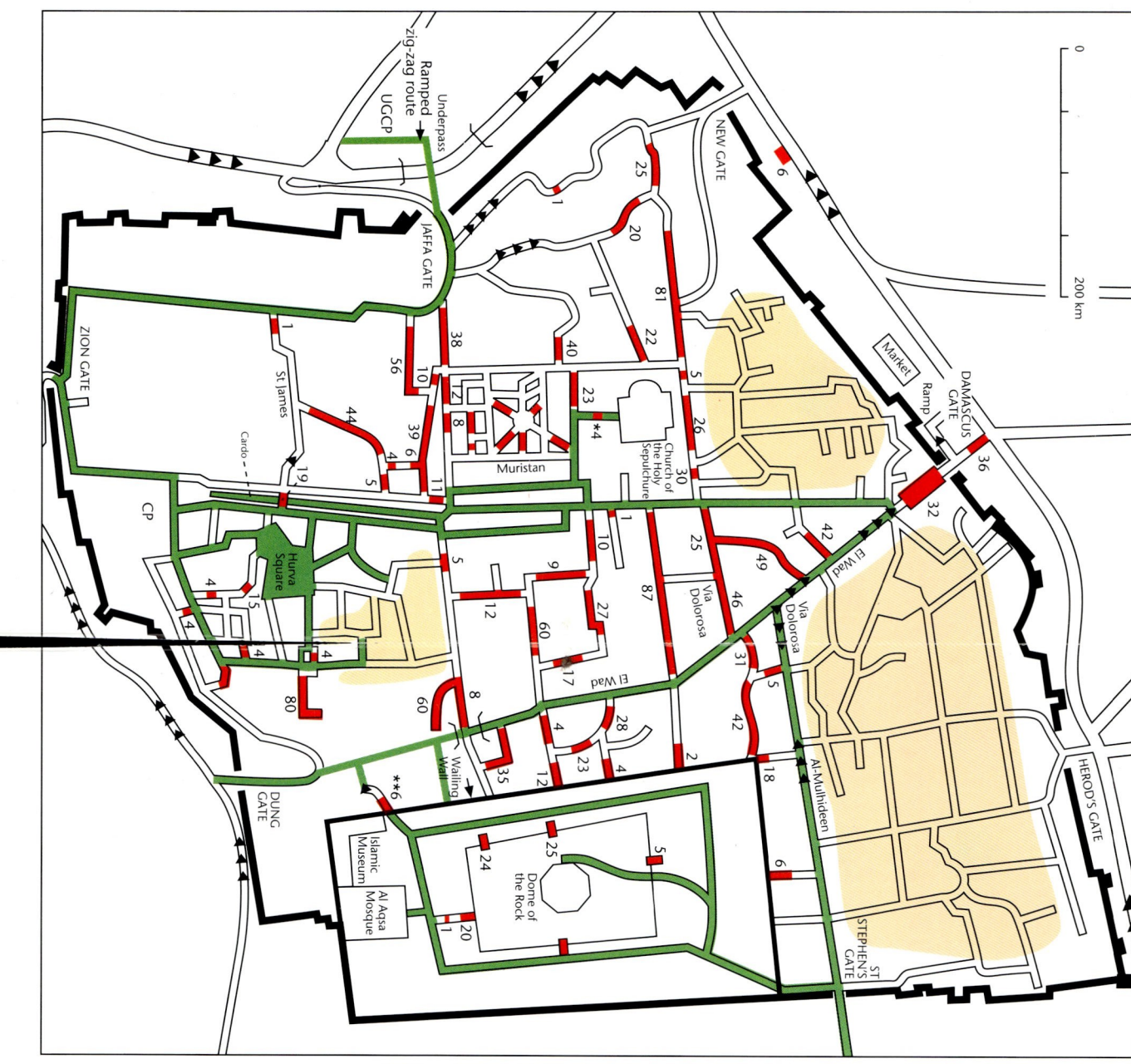

Jerusalem Old City Step Map

A GUIDE FOR THOSE WHO HAVE PROBLEMS GETTING AROUND

Access in Israel

& THE PALESTINIAN AUTHORITY

Research and survey work carried out by
Pauline Hephaistos Survey Projects

Written by Gordon Couch and the PHSP team

Quiller Press
London

The other guides in the PHSP series are:
Access in Paris
Access in London
These are available from bookshops or from **Access Project, 39 Bradley Gardens, West Ealing, London W13 8HE**, *e-mail:* gordon.couch@virgin.net. There is no charge but people are requested to make a donation towards the considerable research and publication costs.

Access in Paris was published in 1993, and there is a 1997 supplement. *Access in London* was published in 1996, also has a 1997 supplement. For updated information, look in the website www.disabilitynet.co.uk under information and access guides. From time to time we will insert new information and corrections on to that website.

The suggested contribution for one of the guides is around £10 or US $15, plus postage. If you're sending money from abroad, please send cash. Cheques drawn on foreign banks cost a disproportionate amount to put through a bank account. If you have a British bank account then cheques should be payable to 'Access Project'.

Other information sources include:

RADAR 12 City Forum, 250 City Road, London EC1V OAF *website:* www.radar.org.uk *email:* radar@radar.org.uk Tel: 020 7250-3222 Minicom: 020 7250-4119 Fax: 020 7250-0212.

Access-Able Travel Source *website:* www.access-able.com

Global Access *website*: www.geocities.com/Paris/1502 titled Disabled Travel Network

---

Note that a **LARGE PRINT** version of the book can be obtained from
Access Project, 39 Bradley Gardens, West Ealing, London W13 8HE
e-mail: gordon.couch@virgin.net

First published 2000 by Quiller Press Ltd
46 Lillie Road, London SW6 1TN
ISBN 1-89916-361-1

Copyright 2000 © Pauline Hephaistos Survey Projects

Line drawings and design: Graham Hiles
Printed by Colourcraft, Hong Kong

All rights reserved. No part of this book may be reproduced or transmitted, in any form or by any means, without prior written permisssion of the publishers.

The guide is based on survey work carried out during 1998/99 by members of Pauline Hephaistos Survey Projects (PHSP).

What we try to do is:

- provide practical and well-researched information for those wishing to travel, based on the first-hand experience of disabled travellers;
- set new standards in terms of a clear and concise presentation of access information; and
- act as a catalyst for change, both by making people more aware of what needs to be done, and by showing what is currently possible.

Over the years, the group has produced seventeen access guides, and this is the third edition of the Israel/Palestinian areas book. Virtually every site, sight and hotel described in the guides has been wheeled into or walked over by one of our survey teams, so that all the information is based on visits and on what we have seen – not just what we have been told.

The group of surveyors included a variety of people each with different abilities and disabilities. We come from several universities and colleges; from St Paul's School in London and from Lord Mayor Treloar College near Alton in Hampshire. A few of the group are 'post-student' age and working in a variety of jobs.

The PHSP name is a bit of a mouthful. Pauline arises from St Paul, and some of us come from a Christian group attached to St Paul's School called the Pauline Meetings. The Hephaistos part of the name arises from the god who was the smithy in Greek mythology, and the equivalent of the Roman god Vulcan. Hephaistos was a son of Zeus, who was foolish enough to defend his mother, Hera, during some major row with Zeus. Zeus kicked Hephaistos off Mount Olympus and, after a long fall, he landed at the bottom and broke his leg. In frescoes he is shown with one leg facing one way, and the other turned through 90°. He has been adopted by some as the Greek god for disabled people, and gave his name to a school near Reading which a number of the group attended before its closure.

© Pauline Hephaistos Survey Projects

The information in this guide is incomplete and if you can supplement or correct it, please contact Access Project at the address opposite.

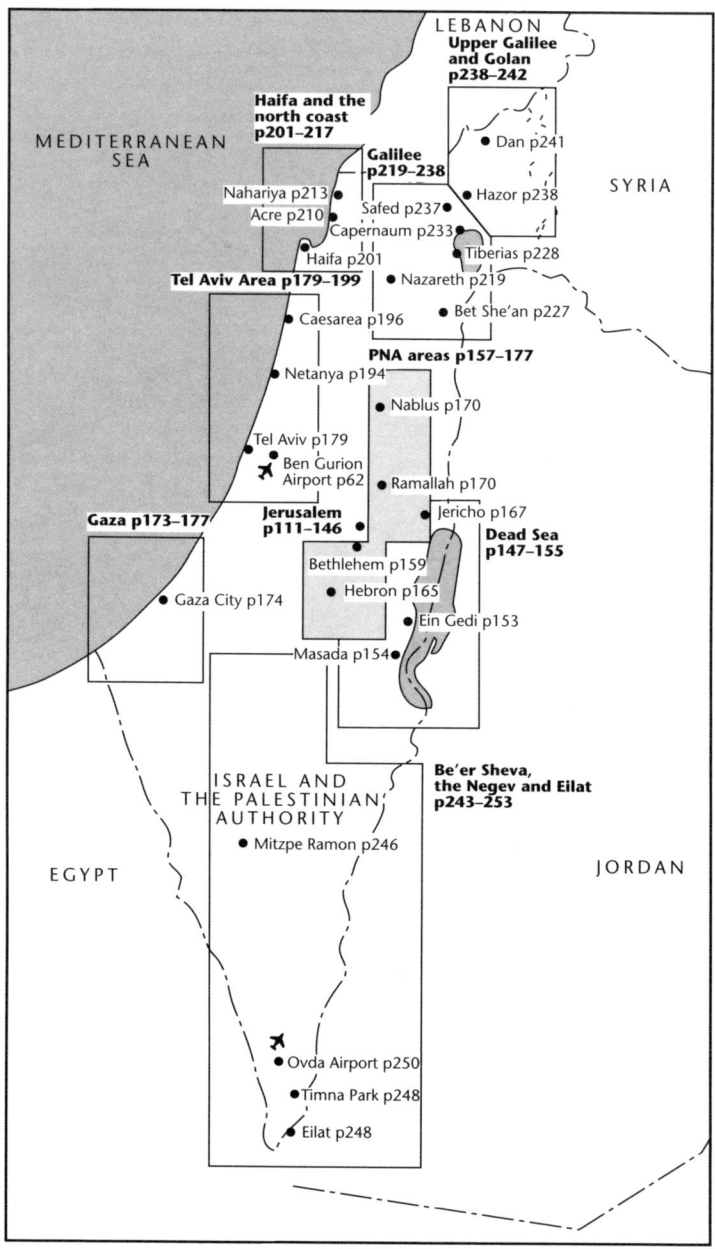

Contents

Introduction
How the guide is arranged 10
Units and definitions 11

General information
Information sources 17
Adapted transport 33
Car hire 35
Currency 42
Insurance 45
Maps and guides 50
Place names 57

Travelling and getting around
By air 60
Getting around 66

Accommodation
Jerusalem 74
Dead Sea 79
PNA areas 84
Tel Aviv and the Med' coast 87
Galilee 93
The Negev and Eilat 103
Kibbutz fly-drive packages 107

Jerusalem
The Old City 114
Temple Mount/Haram al-Sharif 116
Via Dolorosa 118
Western Wall 119
Church of the Holy Sepulchre 124
David's Citadel 125
Mount Zion 128
East Jerusalem 130
Mount of Olives 131
West Jerusalem 134
Givat Ram 137
Yad Vashem 143

Dead Sea region
En route from Jerusalem 149
Ein Gedi 153
Masada 154

PNA areas
Bethlehem 159
Hebron 165
Jericho 167
Ramallah 170
Nablus 170
Gaza 173

Tel Aviv and the surrounding area
Tel Aviv 179
Jaffa 190
Around Tel Aviv 192
Netanya 194
Caesarea 196

Haifa and the north coast
Central Haifa 203
Carmel Centre 205
Western Haifa 206
South of Haifa 209
Acre 210
Nahariya 213
Akhziv 214
Rosh Hanikra 215

Galilee, Upper Galilee and the Golan
Nazareth 219
Cana 223
Meiron 223
Megiddo 224
Mount Tabor 224
Shibli 225
Sepphoris/Zippori 226
Bet She'an 227
Tiberias 228
Tabgha 232
Capernaum 233
Yardenit 236
Hammat Gader 237
Zefat 237
Upper Galilee and the Golan 238

Be'er Sheva, the Negev and Eilat
Be'er Sheva 243
Mitzpe Ramon 246
Eilat 248

Our top twenty sights 254

Design advice 255

Symbols 264

Index 272

Acknowledgements

The project has involved a considerable number of people, without whom the guide would never have been researched and written. The various activities have included:

- ensuring that the necessary financial basis was secure, for which we are particularly grateful to the trustees of the charitable trust, to past members and friends of the group who have contributed by covenant and to various charitable trusts and companies who have sponsored or supported us;
- careful preparation and planning of what was to be visited and ensuring that the surveyors were well briefed about what to look for;
- undertaking the practical research, by visit;
- writing, proof reading, editing, preparing diagrams and symbols and the host of meticulous and time-consuming activities that are necessary in putting together the text of such a guide;
- publishing, distribution and publicity.

We would like to express our thanks to all of the following, in their different roles, some large, some small, including the foot and wheel work, writing and proof-reading:

Steve Bovey, Gordon Couch, Nicky Drake, Rob Droy, Polly Ferguson, Tom Glennie, Alan Kerr, Kate Leach, Heike and James Lengenfeld-Brown, Rory Mee, Herminé Nalbandian, Janet Stafford, Rob Stanier, Nick Tjaardstra and particularly to James Ross, Justin Irwin and Nick Windsor for their efforts during the final stages.

Past members and friends of the group who have made donations and covenants and who gave us the confidence to commit ourselves to the project:

Adrian Rates, Roger Ayers, Dave Allport, Tim Atkinson, Dave Aubrey, Clive Barter, Matthew Boulton, Neil Brown, James Clay, Ian and Rachel Copeland, Gordon Couch, Richard Donaldson, Polly Ferguson, Tom Ferguson, Robert Gibbs, Alex Gordon-Brander, Harry Gostelow, Paul Haines, Tom Kiggell, Duncan and Debbie MacConnol, Mayo and Thalia Marriott, Richard Marshall, Geoff Matthews, Andy Pao, Adrian Rates, Ben Roberts, Janet Staffford, Rob Stanier, Roger Stone, David Wallace, Matthew Woodeson, Mark Worledge.

The trustees of the charitable trust which finances the activities:

Dave Aubrey, Isabel Baggott, Gordon Couch and Mukesh Patel and their honorary auditor Peter Stevenson.

Our sponsors, who provided essential supplementary finance to the charitable trust:

Allchurches Trust
Burdens Charitable Foundation

David Uri Memorial Trust
Mark and Indi Hutchins

Pauline Meetings Centenary Service collection
Selwyn College Cambidge, JCR

Sobell Foundation
University College, Durham, JCR

We would also like to thank various friends in Israel and the Palestinian areas for help, advice and assistance, including:

Helena Aharon, Zainab Al-Kurd, Alon Borman, Zvika Gur, Ibrahim Jaber, Sara Hopenfeld, Shoshi Leket, Amnon Lipzin, Amit Netzer, Betty Majaj, NiraQ, Lana Rabadi, George Rishmawi, Michael Roitman, Jody Sirota and Arik Vamosh.

We would like to express our thanks to Quiller Press, and to Jeremy Greenwood in particular, for publishing the guide and ensuring its distribution through bookshops. Also to Graham Hiles for providing the page layouts and artwork.

Preface

In writing anything about the Holy Land, one is in danger of treading on someone's toes. Our particular guide has no political, racial or religious axe to grind, and we have tried to be as even-handed as possible. Calling our guide *Access in Israel and the Palestinian Authority* doesn't imply any recognition of territorial rights which are the subject of discussion, negotiation or controversy. The outcome of the Oslo Peace process, and the negotiations between the Israeli government and Palestinian representatives will affect a number of issues, some of which will have an impact on the visitor. Similarly, the outcome of discussions between the Israeli and Syrian governments may affect access to areas in the Golan Heights in the future.

We are indebted to the Israeli Government Tourist Office and the PNA Tourism Ministry for advice, and the Awqaf administration for giving permission for wheelchair access into the mosques on Haram al-Sharif.

Our viewpoint as a group of British, mainly Christian, visitors is bound to be biased (perhaps unknowingly), and we apologise if we have failed to give sufficient weight to Jewish of Muslim interests and viewpoints in our survey.

We hope that the Guide will not only be useful as a 'guidebook' for those who live locally and for visitors, but that it will provoke action to improve access for disabled people.

Abbreviations

~	approximately
+	steps up
–	steps down
[..cm]	the height of a single step
–	a threshold, where there is a step up immediately followed by one down
AD	Anno Domini (the basis of the Gregorian calendar, alternatively expressed as CE)
AT	Alternative Tours
ATG	Alternative Tourism Group
BA	British Airways
BC	before Christ (also expressed as BCE)
BCE	before the Common Era (also BC)
CE	Common Era (also expressed as AD)
CP	car park
D	door width, in cm
Fax:	fax number
GF	ground floor
GFB	ground floor bedroom
H	height in cm
HI	Hostelling International (the international youth hostels association)
HR	handrail
IGTO	Israeli Government Tourist Office
IH	Israel Handbook with the Palestinian Authority areas, 1999.
IHA	Israel Hotel Association
L	length in cm
LP	Lonely Planet, Israel and the Palestinian Territories, 1999.
MP	Mobile Post
MSCP	multi-storey Car Park
OUP	Oxford University Press
PHSP	Pauline Hephaistos Survey Projects
PNA	Palestinian National Authority
POB	Post Office box
RADAR	Royal Association for Disability and Rehabilitation
RG	Rough Guide to Israel and the Palestinian Territories, 1998.
SATH	Society for the Advancement of Travel for the Handicapped
ST	Clear side transfer distance alongside toilet (cm)
Tel:	telephone number
UGCP	underground Car Park
UNRWA	United Nations Relief and Works Agency for Palestinian Refugees
W	width in cm
WW1	World War 1
WW2	World War 2
YH	Youth Hostel

16thC, 19thC are used for 16th century, 19th century etc.

Introduction

It is impossible to sum up the appeal and sheer excitement that can be generated by a visit to the Holy Land. For many it is the trip of a lifetime for which they'll save and sacrifice, and one which will bring unique opportunities and experiences. People may come to visit family and friends, or because of interests in business, in history or because of the fascinating (and frustrating) politics involved.

This is a guidebook that describes accessibility, and details the various barriers to access in different places. The information will be of use to a wide range of people with disabilities, including those who use wheelchairs. *A listing does not necessarily imply that a site is step free or is easily visited.* **There will be a description in the guide so that the reader can decide whether a visit is practicable.**

Current events and recent history have made even the naming of this book quite difficult. In 1993 the Oslo Peace Accords were signed between representatives of those living in the area, Israeli and Palestinian. Since then, progress towards a just peace has been slow and sometimes seemingly non-existent. In 1999, a new Prime Minister was elected in Israel, bringing new hope for progress towards both peace and justice. Until the resolution of this process, and the establishment of a Palestinian state, we are calling this book *Access in Israel and the Palestinian Authority*. In the text we shall sometimes use a shorthand, simply referring to the *Holy Land* or in some places just '*the Land*'.

All the views expressed are those of the PHSP survey teams and relate to the places we went to at the time of our visit. We've tried to include sights of interest to a wide range of visitors; Jews, Christians, Muslims, historians, archaeologists and even sociologists and business people. We recognise that however hard we try, we're bound to be slightly biased in our approach, because most of the surveyors are Christians, and are of student age. This means that we may not fully appreciate everyone's priorities. You will make your own judgments about what you want to see and visit. We have felt free to make comments if places were of particular interest to us, but most of these views are the personal ones of different surveyors.

What this guide is about

This guide is specifically an ACCESS GUIDE FOR DISABLED VISITORS. Its aim is to help those who have any kind of mobility problem, ranging from someone who's had a recent illness or accident, to someone who has a chest or heart condition, or someone who uses a wheelchair. We assume that people will use it in conjunction with conventional guide-books and maps, and it's helpful to get two or three

of these before you travel, to read up about the places you'll see and visit.

The idea of visiting a country thousands of miles away may seem daunting to someone who has a disability and who can't walk very far or climb many steps, or to someone who uses a wheelchair. We hope, however, that the information given in the guide will enable and encourage many people to make the trip who would otherwise have thought it impossible.

The research and survey work for the Guide was carried out in 1998/99 by disabled people, several of them in wheelchairs, together with a number of able-bodied friends. We made several trips to Israel to get first-hand information, and practically all the places included in the guide (public buildings, sights, hotels etc) have been walked into and wheeled over by one of our survey teams. A few of the descriptions arise from our earlier surveys in 1980 and 1987, but when this is the case we specifically say so by putting the date in brackets. We've tried to be both accurate and objective. Things change with time, and our descriptions relate to what we saw when we visited in either 1998 or 1999. If some features are of especial importance to you, particularly in connection with accommodation, it's essential to check these directly with the hotel or site when making reservations or arrangements. There may be aspects of the facilities of interest to you that we have not fully covered. If we measured and described everything and took everyone's needs into account, our guidebook would need to be at least ten or twenty times as big, which would make it impossibly expensive and not very user-friendly.

There's so much to see and do, that it's important to plan your trip carefully, particularly if you have problems getting around because of disability or recent illness. **There are a great many places of relatively easy access (ie that you can get to by car, and where you can walk or wheel more or less on the flat).** There are others where access is difficult and a few where it is virtually impossible. Don't feel cheated if you only go into the sights with easier access, because if you visit most of those, you'll have seen quite enough to make the trip memorable and worthwhile. To us, almost as important as going into the specific buildings, was the sense of "being there", in Jerusalem and Galilee, on Carmel and Tabor, at Abraham's tomb and Megiddo, and in and around the Dead Sea and on the Mediterranean coast.

Going with an organised group vs independent travel

One thing that we had not expected, and which may colour your approach to planning a visit, is that a high proportion of tourism in the Holy Land is in the hands of tour operators which are (naturally) mainly run by Jewish companies. Independent tourism is not the norm, and individual tourists do not attract some of the discounts in cost that the tour operators can obtain. **It is, however, perfectly possible for the independent traveller with one or two friends to make all the arrangements for a wholly satisfying and exciting visit**. You may visit slightly fewer places, but you'll meet more people, and there'll be more surprises – both of which are among the joys of travelling. The information in this guide is intended to help independence – but the content can also help those using a tour operator, enabling them to ask the right questions.

Many travel agents and tour operators do not readily understand the needs of people with disabilities. Levels of awareness and understanding of disability in Israel are much lower than in most European countries and in the USA. You can get an operator to book/organise your accommodation, using the information from this guide, subsequently checking directly with the hotel over necessary details. You need to ask them whether the accommodation has been visited and assessed by a tour company representative (and if so, what are the details), or whether they are relying on information given by the hotel. The comment/information that 'the room/s have been used before by disabled people' is of such limited value as to be almost meaningless, since people's abilities and needs differ greatly.

Using an agent, you might be able to get some of their company discounts, assuming that you book your flights through them and possibly your hire car as well. You are then a serious enough customer to warrant some attention. You might also want to use a local tour company to organise particular visits on specific days, such as to the more difficult places including parts of Jerusalem (where driving and navigating can be slightly more than a challenge), and also to some PNA areas.

There are real advantages in being part of a large group, and some pilgrimage parties will undoubtedly gain enormously from the experience of fellowship and shared experience and worship, in and near the various holy places. **Also, there are specialist operators who are experienced at organising visits for people with disabilities, and who may be able to facilitate a visit which would not otherwise be possible.**

Normal package tours, based on coach travel in unadapted buses, may impose strains on disabled visitors and/or their friends. The idea of selectively using taxis and hire cars has immense advantages, and for a group of people it isn't impossibly expensive. One possibility is to be part of a group, but with a good deal of time to wander and sightsee on your own or with two or three friends. You may be able to negotiate some mini-packages with specialist operators. An idea for this could be to spend three days with adapted transport in Jerusalem – and maybe for a longish trip into the Negev – and then you might use your own hire car for the Galilee and Acre. There are fly-drive packages which use kibbutz inns that should be of particular interest to a group including one or two disabled members. The possibilities are endless.

Something you'll have to get used to is that arrangements sometimes don't work out, and information you are given may be wrong! There can be a certain vagueness in attitudes to time and organisation. The almost offhand, approach to everything became understandable when we were there in the summer. When the temperature was 40°C plus, we found our own approach to both time and organisation became much more laid back.

On the question of information, we were caught out many times at potential sources of authoritative information. **Many people do not seem to understand the concept of information.** We met this time and time again when researching the guide. The question "Where do the buses go to from here?" (Information) was nearly always countered with "Where do you want to go?" It was certainly not helpful when writing a book, and would not be so if you were wanting to make a decision about where and when to go.

You need to think carefully about what kind of visit you want, and much depends on who you are travelling with. Are you with your family, or with a small group of young people? Do you want to spend time on the beach, or are you going on what is primarily a pilgrimage? Do you find dealing with hassles and difficulties is a positive challenge, or do you ideally want an easy time, and to let others worry about any problems? All these are things which visitors will have to work out for themselves.

A brief history

The Holy Land is an area that thousands of people would love to visit for all sorts of reasons. **The Land** is of immense importance to the followers of three major world religions (Judaism, Christianity and Islam). The area is also important to those with the Bahai faith.

It has been a centre of the greatest historical significance for thousands of years, partly because it was on the main trade route between Africa and Asia. It has been invaded and conquered many, many times and there are dozens of archaeological sites of unique interest dating from very early times. It was the home of God's chosen people, the Hebrews, who were conquered and exiled both in 586 BC/BCE and again in 70 AD/CE. The Romans had an enormous impact on the country some 2000 years ago, and following the Jewish revolt against Roman occupation, the Jews were scattered, forming the Diaspora in many far flung parts of the world. When Constantine legalised Christianity in the Roman Empire, it became the Holy Land, and the remains of some of the early churches from this Byzantine era still exist. With the rise of Islam, Christians in the Land were evicted. Later, the Crusaders came, and battled over the Land for some two hundred years, before finally being thrown out by an Egyptian dynasty, the

Mamluks. Later again, the Turkish Ottomans took over, but it was not until the 19thC that significant Jewish resettlement in the area started. Following WW1, the British were given a Mandate under the League of Nations to govern the area. Jewish immigration increased, particularly during and after the persecution of Jewish communities in the places under control of the Nazis.

Just after WW2, the new United Nations proposed that the country should be partitioned between the recently arrived Jewish immigrants and the indigenous Arab Palestinian population. No agreement was reached, and the British left on the 14th of May 1948, unable to control mounting levels of terrorism and violence. The Israeli leader David Ben Gurion declared the independence of the State of Israel. After several wars with Arab neighbours, and a great deal of pain, terror and destruction throughout the area, Israel was able to make peace deals, first with Egypt and later with Jordan. The situation of the Palestinian peoples is not yet resolved. They remember the 14th May 1948 as al-Nakba (the catastrophe). Many were displaced during the fighting after the establishment of the state of Israel. Others were displaced in 1967. Some have become Israeli citizens, but many more are now living as refugees in various parts of the Middle East. Some are in camps in both Gaza and on the former West Bank. One quarter of the world's refugees live in the area in and around Israel.

Whatever view you take about the history of the area over the last 50 or 60 years, and the justice or injustice of the actions of both Jew and Muslim, Israeli and Palestinian, it is a fascinating place. There have been new social forms such as the kibbutz and moshav communities; there are modern cities and ancient cultures; there are longstanding residents of the area, including Jews, Palestinians, Bedouin, Druze and Bahai's. Some have been dispossessed of their land and homes by recent events. Israel has established its own culture and democracy. It has welcomed immigrants in their thousands from all around the world, initially mainly from Europe and Middle Eastern countries, and recently in considerable numbers from the former Communist areas. Palestinian communities are spread throughout the area, some within Israel, some in the pre-1967 West Bank, partly now under Palestinian National Authority (PNA) control; some are in Gaza, and others are in neighbouring countries, particularly Lebanon.

The main centres of interest

There is great interest in various social structures in the area, in its recent history, in the geography (which is unique) and it is a historian's paradise, with archaeological sites everywhere. There are modern cities, industrial and business opportunities, and huge refugee camps, all within a hundred kilometres of each other. "Tel Aviv plays, Haifa works and Jerusalem prays" is a popular summary of Israel's three largest cities, and while there is no equivalent summary of the character of the Palestinian areas such as

Gaza, Jericho, Bethlehem, Ramallah, Nablus and the disputed land in east Jerusalem, each has its particular flavour.

The four holiest Jewish cities in Israel are said to represent the principal elements of creation. They are Jerusalem (fire), Hebron (earth), Tiberias (water) and Zefat (air). Jerusalem is the site of the Temple, and of the traditional rock on which Abraham was to have sacrificed Isaac (now covered by the Dome of the Rock). The only remains of the Temple are the Western Wall or HaKotel Hama'aravi and it is the holiest site in the country for Jews. There are people praying there all through the day, and it is a busy place at sundown on *Shabbat*. Hebron is home to the tombs of Abraham, Isaac and Jacob. Its recent history has been particularly troubled (see other guidebooks), and it is now a largely Arab/Moslem city but with a heavily guarded Jewish Yeshiva right in the city centre. Tiberias has the tombs of several key Jewish Rabbis, including that of Me'ir Ba'al Ha-nes which has both Ashkenazi and Sephardic sections, and is one of Judaism's most holy sites. Zefat is a centre for Jewish mysticism.

There are three main centres of interest and pilgrimage for Christians. These are Bethlehem, the traditional site of Jesus' birth, Nazareth and the Galilee, where he was brought up and where much of his ministry took place, and Jerusalem, where he was crucified and resurrected. Other sites of interest are connected with the growth of the early church, and then with subsequent attempts by the Crusaders to control the area by military conquest.

For Moslems, the mosques on Haram al-Sharif (The Noble Sanctuary) on Temple Mount are the third and fourth most holy Islamic shrines after Mecca and Medina. Al-Aqsa is a large active place of worship. The Dome contains the rock from which, in Islamic tradition, the Prophet Mohammed launched himself heavenward to take his place alongside Allah. Al-Aqsa means 'the distant place' (from Mecca).

All of the sites and shrines arising from the period before the time of Jesus are holy to those of all three monotheistic faiths. These include, in particular, the tombs of Abraham, Isaac and Jacob at Hebron, as well as numerous other places described in various Old Testament stories.

Geographically, the places of greatest interest are the Dead Sea, which is unique and amazing, and is the lowest place on earth; Mount Hermon in the north and the Negev Desert in the south. There are also the coastline resorts, both along the Mediterranean and right in the south at Eilat, and many visitors come simply to enjoy the sun and sea, especially during the winter.

Is it safe?

The whole area has lived under threat for more than half a century, and in some places there is an uneasy co-existence between Jew and Arab. Because of what we read in the newspapers and see on TV, the first question most people ask is *"Is it safe?"*.

In a sense, there is no absolute answer. One can ask, *"Where is safe these days?"* Hundreds of thousands of visitors go to the area every year with no security problem of any kind, so we think you should feel at least as safe as if you were visiting New York or London or even the Spanish coast. We've spent a lot of time in the area in that everywhere described in the guide has been visited, and we have felt absolutely safe. **Far too many people miss out on travelling because of perceived risks that are in fact little greater than the chance of an accident in the home or when using the roads in their neighbourhood.**

Partly because of the tight security, levels of street crime tend to be lower than those in Europe and North America. The biggest risk you will take does not arise from the possibility of terrorist activity, but relates to the appalling toll of road accidents. We understand that over the last fifty years, more people have been killed on the roads in Israel than have been killed in all the wars that have taken place in the area – which is a somewhat chilling statistic.

You'll certainly have to get used to seeing soldiers about the place carrying guns. You will encounter some road blocks and even searches, if security is tight while you're there. The controls are part of the process of policing people's movement between Palestinian National Authority (PNA) areas. On the whole none of it makes much difference to the tourist except sometimes to cause some delays in travelling around.

You may need to take advice on the security situation in obviously sensitive areas if there is the threat of trouble, but the chances of any hassle are incredibly remote. Bear in mind that the advice given by some Israelis may be very different from that given by Palestinians, and even your travel agent may exaggerate the risks involved in visiting particular places. If you want to go to PNA areas, take advice from Palestinians. We visited Hebron and Gaza, both thought of as possible trouble spots, and we not only had no problems, but felt warmly welcomed. We also visited Bethlehem, Jericho, Ramallah and Nablus. **A degree of caution, awareness and sensitivity are essential, but there is absolutely no need to be paranoid over the question of safety, provided you are sensible**.

Words of warning

Disabled people want to travel like anyone else. The advent of cheap air fares has made it possible for a great many people to visit interesting and far-away places, and airlines are generally helpful in carrying disabled passengers including wheelchair users. However, the regulations and provisions differ from airline to airline and this can present problems, although it has all become somewhat easier and more commonplace during recent years.

> ## Key constraints
>
> **Remember that accommodation listed by others as being 'accessible' may or may not be suitable for you.** There are no proper standards applied, and a profound and general ignorance of the specific needs of disabled people. The information in this guide will give you a good starting point for planning and negotiating, and remember that there *is* usable and accessible accommodation out there.
>
> If you can't get into a conventional car or on a bus, then getting around may present problems. **The amount of adapted transport is limited**, see p33, and see also the details about specialist tour operators p31 who have experience of planning visits for disabled visitors.

Many high street travel agents, even now, have no knowledge or experience of making arrangements for disabled people, and they neither appreciate what questions to ask, nor the need to crosscheck vital details. It's no good just sending off a letter or fax and assuming that all will be well when you are told that the hotel is 'accessible'. A clear and descriptive response is needed showing that the recipient understands what is required, with factual details about distances and steps, and about the bathroom design, door widths and bed height etc. Unless you are dealing with one of the small number of companies who understand disability and know what they are doing, make your bookings in good time. Then you can ensure that all the important questions have been both asked and answered by the people directly involved. Ask your travel agent for copies of the replies received from both airline and hotels confirming that the arrangements meet your needs, and then you can assess the need to contact them directly yourself for clarification. You may find it helpful to show your travel agent the section towards the end of this book on *Design advice*, since this may clarify some of the issues, and the questions to be asked.

It is worth emphasising that things are changing, but in travelling to the Holy Land you are taking a step back into the kind of world (in terms of both facilities and attitudes to disabled people) that existed in Britain and America back in the 1970s. Awareness is generally only just dawning, so don't expect the kind of facilities or attitudes that you may have become accustomed to.

It is often the case that wheelchair users receive the most attention as they present the most visible potential problems in terms of access, and that people with other disabilities may get overlooked. It's very important that people with visual and/or hearing impairment, amputees, those with a bad heart or who are arthritic, and the mum travelling with two young kids, get the same kind of consideration.

In both Israel and the Palestinian areas, you'll have to get used to the different and more casual lifestyle. Adapting to a country's ways is part of the enjoyment of travelling, so don't be put off; but equally don't expect life to be like it is at home. It is an area of contrasts, and you may find some things run meticulously to time, so that in some places if you don't turn up to dinner at exactly the right moment you don't eat! Equally, with many other things, they happen when they happen if you're lucky, and it may just turn out that everything is closed on the day you want to go there. There are not only numerous festivals and holidays but strikes in Israel are quite common (in our experience). These can shut down various services, including tourist offices and some of the places you might want to visit.

You'll have to get used to coping with relatively rough surfaces and conditions. There are hilly streets, steps, crowds and bad pavements. A chair user should almost expect to get maintenance problems with their chair. Make sure that it is in good repair, and take a basic repair kit as a precaution. Carrying a spare inner tube may be a good idea. If you will need help getting on and off conventional coaches, then it may even be sensible to bring your own ambulance/transfer chair which can help with loading and unloading.

Views on accessibility in the Holy Land from two chair users

Arik Vamosh is a war veteran, disabled in 1973, and a wheelchair user as a result. "One of the factors that made it difficult for me to tour Israel for many years was the *everybody in Israel is friends* approach, prevalent among the Israeli public. This cultural phenomenon, characterised by the *What's the problem? We'll help you!* offer, although it appears positive, is negative in the context of the disabled. Instead of making all public places accessible, enabling everyone an independent and dignified entrance, the attitude fosters a dependency that eventually results in disabled people shutting themselves up at home.

A generation ago, visiting natural sites required enlisting an auxiliary force of family and friends who could drag me over innumerable obstacles. A trip to the waterfalls in the Golan imposed on my friends the gruelling task of pushing my wheelchair with me in it, several kilometers – often on two wheels.

Has the situation changed? Not much.
Despite the great progress with the development of natural and historic sites, preserving them and equipping them for visits by the general public, only a handful of them are accessible to the disabled. Unfortunately Israel is still half-way between the third and the first worlds in its policies *vis à vis* the disabled" ***(published in the Eretz magazine, 1999).***

Howard Chabner is an American chair-user who has visited Israel in 1978, 82 and 97 "Access in Israel is poor compared to the United States. The Israeli preference for improvisation and ad hoc solutions over planning, which has served the country so well in many areas, is partially responsible for this situation. Accessible ground transportation is limited and accessible hotel rooms are few. Major road intersections often lack kerb ramps. Because of the poor state of access and knowledge about it, if you use a travel agent, make sure that they specialise in accessible travel. It is very important to be aware that very few restrooms (toilets) anywhere in Israel comply with American or European standards. Many are too small, grab bars are poorly placed and these often protrude into the side transfer space. Toilet height is usually at the lower end of the US range, and toilet seats are often made of flimsy plastic. Some bathrooms in hotels have a tile floor with a drain in the main area, but even these are not designed with a fold down seat and flexible shower head to facilitate showering" **(published on the Yad Sarah site on the internet, dated 1997).**

How the guide is arranged

A wide range of information is presented and it is worth explaining where to find things, in order to make the best use of the guide. **WE HAVE TRIED TO IDENTIFY PARTICULARLY ACCESSIBLE SIGHTS AND ACCOMMODATION, BUT WE'VE ALSO INCLUDED DESCRIPTIONS OF OTHERS. YOU WILL MAKE UP YOUR OWN MIND AS TO WHETHER YOU CAN OVERCOME THE OBSTACLES INVOLVED.**

The two most useful tools in finding your way around the book are the Contents list, and the Index. The guide starts with a range of general information, highlighting various sources that are of particular interest to disabled travellers. The discussion on travel covers both getting to Israel, and getting around once you are there. The accommodation section concentrates mainly on places which are broadly accessible (more so than others, anyway) and towards the lower end of the price range.

The sights in and around Jerusalem are then described, followed by those around the Dead Sea and in PNA areas. Then the Mediterranean coastal strip with both Tel Aviv and Haifa are described; then Galilee and the north; and, finally, the Negev and Eilat in the south. You will find that most of the prominent sights and places are listed in the Index.

It has been assumed that this book will be used in conjunction with maps and conventional guidebooks, and we refer to various guides and maps in the text, in particular the Lonely Planet Guide *Israel and the Palestinian Territories*, and the *Israel Handbook with the Palestinian Authority areas*. Also we found the Rough Guide to *Israel and the Palestinian Territories* to be particularly helpful. In the text we have referred at different times to all three, abbreviating the Lonely Planet to LP, the Israel Handbook to IH and the Rough Guide to RG.

Units and definitions

Measurements

We have given measurements in centimetres (cm) and metres (m). Although these are the units increasingly being used internationally, both Americans and British people often think in Imperial measures. To convert metric measurements to Imperial units, use the following guidelines:

10 centimetres is about 4 inches (2.5 centimetres=1 inch)

1 metre is about a yard

1 litre is about 2 pints

1 kilo is about 2 pounds

The diagram on p27 gives the approximate dimensions of a standard wheelchair. Chairs vary considerably in size so it's worth checking the exact dimensions of yours to relate to the measurements given in the guide.

Steps

Steps are listed by number, with + indicating steps up and − indicating down. The word steps is normally only used once during a description of a site, and subsequently steps are simply indicated by +2 or −6 as appropriate. Where there are single steps, their height is of particular importance and we have measured the height in centimetres, indicated thus +1 [12cm]. This means one step, 12cm high.

Where there is a threshold, with a step up followed immediately by a step down and only a tiny gap between them, we have indicated this by using the sign ±. Again, we have indicated the height of the barrier using the format [15cm, 6cm] which would mean a step up of 15cm, and that there is only 6cm down on the other side. High thresholds can be particularly difficult for chair users.

Toilets

Our definition of a **unisex wheelchair toilet** is one where the door opens outward; the door width is greater than 70cm and the side transfer space is greater than 70cm. If there is a cubicle inside the men's or women's toilets meeting the same specification (D70+ ST70+) then it is called a **wheelchair cubicle.** If the cubicle does not quite meet the criteria, but is adapted for a chair user, then we call it a **unisex adapted toilet**, or an **adapted cubicle**, and we give the appropriate measurements and information.

Lifts

A **lift** is in a lift shaft, with doors, and a cabin which can be large or small. It goes up and down between the floors of a building.

An **open lift** is a small rectangular vertical lift, usually to take one chair user at a time and bypassing just a few steps – often added in a building as an afterthought.

A **platform stairlift** goes up stairs (attached to the wall) and has a platform which can take a wheelchair, and its occupant.

Measurements are given in centimetres (cm) for lift measurements: door width (D), cabin width (W) and cabin length (L). On this basis, you can decide whether the lift is large enough for you to use. Similarly, with toilets, we have given the door width (D) and the space for side transfer (ST) from the toilet seat to the wall. With bedrooms we normally state the door width as Dxx, the bathroomDxx as the width of the bathroom door and give the ST space also in cm.

Movable chairs and tables

In cafés, restaurants and dining rooms we have not said each time that the chairs and tables are movable. It is assumed that they are movable, and therefore more convenient for chair users and for others. **Where they are not movable, or if the seats and tables are high up or might cause a problem, we have said so.**

Symbols

Some years ago the use of a symbol to denote facilities for disabled people was agreed internationally and everyone is now familiar with the 'wheelchair' sign. In principle, the sign is used in accordance with criteria such as flat or ramped access; doors wider than 80cm, the provision of a large lift and so on. Unfortunately in practice it has been misused so widely so as to become virtually meaningless, particularly when used in guide books and listings, and on signposts. The assessment of accessibility is made by so many different people with varying perceptions of disability that some places listed as accessible have steps at the entrance or other obvious barriers. **Our approach is essentially descriptive, and we leave readers to make up their own mind about what is accessible for them.**

Symbols are used here to highlight certain data about access, and there is a key in Arabic, French, German and Hebrew. We hope that a system like this will soon be used to summarise important access data in conventional guide books.

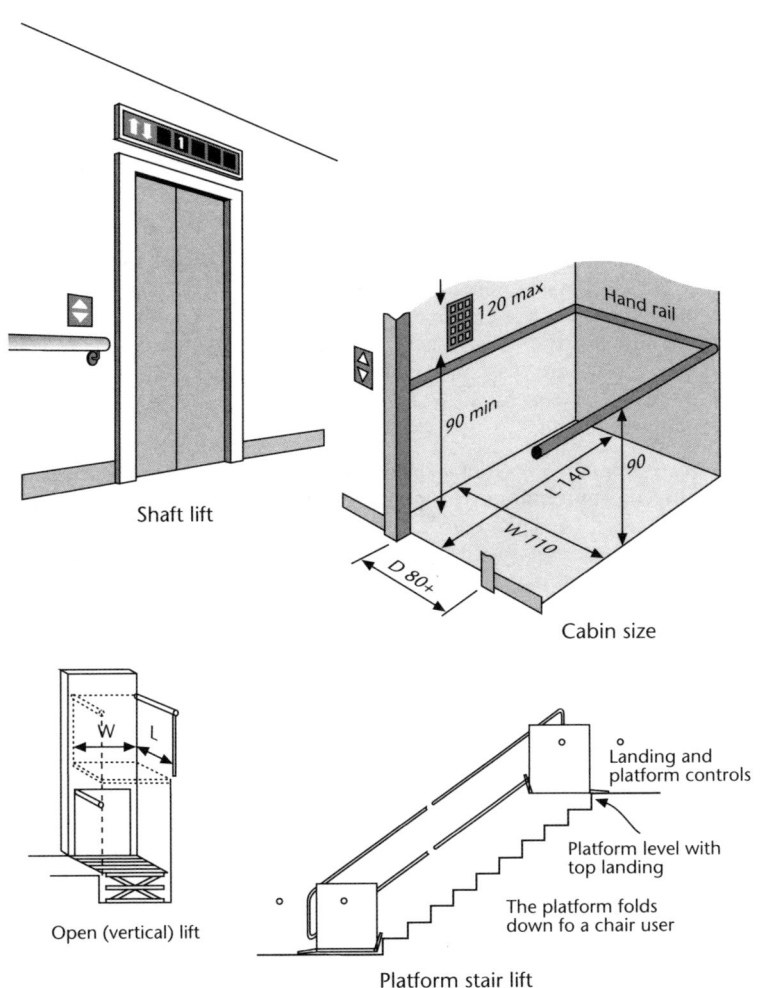

Different kinds of lift

Disability terms

Throughout the book we have used positive language about disability, and tried to take a positive attitude to obstacles. The barriers are there to be overcome, not simply accepted, and for a long time we have been part of the movement involved in breaking down barriers. Members of our group have a variety of disabilities and as a result are handicapped by the world around them.

We talk about disabled people and not 'the disabled'. When people refer to a 'disabled toilet' they imply that the cistern doesn't work, and not that it is big enough for a chair user. We have used the terms **wheelchair toilet,** or **adapted cubicle,** to describe a valuable facility. Amazingly (we think) we found places where parking, entrances and other facilities are still described as being for 'invalids'. Emphatically, we do not regard ourselves as being invalid or ill.

The use of language changes, and there is, of course, a danger in worrying too much about precise political correctness. Nonetheless a sensible use of language can help to change attitudes, and to increase understanding, especially if it causes people to ask, 'Why did you say it that way?' RADAR (see p20) issue a briefing on the use of disability terms, and will send a copy if asked.

Endpiece

We obviously hope that the information in the guide will be useful, but it can't solve all possible problems. What we provide is basic and factual, and YOU must decide what is sensible and practical to attempt. We've listed other resource centres and sources of information that you may usefully contact. For most people it will be important to plan a visit for a time when the weather is reasonable (ideally NOT during the summer, unless you can cope with extreme heat); to ensure that their accommodation is satisfactory, and in a reasonable location; and to organise how to get around. The easiest way for most disabled visitors to get around is either to hire a car, or to make use of the specialist tour organisers.

Ultimately to have a successful and adventurous holiday anywhere, what you'll need is some forethought, determination, patience and a good sense of humour!

Have a good trip

We have been visiting the area regularly for more than twenty years, and while many things need to change, both facilities and attitudes have improved during that period. We have enjoyed the visits enormously, and have learned that the few frustrations encountered are far outweighed by the unique and amazing experiences to be encountered in 'the Land'.

Speciality foods

One of the great joys of travelling is the opportunity of trying new and different foods which are 'native' to the area involved. In the Holy Land there are all kinds of foods, some of them originating from Jewish culture and practice, some with their roots in Arabic Middle Eastern culture.

Among the things you can encounter in the Holy Land are:

- **various forms of bread, such as the**

bagel, a bread ring with a chewy texture which is boiled briefly before baking;
matza, an unleavened bread more like a dried biscuit which is eaten during Passover
pitta, a round flat hollow bread which can be stuffed (for example as a falafel) or which can be used with dips.

- **Middle Eastern specialities, such as**

falafel, deep fried chickpea balls, often served with salad in a pitta bread,
fuul, an Egyptian brown fava bean stew;
maqluba, layers of meat, vegetables and rice, served upside down;
sfiha, Palestinian pizza baked with minced meat and onion;
shashlik, lamb and vegetable kebab grilled on a skewer;
waraq dawali, stuffed vine leaves.

- **Jewish specialities, such as**

blintzes, pancakes, often stuffed with cheese;
cholent, a sabbath stew cooked slowly overnight with beef, vegetables and dumplings;
kreplakh, ravioli-type stuffed pasta, eaten in chicken soup;
latkes, fried patties of potato;
schnitzel, veal or poultry steaks covered with matza meal and fried.

General information

> This chapter covers:
>
> - **Information sources, particularly those for disabled people**; Adapted transport; Calendars in use; Car hire; Climate; Communications: Converting to metric units; Currency and deposits; Electrical supply; Holiday helpers; Insurance; Local customs; Maps and guides; Medicalert; Medical requirements; Newspapers, radio and TV; Package tours; Passports and documentation; Sympathetic Hearing Scheme.

Information sources

We start with a listing of the main sources of general information about the area, particularly for the visitor, and then with a listing of sources which may have specialist and up-to-date information for the disabled visitor.

These days, one of the best ways of finding the right contacts who can help with information is to use the internet. While there is a great deal of junk and misinformation on the web, some of the best sites take trouble to keep their information up-to-date, and you can learn a great deal from them.

A guidebook like this is only a 'snapshot' which can give information which was available to us before publication. One of the advantages of web sites is that they can contain up-to-date information which was simply not available when we did our research. Equally, many websites are not properly maintained and contain old telephone numbers and other misleading information. The information on the web about access is generally of very poor quality, and we would recommend checking carefully if access details are important.

The most obvious information sources are the **Israel Government Tourist Office (IGTO)** which has branches in many countries, including Britain, Canada and the USA, and the **PNA Ministry of Tourism**. They will have good general information, but they are **not** knowledgeable about access issues. The **Israel Hotel Association** publishes a hotels list which includes a key with the information 'DIS' which means that there are facilities for disabled visitors. Unfortunately, no standards are applied, and different hoteliers use different criteria, so the listing includes a few that are really good, some that would be OK for some disabled visitors, and some that are pretty awful. The listing is therefore of limited value in relation to access, but the price and contact details are useful and accurate. The IGTO publishes *A visitor's companion* which is a useful compendium of facts and advice.

18 GENERAL INFORMATION

The main IGTO offices in Britain and North America are at:

- UK House, 180 Oxford Street, **London** W1N 9DJ *e-mail:* igto-uk@dircon.co.uk *Tel:* 020 7299-1111 *Fax:* 020 7299-1112.

- 800 Second Avenue, **New York** NY 10017 *e-mail:* info@goisrael.com *Tel:* (212) 499- 5650 *Fax:* (212) 499-5655.

- 5 South Wabash Avenue, **Chicago** IL 60603-3073 *e-mail:* igtochicago@aol.com *Tel:* (800) 782-4306/(312) 782-4306 *Fax:* (312) 782-1243.

- 6380 Wilshire Boulevard #1718, **Los Angeles** CA 90048 *e-mail:* drorigto@priment.com *Tel:* (213) 658-7462 *Fax:* (213) 658-6543.

- 180 Bloor Street West, Suite 700, **Toronto**, Ontario M5S 2V6 *e-mail:* igto@idirect.com *Tel:* (416) 964-3784 *Fax:* (416) 964-2420.fl

There are also offices in Australia, Austria, Denmark, France, Germany, Holland, Italy, Japan, Korea, South Africa, Spain, Sweden and Switzerland.

The **Palestinian National Authority (PNA) Ministry of Tourism**, POB 534, Manger Square, Bethlehem *website:* www.visit-palestine.com *Tel:* 02 274-1581 *Fax:* 02 274-3753. The Gaza office can be contacted on *Tel:* 07 282-9461 *Fax:* 02 282-4856, and the Jericho office on *Tel/fax:* 02 992-1229. There is a much more extensive site run by **The Alternative Tourism Group (ATG)** at *website:* www.patg.com which has numerous other links to Palestinian sites including www.palestine.net and to the **Birzeit University** *website:* www.birzeit.edu in Ramallah.

The **Israel Hotel Association** is at 29 Hamered Street, POB 50066, Tel Aviv *website:* www.israelhotels.org.il *e-mail:* infotel@israelhotels.org.il *Tel:* 03 517-0131 *Fax:* 03 510-0197.

On the internet, *there are websites* at:

- www.netvision.net.il/php/yosibeck the **Center for Information on Israel**. As one might expect, there's not much access or disability information and what there is does not conform to any consistent standards. We did not get the impression that the site is kept regularly up-to-date;

- www.iGuide.co.il is a **Guide to the Israel Internet** sponsored by the leading service provider in Israel, netvision. It includes a classified directory of sites and a complete listing of all domain names in the Israeli internet;

- www.hebron.org.il represents the views of Jewish settlers in Kiryat Arba (**Hebron's suburb**), and has links to other Jewish sites;

- www.inisrael.com **Interactive Israel**, which includes information about travel agents; hotels and about the major towns and cities but, as with others, with little access information;

- www.infotour.co.il **Israel Tourism and Recreation** the official Ministry of Tourism site which includes long listings of travel agents, car rental companies and up-to-the-minute news;

- www.maven.co.il describes itself as **Maven, the Jewish Portal**. It includes a range of subjects, including travel and tourism, entertainment, and Judaism. It has pages on Jewish festivals;

- www.virtualjerusalem.com **Virtual Jerusalem** is news-based, and includes a great deal of information of interest to the Jewish community and a page entitled 'Ask the Rabbi'.

The **Palestine Academic Society for the Study of International Affairs (Passia)**, 18 Hatem Al-Ta'i Street, Wadi al-Joz, PO Box 19545, Jerusalem *e-mail:* passia@palnet.com *Tel:* 02 626- 4426 *Fax:* 02 628-2819 maintains an independent financial and legal status, and is not affiliated to any government, political party or organisation. Its office is located just off Ibn Jubier in East Jerusalem. Passia encourages Palestinian-Palestinian, Palestinian-Israeli and Palestinian-International dialogue and discussion. It holds regular Interfaith Dialogue meetings, and seminars on International Affairs and Civil Society Empowerment. **It produces a comprehensive and valuable directory of Palestinian organisations and contacts, ranging from NGOs, charitable organisations, hotels and car hire companies to a comprehensive listing of PNA government departments, and a critique of the policies being followed.**

In addition, there are several reputable organisations with whom we have not been directly in contact, but who may be helpful with particular information. These include:

- up-to-date information is to be found at *website:* www.btselem.org from an active Israeli human rights organisation **B'Tselem**;

- **Jerusalem Media and Communications Centre**, Ghassan Khatib, 5 Nablus Road, Sheikh Jarrah, POB 25047, Shu'fat, Jerusalem *website:* www.jmcc.org *e-mail:* jmcc@jmcc.org *Tel:* 02 581-9777 *Fax:* 02 582-9534. This was started by a group of Palestinian journalists and researchers to provide information on events in Palestinian areas;

- the **National Parks Authority**, 35 Jabotinski Street, POB 3577, Ramat Gan 52511 *e- mail:* npa-il@internet-zahav.net *Tel:* 03 576-6888 *Fax:* 03 613-2656 who administer more than forty parks and sites throughout Israel. At some of them, efforts have been made to improve access, and to provide facilities for disabled visitors;

- *website:* www.igc.org/igc/issues/me is the site for the **Peace Net Middle East**.

Guidebooks are a really good source of information, and these are discussed under *Maps and guides* later in this chapter. Note that information relating to access is largely missing, although some include good plans of the various sites which will show how big the place is, and possibly where there are steps.

Information sources for disabled travellers

In the UK, various organisations can give advice about taking holidays, and these include:

- the **Disability Net** *website:* www.disabilitynet.co.uk is run by a voluntary group in the UK called Muscle Power. It contains a wide range of information and contacts. You will find part of the text of our other Access guides to London and Paris on this site (under Information and Access/Access Guides);
- **Holiday Care Service (HCS)**, 2nd Floor, Imperial Buildings, Victoria Road, Horley, Surrey *e-mail:* holiday.care@virgin.net *Tel:* 01293-774535 *Fax:* 01293-784647. HCS is the central source of travel and holiday information in the UK for disabled or disadvantaged people. It provides some brief information sheets about foreign countries. They publish an information sheet on getting support for travelling, and offer their own insurance policy for disabled travellers;
- **RADAR** 12 City Forum, 250 City Road, London EC1V 8AF *website:* www.radar.org.uk *e-mail:* radar@radar.org.uk *Tel:* 020 7250-3222 *Minicom:* 020 7250-4119 *Fax:* 020 7250-0212. RADAR is the central coordinating body for all voluntary groups concerned with disabled people in the UK. It provides advice and information on a variety of subjects, including access, housing, benefits and holidays. It produces an extensive publications list. Because of lack of resources, RADAR is no longer publishing its various guides to travelling abroad; however, they have a number of useful booklets, including Holiday Fact Pack, published in 1999 with information both on insurance and on organisations involved in holiday opportunities for disabled people;
- **Tripscope,** Alexander House, 247 High Street, Brentford, Middlesex TW8 0NE *website:* www.justmobility.co.uk/tripscope *e-mail:* tripscope @cableinet.co.uk *Tel:* 08457-585641 (with a local call rate from anywhere in the UK), offers a wealth of practical information on travelling. If you are flying, and need special services, such as oxygen, talk to Tripscope. They can advise about accessible ways of getting to the airport, about the facilities offered by different airlines, and about insurance requirements. They are experienced and friendly. Advice is free, and is available during normal working hours.

In the USA, there are many groups and organisations:

- a site with quite an extensive listing, and with good links is **Access-**

بسم الله الرحمن الرحيم

| The Administration of Awqaf & Islamic Affairs - Jerusalem | دائرة الاوقاف والشؤون والمقدسات الاسلامية العامة - القدس |

الرقم :

التاريخ: ٩ /جمادي الاخره/ ١٤٢٠
١٩٩٩/١٠/٩

لمن يهمه الامر

يسمح للزوار اللذين بحاجة الى كراسي متحركة للتنقل داخل الحرم الشريف بالدخول مع الكراسي الخاصه بهم، وسوف تقدم لهم كل مساعدة من قبل العاملين في الحرم الشريف لتسهيل الزيارة.

والسلام عليكم،،

مدير اوقاف القدس

المهندس عدنان الحسيني

نسخة / للملف العام

/ ع ح ٩

تلفون ٦٢٨٣٢٩٢ و ٦٢٨٣٣١٣ و ٦٢٧١٥٦١ ص . ب ١٩٠٠٤ فاكس ٦٢٨٥٥٦١

Jerusalem Old City Step Map

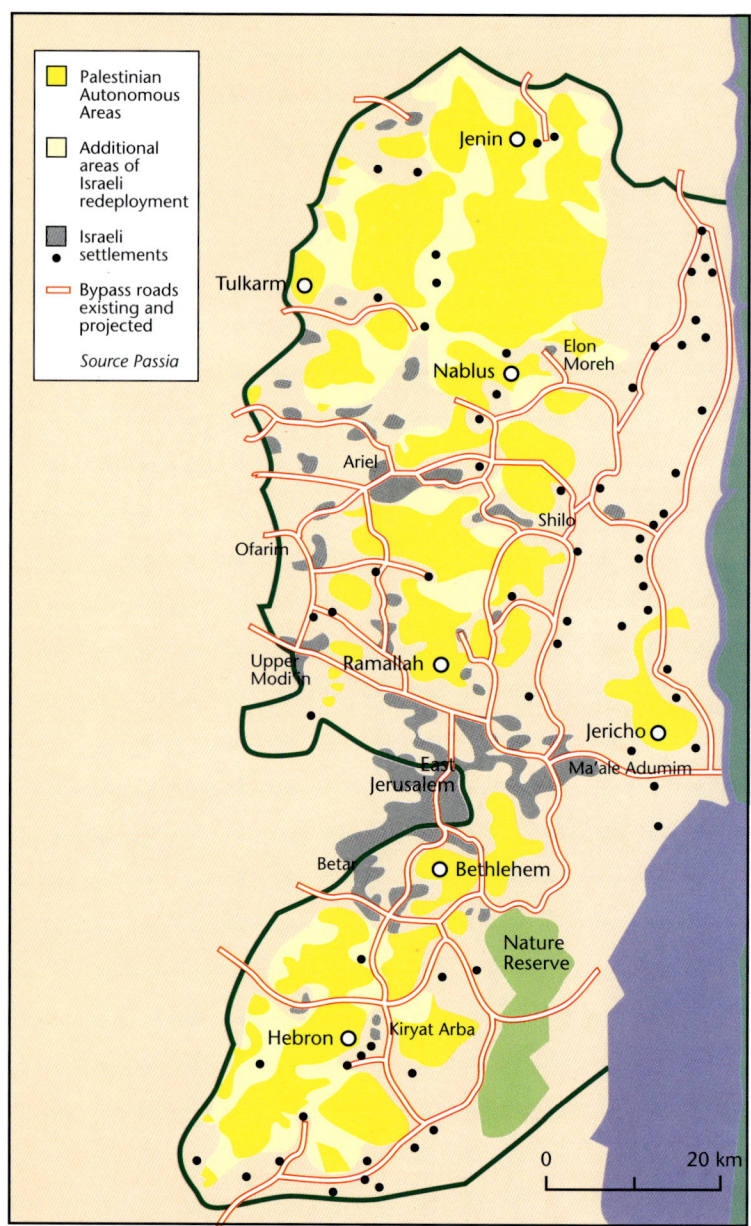

Areas of PNA autonomy on the West Bank. Details are under negotiation

PHSP surveyor looking over the Old City

26 GENERAL INFORMATION

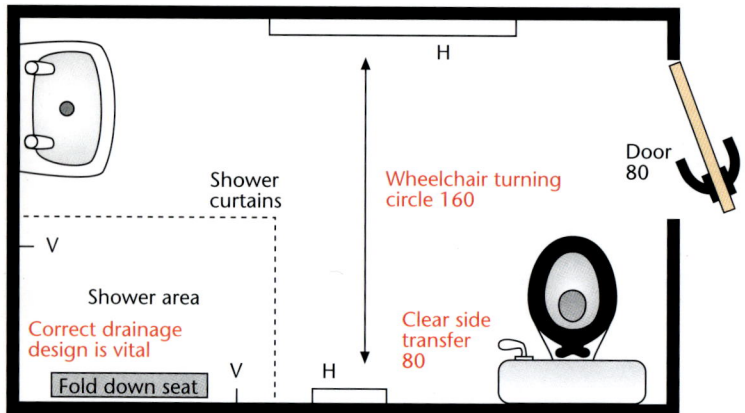

Overall dimensions 250 x 180 (150 cm min) (not drawn to scale)

H = horizontal grab bar
V = vertical grab bar

Dimensions in cm

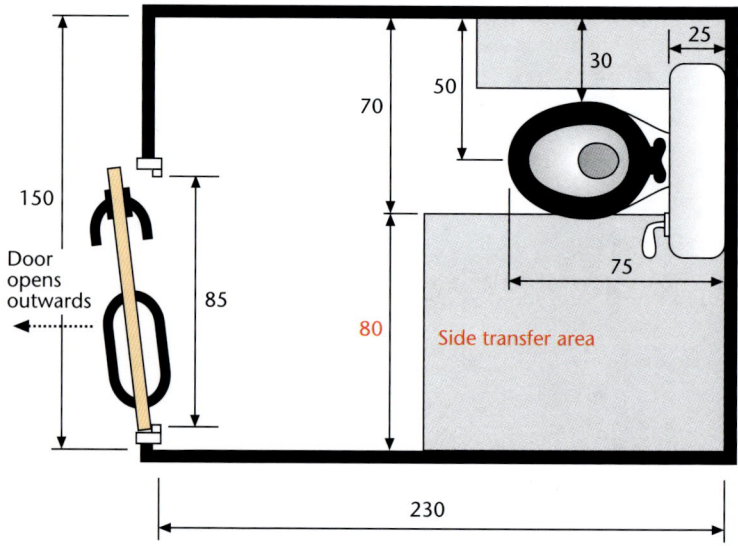

Recommended bathroom and toilet layouts

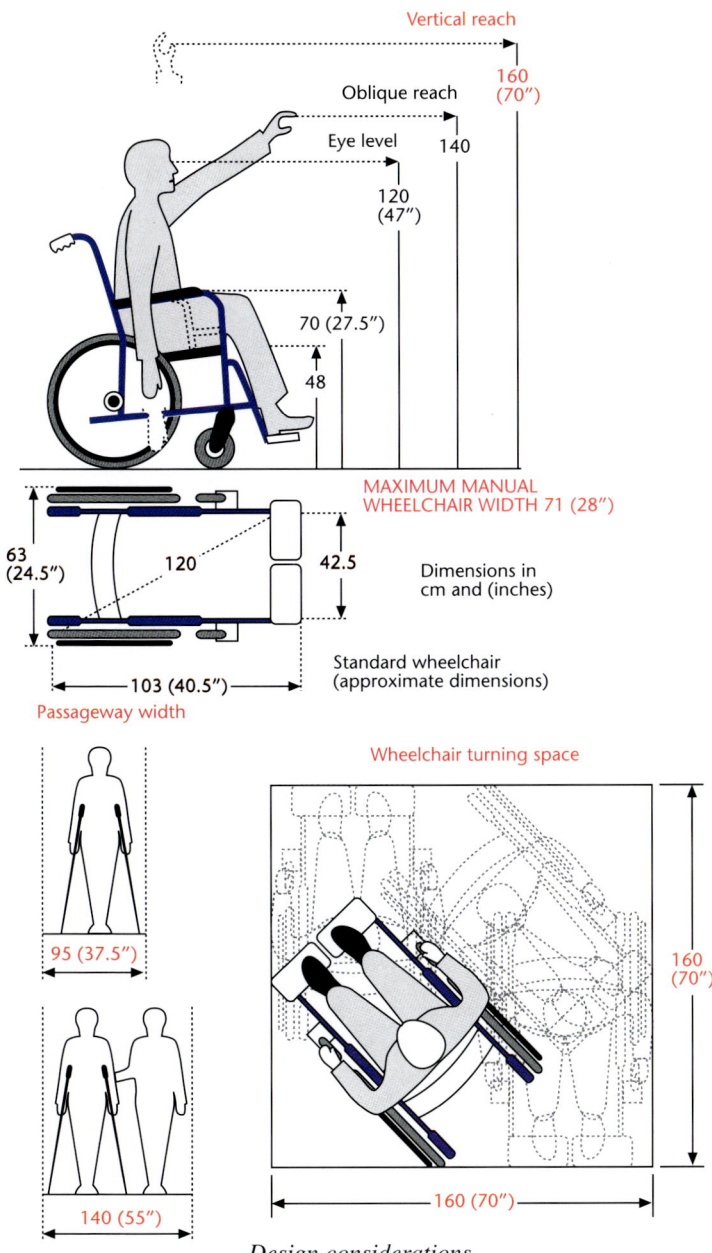

Design considerations

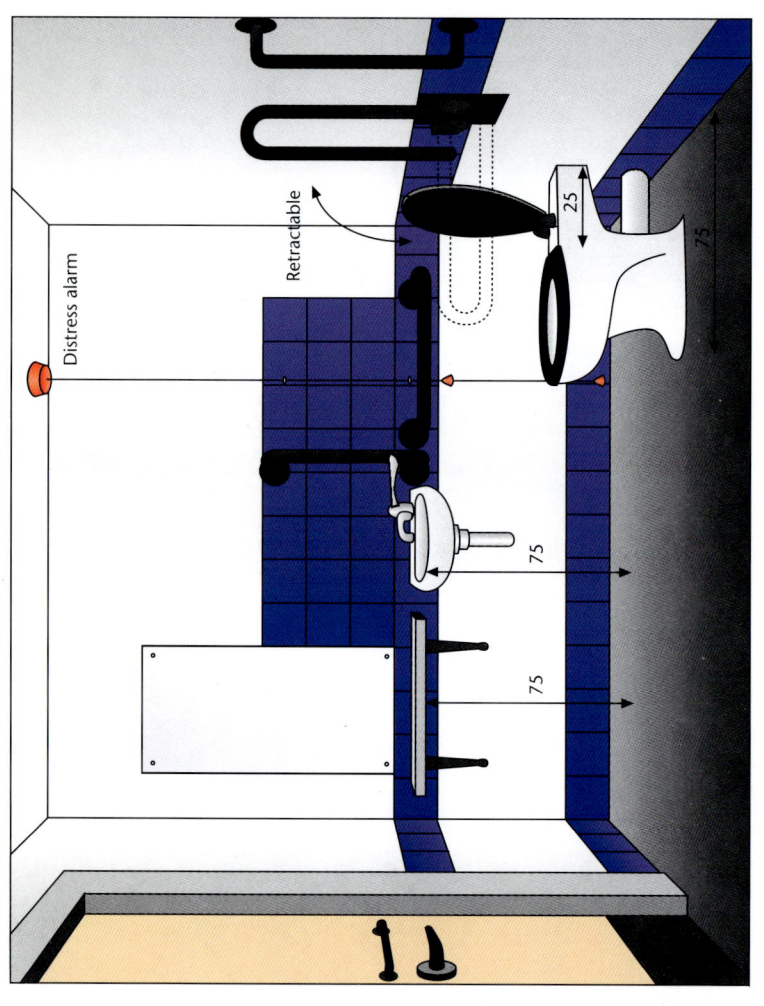

Design criteria for a disabled person's toilet

Ability *website:* www.access-ability.co.uk has some good contacts listings, for the UK, USA and Canada

- Note especially **Access-Able Travel Source** *website:* www.access-able.com which has gathered a huge amount of practical information and advice. It is run by Carol Randall who has extensive contacts, and keeps everything well up-to-date as far as is possible. Access-Able is incorporating **Travelin' Talk** *website:* www.travelintalk.net into their site. Travelin' Talk is a worldwide network (though mainly from the US) of people with disabilities who offer travel information and emergency assistance to one another;

- **Access for Disabled Americans,** 436 14th Street #200, Oakland, CA, USA, *website:* www.maxpages.com/disabledaccess *e-mail:* Psmither@aol.com *Tel:* (510) 419-0523 *Fax:* (510) 419-0768 publish a regular newsletter and an *Around the World Resource Guide*;

- **Global Access** *website:* www.geocities.com/Paris/1502 titled Disabled Travel Network, has an extensive listing of links, and provides a site where disabled travellers can share their experiences. They list our other guides, so they must be good;

- **IMAT (International Association for Medical Assistance to Travellers)** 417 Center Street, Lewiston, NY 14092, USA *Tel:* (716) 754-4883. IMAT tries to coordinate a group of doctors around the world to provide assistance to travellers who require medical attention while away from home. This could be of immense value to some people. They are a voluntary group and operate on the basis of donations only;

- **INDIE, the Integrated Network of Disability Information and Education** *website:* www.indie.ca which also has extensive contacts and disability organisations listings;

- **Mobility International**, PO Box 10767 Eugene, OR 97440, USA *website:* www.miusa.org *e-mail:* info@miusa.org *Tel:* (514) 343-1284 *Fax:* (514) 343-6812. A non-profit organisation that promotes international educational exchange and travel. They maintain information sheets on many areas in the world and have some sixty regional offices in different places;

- **MossRehab ResourceNet** *website:* www.mossresourcenet.org has some pages relating to accessible travel. The Moss Rehabilitation Hospital was for a long time one of the leading sources of information in the US for disabled travellers;

- **SATH (Society for the Advancement of Travel for the Handicapped)**, 347 Fifth Avenue, Suite 610, New York, NY 10016, USA *website:* www.sath.org *e-mail:* sathtravel@aol.com *Tel:* (212) 447-7284 *Fax:* (212) 725-8253. Organises an annual conference on disability travel in the US and abroad. Publishes access information through a quarterly magazine *Open World*, and on its website. Works with the American Society of Travel Agents and National Tour Association as well as serving on corporate advisory boards and federal regulatory committees.

Getting the right information is a question of who within the group you contact has the practical knowledge that you are after.

In the Holy Land

The main organisations with whom we have had contact are:

Ezer Mizion, 25 Yermlahu Street, Jerusalem *e-mail:* ezer-m @netvision.net.il *Tel:* 02 500-2111 *Fax:* 02 537-4881 runs a number of programmes for children with cancer, and provide other support services for people with disabilities when possible. They provided us with transport to get from the airport to our hotel in Tel Aviv when Yad Sarah (see below) were unable to help. It's probably best to talk to Yad Sarah first, but there are some requests that Ezer Mizion may be able to help with.

MILBAT, The Israel Centre for Technology and Accessibility, Tel Hashomer, Ramat Gan, 52621 *Tel:* 03 530-3739 *Fax:* 03 535-7812. This organisation is the centre for information for disabled people about equipment. It was set up to provide much needed support to Israeli veterans injured in the various wars. When we visited in 1998 it seemed clear that they were underresourced, and that they were trying to cope with a massive workload with only a tiny number of staff. They are, however, both friendly and, wherever possible, helpful. They issue some information leaflets for disabled visitors about accessible accommodation and adapted transport, but some of the information was unspecific and much of what we saw was out-of-date.

MILBAT have close contact with a wide range of reputable suppliers and can give advice concerning equipment repairs, transportation and medical assistance. This service is available in principle to Israelis and Palestinians as well as tourists. They also offer information on recreational activities for disabled people such as Jeep tours, water skiing, kayaking and horse riding etc. The have a lot of equipment on site but an appointment is essential.

Umbrella Organisation of Associations for Disabled People in Israel (UOAD), 68 Eben-Gvirol Street, POB 16636, Tel Aviv 61166 *e-mail:* mim@netvision.net.il *Tel:* 03 695-4208 *Fax:* 03 695-4207. UOAD operate an extensive programme to promote an increase in the employment prospects for disabled people. This is done through information and counselling centres, and by informing employers about people's abilities and encouraging an increase in the opportunities available. It is also promoting the provision of more accessible transport. Advice and help is available to visitors wherever possible, but as with other Israeli organisations operating in the field of disability, UOAD is grossly overstretched in undertaking the work it does.

Yad Sarah, Kiryat Weinberg, 124 Herzl Boulevard, Jerusalem *website:* www.yadsarah.org.il *e-mail:* info@yadsarah.org.il *Tel:* 02 644-4426 *Fax:* 02 644-4423. Yad Sarah is a unique, community-based non-profit, non-discriminatory organization whose 6,000 volunteers and the small number of professional staff provide, via 85 centres located throughout Israel, free homecare, support services to residents in need of temporary or permanent assistance. Details of the branches are given on their website.

Visitors can borrow equipment that they may need from Yad Sarah against a refundable deposit, exactly as Israelis do. You can borrow anything from a walking stick to a hospital bed and from a breast pump to an oxygen concentrator. You must bear in mind, of course, that such negotiations take time, and the offer of a loan is conditional on the availability of the equipment you want. In the Jerusalem area, they can help to equip your hotel room to make your stay more comfortable, for example by raising the bed or providing a commode. This would be subject to the policy of the hotel, and **Yad Sarah request a month's notice** of people's requirements.

Visitors in wheelchairs can use Yad Sarah special transportation vans for a fee in the same way as Israelis, and this can include travel to and from the airport. Such transport can certainly be helpful, but it would probably be difficult (if not impossible) to plan a touring holiday using it. Because of the nature of the organisation, there are many calls on its resources, and providing transport for visitors will not be its main priority.

The people there are both friendly and helpful. In 1999 the key person was Joram Seela. We asked for transport from the airport to our Tel Aviv hotel during our visit in April 1999. As we were arriving on Friday evening, during Shabbat, Yad Sarah were unable to help, but they put us in touch with Ezir Mizion who were, and we were driven in some style into the centre of Tel Aviv at about 160 km/h!

Specialist tour operators

In 1999 there were just a few companies in Israel and the Palestinian Territories who specialise in organising visits by disabled people. We have met or spoken to all the major players in the companies mentioned here, but we have not used their services specifically, so we have no way of comparing what they offer in terms of value for money. Commonsense says that individually tailored tour visits using accessible transport are likely to be more expensive than a standard package. **On the other hand you get the experience of people who know what they are doing and who are likely to be both friendly and helpful.** This saves money, and you will almost certainly not encounter any real disasters *en route*. The two greatest problems in Israel are finding accessible accommodation at a reasonable price (and in the right place!) and finding accessible transport. These are the two aspects that a local operator who knows what they are doing can sort out for you. They will also have practical knowledge about the needs of disabled travellers.

Magister Tours 18 Hagalim Boulevard, Herzlia 46725 *e-mail:* magister@netvision.net.il *Tel:* 09 951-3001 *Fax:* 09 951-3002. A recently established division of Magister Tours specialises in tours for disabled visitors. It is run by Zvika Gur who is himself a wheelchair user. They offer a range of options in terms of touring, with accessible lodging and transport with lift access. They will customise tour itineraries to meet individual needs, and can organise the framework for historical and religious tours, spa treatments and visits to practically any of the places described in this guide. They can organise a car with hand controls, holidays near beaches and swimming pools, challenging sports and activities and visits to the shops, as well as all the sights, shrines and places of historical interest.

Shartours *e-mail:* sharturs@inter.net.il *Tel:* 09 862-1343 *Fax:* 09 862-3082. The company claims to be experienced in the business of organising tours which meet the needs of disabled travellers. However, we had considerable problems in getting any response out of them when they were asked for slightly more detail. It took several phone calls and faxes just to elicit a bland reply which simply said something like "We can do it". We have still not managed to get an address for where they operate from, or to see a brochure. They may be OK, but they sure were difficult to get information from, and when we did, it was vague!

Tourism for People with Special Needs *e-mail:* meieli@zahav.net.il *Tel:* 06 628-8059 *Fax:* 06 628-9247 is working in conjunction with **Keli Tours**, 19 Hacharoshet Street, Keidar-Centre, Ra'anana 43656 *e-mail:* ekedmi @netvision.net.il *Tel:* 09 740-9490 *Fax:* 09 740-9408. The manager is Eli Meiri. They can offer a wide variety if tours, including destinations in Israel, the Palestinian Territories, Jordan and Egypt. They say that they can provide accessible lodging, and transport with a lift and wheelchair clamps. They organise historical and religious sightseeing tours, spa visits for medical treatment, and even visits to centres that manufacture equipment for people with disabilities. Special and appropriate tours can be arranged for people with visual and/or hearing impairment.

In the UK there is:

Especially Made Tours, c/o Janet Stafford, Torch Trust for the Blind, Torch House, Hallaton LE16 8UJ *website:* www.especiallymadetours.co.uk who offer occassional tours for people with various special needs. They have a lot of experience in organising such visits and have done their homework in terms of making sure that the facilities are practical. Their visits are also very reasonably priced.

In the USA there are:

Accessible Journeys, 35 West Sellers Avenue, Ridley Park, PA 19078, USA *e-mail:* sales@disabilitytravel.com *Toll free:* 1 800 TINGLES *Tel:* (610) 521-0339 *Fax:* (610) 521-6959 have extensive experience in organising travel for people with special needs, and have previously organised visits to Israel.

Travel Aides International, 14885 Snowberry Circus, Magalla, CA 95954, USA *e-mail:* travel@c-zone.net *Tel:* (530) 873-2977 is a business to both assist and travel with people with disabilities. They operate a travel agency, one of whose destinations is the Holy Land, and can provide medically qualified companions.

For those interested in tours which centre on Palestinian areas, there is:

The **Alternative Tourism Group** PO Box 173 Beit Sahur, near Bethlehem *website:* www.patg.com *e-mail:* atg@p-ol.com *Tel:* 02 277-2151 *Fax:* 02 277-2211 offer a range of possible tours and visits, particularly for those who want to be with Palestinians. They can organise a stay in a family home with guest rooms. We were taken to two such homes which had basically flat access. Neither was purpose-built for a chair user, and in both the bathroom was rather cramped with D65, but for an able chair user this would be a fascinating way to spend some time (see further details on p157). They have less direct experience of disability than some of the other operators listed here.

Adapted Transport

There is currently very little adapted transport available in Israel (minibuses with tail-lifts, cars with hand controls, etc). Eldan Rent-a-Car have just three cars with adaptations for hand controls.

Three companies with minibus/vans with a tail-lift are:

- **Hesseit**, POB 470, Kfar-Saba 44103 *Tel:* 09 742-5432 *Tel/fax:* 09 742-7177 have eight adapted vans with lifts. These are only available for hire with a driver at a rate of about $300-350/day (probably defined as an eight-hour day). The vans cannot be used in PNA areas.

- **Orthopedit Rehabilitation Accessories**, PO Box 2276, Kfar-Saba, 44425 *e-mail*: orthoped@internet-zahav.net *Tel:* 09 766-2627 *Fax:* 09 766-2688. They can offer full-size vans which can take two chair users, and three others, and a safari which can take one chair user and two others. The minimum age for driving these vehicles is 24, and on the insurance you would have to pay the first $800 of any damage. They have quoted us a rental charge for these vehicles of some $140 per day. For the Mercedes, it is slightly higher at $180/day. They also say that the cost of renting a vehicle with a driver is nearly $50 per hour. The vehicles **can** be used in PNA areas.

- **Zer Services Ltd**, *Tel:* 03 732-1132 *Fax:* 03 573-1037. They have adapted vehicles which can be used only with their driver, and cost about $400 for an eight-hour hire.

Nazarene Tours Ltd, PO Box 86, Nazareth 16100 *Tel:* 06 645-2171 *Fax:* 06 657-1524 can offer an accessible bus which can carry up to ten chair users, and sixteen other people, all for $500 per day. A good offer for a group of people.

The prices quoted are simply those given to us in reply to our general enquiry. More detailed negotiations are clearly needed before renting a vehicle as there may be some distance from the hire company offices to where you are staying, and you need to clarify when the charges start. Distances in Israel are generally quite small, so unless you are going down to Eilat, or the Negev, there should be no extra charge for the distance travelled. The question of being able to enter PNA areas is clearly important if you want to visit Bethlehem, Jericho, Nablus, or other places under PNA control.

Calendars in use

There are three main calendars in use which determine the day, month and year. In addition there are several other recognised ways of calculating the date. The main systems are:

- the Jewish Calendar, dating from creation 5761 years ago (designated AM or Anno Mundi);

- the Gregorian Calendar based on the birth of Christ (which is the system used in Western Europe and the US). This gives rise to the abbreviations BC (before Christ) and AD (Anno Domini, In the year of our Lord – ie after Christ's birth)

- the Islamic Calendar, used by many Arabs starts in 622CE (AD) when Mohammed fled from Mecca to Medina. It is called AH or Anno Hegirae.

The equivalent year to 5761 is 2000 Gregorian and 1378 Islamic, although it is only the Gregorian calendar that has New Year on January 1st. Both the Jewish and Muslim calendars are based on phases of the moon in which each month begins and ends with a new moon. To make up the difference between a year of twelve lunar months and a solar year of 365-366 days, the Jewish calendar adds on a month every three or four years. The Muslim calendar does not include such leap years and consequently regresses against the Western Gregorian calendar by approximately eleven days a year. What this means in practice is that both Jewish and Muslim festivals fall on different days on the Gregorian calendar every year. Guidebooks and diaries will give these dates for the next few years, but be warned that the dates of Muslim holidays are fixed according to actual sightings of the new moon, so the predicted dates arc only approximate. The basis for the various dates is well explained in the RG.

Both Jews and Muslims use the term Common Era (CE) when referring to Gregorian years. Thus Before the Common Era (BCE) is used for before the time of Christ. In the West, the reference is more normally to AD and BC. We have generally used the 'Common Era' convention in the guide, except in some cases when referring to Christian sites or historical events of particular Christian significance. The Julian Calendar used by Orthodox Christians runs thirteen days behind the Gregorian, while the Armenians use another variation.

There are a lot of festivals, and the different calendars can result in confusion, particularly when finding out whether a place you want to visit is open or not. There are all the Jewish and Islamic festivals, and the Christian ones based on three different calendars. There are at least three different New Year celebrations. Unquestionably, whether you're Jewish, Christian, Moslem, or of no particular faith, it can be exciting to be around at one of the major festival times. The festival dates for the coming year can he obtained from the IGTO or from the Christian Information Centre. They are also published in some of the guidebooks. During the more important religious holidays, the sites you want to visit may be closed. There are also important secular holidays, and Israel has its Independence Day, while Palestinians keep both Fatah Day and Independence Day as public holidays.

Because of all these different festivals and public holidays, it is important to take advice about what may be open at particular times. There are large-scale closures of Jewish sites during Pesach/Passover, and Islamic sites are likely to have restricted opening times during Ramadan.

One bizarre variation we encountered while in Jerusalem during the (Gregorian) Easter weekend in 1999 was that Israel introduced Summer Time on the Thursday night, so that the clocks went forward by one hour. The Palestinian National Authority (PNA) areas however, did not change their clocks on the same day, so that as we were staying at a Guest House partly staffed by Palestinians, nobody quite knew what time it was! It illustrates the need to be very relaxed about time, and to be prepared to 'go with the flow' rather more than one might when at home.

Car hire

Hiring a car makes a visit to the Holy Land possible for many disabled people. If you can afford it (and obviously provided someone in the group can drive) the use of a car will make it possible to visit many places that you would not otherwise see. Your own car gives you the freedom to do things at your own pace and in your own time, and you can collect and return it at the airport. **For a family, or group travelling together, car hire need not be expensive**. It would almost certainly be less expensive than using specially adapted transport, see p33, which is the only other alternative to getting on and off buses and coaches. Negotiating the hire may be a somewhat complex exercise if you want to get the best deal as there are several factors to take into account.

Of the major car hire firms operating in Israel **only one offers adapted cars with hand-controls** and that is **Eldan Rent-A-Car**. These must be booked well in advance as there were only three adapted vehicles in the country at the time of the survey.

Eldan International Reservations:

London 136B Burnt Oak Broadway, Edgware, Middlesex, HA8 OBB *Tel:* 020 8951-5727 *Fax:* 020 8951-5786.

New York Suite 2004, 350 Fifth Avenue, NY 10118, USA *Tel:* Toll Free 1-800 938 5000; (212) 629 6090 *Fax:* (212) 629 8253

Paris 51 Rue Richer, 75009, Paris, France *Tel:* (1) 47 70 21 25 *Fax:* (1) 48 24 03 88

Eldan Head Office 20 Hahaskala Blvd, Tel Aviv *website:* www.eldan.co.il *Tel:* 03 565-4545 *Fax:* 03 565-4553

The adaptions on the car are of a standard type. There is a "push/pull lever" on the left of the steering wheel and the gears are automatic. Drivers from Britain should note that because people drive on the right in Israel, these controls are (in a sense) the reverse of what you are used to. Our driver is right handed, and has a much stronger right arm than his left, and as a result had considerable problems with the controls. Those from the USA and other parts of Europe are not likely to encounter this difficulty. There are portable adaptions on the market but they are illegal in Israel, and should they be fitted, you will not be covered by the insurance.

Eldan will hire to drivers over 21, but with an insurance loading for younger drivers. Their cars are insured for driving in PNA areas.

There are several other operators, including Avis, Budget, Europcar, Hertz, Sixt and Thrifty. All have offices throughout the country. If you are renting and returning to the same place (eg Jerusalem, Tel Aviv or more probably Ben Gurion/Lydda Airport) there are other operators who may offer more competitive rates and we suggest that you find out about these through the IGTO or from your travel agent. **All companies say that you must have had your licence for at least one year**. All car hire firms seem to require drivers to be aged over 21 years and have a full clean driving licence. Most have an upper age limit of either 70 or 75.

Younger drivers typically pay more for insurance. An extra charge of typically $3/day is made if there is more than one driver. Theft protection (in addition to collision damage insurance) may involve an extra daily charge, as car theft is quite common in Israel (one of the few crimes that is somewhat prevalent). You can have personal accident and baggage cover for an extra charge, but most visitors will have this insurance already, and there is no point in insuring twice.

One of the more difficult subjects to assess and negotiate is the question of how much 'excess' you carry on the insurance and therefore what you might have to pay, if the car gets damaged. We found that the excess risk that you might have to accept varied from US$300-400 to as much as $1000. With some companies you can pay a fee, typically of around $5-10/day, in order to get a reduction in the excess. **When you are quoted a daily hire rate it is important to clarify exactly what is and what is not included**.

Some rental companies may restrict where you may take the vehicle, and exclude PNA areas. Israeli car number plates are yellow, while Palestinian plates are green. This means that you can attract attention if you are in a car with Israeli plates in a Palestinian area and vice-versa. Don't let this put you off, and just take sensible precautions. Always be aware of where you are. If you want to hire from a Palestinian company, Petra Rent-a-Car operate from Shu'afat (Shufat), just outside Jerusalem. Although their cars have yellow number plates, there is Arabic script all down the side, and they are well recognised within the PNA areas. As we have commented elsewhere, now that the *intifada* is over, the risks involved in driving in PNA areas are minimal, although, as always, you want to keep an eye on the news, and get local advice. All companies exclude crossing international borders and driving in Gaza.

Cars are classified in size from A (the smallest) to E (the largest), and the costs of hire are widely different. The bigger cars cost considerably more. The major firms all have slightly different conditions and rates and offer various special deals at different times of the year. These differences have a considerable effect on what you pay, how much risk you carry and even on where you can go. If you are hiring a car to take a wheelchair in the boot, the companies tend to just assume that you will instinctively know the boot size of a Ford Fiesta or a Seat Ensign (or whatever). In terms of boot size for storing a wheelchair they will, inevitably, err on the side of caution, and may hire you a somewhat larger (and more expensive) car than perhaps you need.

Note that hire company offices may be closed, particularly during Shabbat, and you cannot assume a 24-hour seven day a week service except, probably, at Ben Gurion airport. You pay a small surcharge for pick up and drop off at the airport.

Remember when picking up the car, to check the vehicle for scratch marks and dents and ensure that they are noted by the rental company as you will be held responsible for any subsequent damage. It is also a good idea to check the tyres (especially the spare wheel) and the indicators and lights. You are expected to return the car with a full tank of petrol.

Contact details

Avis Rent-a-car, Avis House, Park Road, Bracknell, Berks., RG12 2EW *website:* www.avis.com *Tel:* 0870-6060100 *Fax:* 0870-9035100. Avis do not hire to drivers aged under 21. They provide insurance cover for driving in PNA areas.

Budget Rent-a-car, 41 The Marlowes, Hemel Hempstead, Herts., HP1 1XJ *website:* www.drivebudget.com *Tel:* 0541-565656 *Fax:* 01442-276100. Budget do not hire to drivers aged under 25. They provide cover for driving in PNA areas.

Europcar, 2nd Floor, Bank House, Park Place, Leeds, LS1 1RY *website:* www.europcar.com *Tel:* 0870-6075000. Europcar do not hire to drivers aged under 21. They provide cover for driving in PNA areas.

Hertz, Swords Business Park, Seatown Road, Swords, County Dublin, Eire *website:* www.hertz.com *Tel:* 08708-448844 *Fax:* 00353-8133416. Hertz do not hire to drivers aged under 21 and do not provide insurance cover for driving in PNA areas.

Petra Rent-a-car, Main Street, Shu'afat, POB 19743, Jerusalem *Tel:* 02 582-0716 *Fax:* 02 582-2668. Petra do not hire to drivers under 24 and you are expected to carry a considerable insurance 'excess'. Insurance cover is provided for driving in PNA areas.

Sixt, 7-11 South Lambeth Place, London, SW8 1SR *website:* www.sixt.co.uk *Tel:* 0800-0566600 *Fax:* 020 7820-9797. Sixt do not hire to anyone aged under 21 and do not provide cover for driving in PNA areas. They can offer cars with roof-racks. Sixt has a tie-up with an Israeli company called Reliable, who advertise car hire at places like Youth Hostels. Their details are: **Reliable**, 64 Gisin Street, Kiryat Arie, Petah Tikva, Israel *website:* www.reliable.co.il *e-mail:* reliable@netvision.net.il *Tel:* 03 921-4222 *Fax:* 03 921-4343. On their website they quote a minimum age for hire of 21.

Thrifty, The Old Court House, Hughenden Road, High Wycombe, Bucks., HP13 5DT *website:* www.thrifty.com *Tel:* 01494-751600 *Fax:* 01494-751601. Thrifty do not hire to drivers aged under 23 and do not provide cover for driving in PNA areas or even in the Old City of Jerusalem. They can offer cars with roof-racks and Thrifty were the only firm we spoke to who offered a waiver to the insurance 'excess' if you are prepared to pay an appropriate daily fee.

Don't expect quite the same smooth service you might get in the UK or the US. Remember, you're going to Israel! Even if the car is pre-booked and pre-everything else, it may take you a while both to collect and return it. It is not, generally, very practical to hire a car just for odd days. If you are unlucky, you might spend a disproportionate amount of the day in the rental office and not much of it driving the car. **We have used car hire extensively and while we have had a few minor hassles, our recent experience has been that things are improving.**

Climate

The climate is more fully described in conventional guidebooks, and if you're disabled you should consider carefully the best time for you to visit. In the summer it can get very very hot, particularly around the Sea of Galilee, the Dead Sea and in the desert areas, with temperatures of over 40°C. If you visit Israel in the summer you'd be well advised to stay in the hilly areas where at least it gets cool in the evenings, eg in Jerusalem, Safed, or on Mount Carmel. The large modern hotels are, of course, all air conditioned, and you may simply want a resort holiday where you can well cope with (and welcome!) the hot weather.

Our advice is strongly not to go in the summer if you want to tour widely, as it will greatly restrict what you can do, and may put impossible strain on your companions. March, April or October are particularly good months for a visit. You may be lucky with the weather during the winter, though there are periodic spells of rain between November and February. We've visited several times during December and have found that the weather has been almost perfect for getting around. Sunny during the day and cool at night. There are occasional flurries of snow in Jerusalem every couple of years, but even in the winter it'll be fairly warm in Tiberias and around the Dead Sea and in Eilat.

Temperatures and climatic conditions vary considerably in different parts of the country because of the differences in altitude and proximity to the sea. There's the coastal plain; the hilly areas around Jerusalem and in the north; the areas below sea level (the Sea of Galilee and the Dead Sea), and the Negev desert to the south each with its characteristic climate. If the weather is likely to be a problem, you'll need to plan your trip with some care and take advice if possible from those who have been to Israel before.

In May and September there's often a period when very hot dry winds known as the Khamsin or Sharav blow from the east, and these can be quite unpleasant. Quoting average temperatures in the 80's means that the maximum will be over 90°F. Temperatures around the Dead Sea are usually higher than at Eilat.

Average temperatures °C

	Jan	Mar	May	July	Sept	Nov
Jerusalem/Bethlehem	6-11	8-16	15-25	19-29	18-28	12-19
Tel Aviv	9-18	10-20	17-25	21-30	20-31	12-25
Nablus	5-20	8-25	10-30	15-30	15-30	5-25
Tiberias	9-18	11-22	17-32	23-37	22-35	15-26
Jericho	11-20	16-23	24-34	28-39	27-36	18-27
Eilat	10-21	13-26	21-35	25-40	24-36	16-28

Remember that the most common illnesses among visitors are sunburn, heat exhaustion and dehydration, and it's a shame to spoil your holiday for the lack of a few basic precautions, such as:

- wearing a hat and using sun protection creams;
- keeping well covered with light cotton clothing;
- avoiding going out at mid-day, though not if you are a mad dog or an Englishman;
- drinking a lot (not alcohol!) even if you're not thirsty;
- taking salt tablets;
- avoiding snacks at roadside stalls and cafés when it is very hot, however appealing they may seem.

The advice about drinking a lot applies at any time of the year. It is only too easy, when out of your normal routine, to drink considerably less than you're used to, when in fact you should be drinking more. Don't begrudge a few shekels for coffee and orangeade. It's money well spent. One or two of our surveyors didn't take this advice and even in December they paid for it hy getting ill. It was simply a question of dehydration.

Communications

Phoning Israel is fairly easy, using the code 00 972 (from Britain) to replace the 0 in the number given as the internal number within the country. In the guide we have quoted the internal numbers, so, for example for a number in Jerusalem, we have given it as 02 987-1234, so that if you are dialling from London, it becomes 00 972 2 987-1234. Currently, the numbers in PNA areas pass through an Israeli telephone exchange, and therefore have the same prefix combinations.

For e-mail, Israeli destinations commonly have the final attribution ".il" while in PNA areas it has recently agreed that the final attribution ".ps" will be used, although at the time of writing, this has not yet been implemented.

There are currently rapid technical advances in international communications, and while conventional phone calls to Israel are quite expensive, there are an increasing number of companies offering international calling cards with cheaper rates. It is also probable that in time an internet-style telephone system will develop, offering much cheaper ways of phoning.

Public phones in both Israel and the Palestinian Territories have been run by Bezeq, the state-run company, and are operated by phonecards which are widely available at both shops and hotels. The network is not particularly well maintained, particularly in PNA areas, and lines are 'out of order' from time to time. There are moves to privatise the system, and a number of new companies have started to operate, so that from appropriate phones using the international codes 012, 013 or 014 you are likely to get a lower rate than using the standard Bezeq code of 00. Mobile phones are very widely used, and Israel has one of the world's highest rates of ownership and use.

Both fax and e-mail provide a cheap way of sending short messages. Remember, however, that e-mail is in its infancy, and the network is still growing. It is essential to get the recipient to acknowledge receipt of an e-mail before you can be sure that the message has got through and has been understood.

If you are travelling around independently, it is well worth considering the hire/use of a mobile phone. It can be very useful for phoning ahead and checking that places are open, and for getting gates and doors unlocked (and even toilet doors opened, possibly), before you arrive. **Solan Communications** offer rent-free mobile phones for short periods with a charge of $0.4/minute for incoming calls and $0.7/minute for outgoing calls. Used carefully (with a stop-watch!) a mobile phone could be invaluable, including the possibility of breakdown and as a contact to and from home in the event of emergency. Be careful though not to hang on for long periods waiting for the right person to answer, and it is very expensive if used for 'chatting'. Sensibly used, a free rental mobile can be of great value. Details from **Solan Communications, POB 173, Ben Gurion Airport, Israel** *Tel:* 03 979-2323 *Fax:* 03 979-2626. While it probably makes sense to pick-up and return the phone at the airport, there are other branches, including:

2 Luntz Street, Jerusalem *Tel:* 02 625-8908
Jaffa Gate, Jerusalem *Tel:* 02 628-0382
13 Frishman Street, Tel Aviv *Tel:* 03 522-9424.

Israel has recently moved from a six-digit number system to a seven-digit base. Unfortunately many printed documents, including people's cards and headed stationery do not reflect this. If you are quoted a six-digit number, then the following may help:

For Jerusalem numbers, try adding a 6 in front of the six-digit number

for Gaza numbers, try adding a 2
for Haifa numbers, try adding an 8
for Herzlia numbers, try adding a 9
for Nazareth numbers, try adding a 6
for Tiberias numbers, try adding a 6.

Jericho numbers beginning "99" now generally begin "23" instead, and Ramallah numbers beginning "99" now begin "29". **There will probably be ongoing changes in the telephone numbering system as the demand for lines increases, and if the PNA areas wish to become independent of Israeli exchanges or to have separate codes**.

Converting to metric units

In the guide we have put nearly all the measurements in centimetres, metres and kilometres (cm, m and km) since these are the units increasingly used internationally. To convert these to feet and inches, use the following guidelines:

10cm is about 4 inches (2.5cm is about 1 inch)

1m is about a yard

1km is 5/8ths of a mile (3km is about 2 miles)

We've given door widths and other measurements in cm and on p27 there's a diagram which gives the approximate dimensions of a standard wheelchair. Obviously chairs vary in size considerably, and you need to know the exact size of yours.

Metric weights and measures are used in Israel and very roughly, a litre is just under two pints, so when you're buying petrol (gasoline) 4.5 litres is about equivalent to a gallon. Solids are sold by the gram or kilogram. There are 1000 grams in a "kilo" and 1 kilo is just over 2 pounds weight.

For temperatures, we have used degrees Centigrade, although readers from the USA will be more familiar with Fahrenheit. To convert:

0°C = 32°F, 10°C= 50°F, 20°C = 68°F, 30°C = 86°F, 40°C = 104°F

Currency and deposits

Israeli currency (shekels – New Israeli Shekels – and agorot) is used everywhere. The exchange rate is published in the *Jerusalem Post* every day. You can now buy your shekels before departure from your own bank, or at Heathrow for example. There is also a useful 24-hour exchange facility on arrival at Ben Gurion/Lydda airport. US dollars circulate fairly freely. Credit cards are widely used, although less so in some Palestinian areas. Remember that using a credit card to get cash can be an expensive way of doing it. You normally pay a transaction charge, and on top of that, interest is charged at up to 30% APR (annual percentage rate) from the time of the loan until you repay both the loan and the interest.

Many prices are set in terms of dollars and if you pay in foreign currency or by using a foreign credit card, you may escape paying local taxes, eg for accommodation and in restaurants. If you are paying cash, US dollars are nearly always the best option for larger purchases. If you want to carry money in the form of travellers cheques, these can provide a safe method, but banks and money changers tend to charge a commission for cashing them.

If you are staying at 'five star' accommodation, then part of the service will probably be good facilities for money exchange, more or less on demand, although the exchange rate may not be brilliant. As in many countries, if you are staying somewhere cheap and depending on a bank to change travellers cheques, you may run into what may appear to be somewhat eccentric opening hours. **Using a bank is a slow process, and may take well over half an hour if you are unlucky**. You queue at one desk, where you show your passport and get an authorisation for exchange. Then you join another queue for the counter where you can get your money. In Jerusalem, there are several money changers just inside the Jaffa Gate, and in other places where foreign visitors go there are an increasing number of bureaux de change. If you are not staying 'five star', it is almost certainly worth having an adequate amount of cash to last for at least three or four days, and provided you take sensible precautions this should be perfectly safe.

Note that if you are offered Palestinian money, which you may be in some places, this consists of old notes and coins dating from the time of the British Mandate. These are quite rare, and are collectors items, so it may therefore be (or seem) very expensive. You can buy PNA stamps, and these make quite an attractive souvenir, as do Israeli stamps, but there is as yet no Palestinian currency. In some parts of the PNA areas Jordanian dinars circulate quite widely.

Make sure your money is carried somewhere safe, and you may be wise to keep it split up in two or three different places. We found that a small pouch for your money and passport kept under your shirt or blouse and held by a string round your neck is particularly effective. They're widely available in travel shops described as a BodySafe and may be more comfortable than a money belt. You need to see what is most comfortable for you. A method of carrying things where the wallet is in some way tied to you makes theft much more difficult. The worst option is to carry your money, cards and passport in a shoulder bag or handbag, and the next worst is to stuff your money in a back pocket. Remember that being in a wheelchair or being a disabled walker is no protection against theft.

Deposits can normally be paid these days by using a credit card number. Hotels normally require a credit card guarantee of payment of the first night of a booking when taking a reservation. Banks can electronically transfer money to a local bank account (for a fee), or you can use a cheque, an International Money Order or MoneyGram obtainable through a Post Office.

Electrical supply

This is standardised as 220 volts AC 50 cycles and so will cause no problems for visitors from Britain. Americans may need to buy a transformer if they want to use electrical items. Remember that if you use an electric wheelchair, the airlines sometimes won't carry the batteries and you may need to organise some batteries and a charger to be available on your arrival in Israel, either through your tour company, through Magen David Adom (the Israeli Red Cross), or through a local organisation for the disabled.

Having an international plug adapter can be useful. Although some British two-pin plugs may work, for example off an electric razor socket, in some places you will encounter an incompatible three-pin system. American visitors may need to convert their electrical equipment to the 50 cycle system compared with the 60 cycles and 110 volts normally used in the US. Get proper advice before travelling.

Holiday helpers

A big problem in planning a holiday can be finding companions who are strong and resilient enough to help get over the various minor problems you'll meet. Much, of course, depends on your degree of disability, how heavy you are and also how well you get along with people! Only you will know all that. If you have friends or family who can go as well, that is obviously ideal, although you must be careful in the planning not to try to undertake too much, especially through the hot summer months. Even if you have a lot of money, finding helpers and escorts to accompany you if you need help is like looking for a needle in a haystack. If your funds are more limited, and you are looking for volunteers, then it's even more problematical.

One approach (in Britain) would be to go through the various organisations like RADAR, SCOPE, the Muscular Dystrophy Group, or the Red Cross. If you only need some limited help while you are in Israel, then undoubtedly the best people to talk to are Yad Sarah. Some specialist tour companies may be able to help, but it may take some time to negotiate something, and don't be surprised if it's difficult.

Insurance

People rarely go on holiday without proper insurance, largely because there are small but out of the ordinary risks involved in travelling abroad. Even though the risk to the individual traveller is very small, the cost of medical treatment and/or of emergency repatriation in the event of an accident can be huge. You hear from time to time about overbooked hotels, Legionnaire's disease, insolvent airline companies, and the work of pickpockets, but remember that bad news always travels fast and often gets exaggerated. The relatively low cost of insurance which includes administration and a profit margin to the insurer, indicates that claims are relatively unusual.

Insurance is offered as part of most holiday package deals, but for the disabled traveller, a careful look at the insurance conditions is advisable.

Key issues

The most important section for almost everyone is that covering health insurance. Some policies still have a clause excluding those with a pre-existing medical condition or disability. Others exclude anyone who has had recent hospital in-patient treatment. The period stipulated can vary from the previous six months, to as much as two years since the treatment. The clauses vary in detail, and it is unfortunately important to read the small print of any policy. Some, quite reasonably, have an exclusion relating to people who are expecting to go into hospital for treatment. **Remember that your travel agent may not understand the implication of a particular clause for you. Also that it is important to tell your insurer in writing of any material facts that might affect the risk being covered.** The probability is that they will simply take note of what you say, and then you will be fully covered in the event of anything going wrong.

The increasing tendency to arrange cover over the telephone leaves the customer at greater risk, as there is no written record of the details you have given, or of the precise cover offered.

Another important aspect of a policy is how the company pays for the necessary health care. The best system for hospital and/or repatriation costs is that the insurer pays for it directly, rather than that you pay and then claim the money back later. What should happen is that you arrive at a hospital where you are admitted. The hospital checks with your insurer that you are covered and then the insurer pays the bills. For smaller sums such as the cost of a doctor's consultation and/or the purchase of medication, it's simpler to pay for these yourself, and keep the receipts for making a claim on your return.

This advice may seem to be boring, but it may also save you from being excluded from claiming a substantial sum of money if something does go wrong.

Policies available

In Britain, there are a number of excellent policies which will provide cover, and some good policies simply say that cover will he given so long as you are not making the trip against the advice of a doctor. Quite how that works if you haven't actually asked your doctor (because you have a stable condition and advice isn't really needed) is a moot point. In most cases, there will be no problem, but for your own protection, it might be worth having some back-up documentation, either by mentioning your disability directly to the insurer, or by dropping a note to your doctor saying that you are going off travelling.

We spoke to Extrasure, who we recommended some seven years ago in our *Access in Paris* guide, and discovered that their approach had changed considerably. They have a Medical Help Line with whom you would have to negotiate, and I was told that ANY medical condition would need to be declared. The list they gave meant that well over half the population would need to inform and consult them before they would assess the premium OR people would be going off only partly covered. We mention this to illustrate the need for doing the necessary homework with any insurer. The probability is that there will be no loading or increase in the premium, unless your condition is genuinely unstable. If, however, you give full information to your insurer, then your cover is cast iron and secure.

For some people, it may be necessary to use specialist companies. For anyone with cerebal palsy, or spina bifida, or multiple sclerosis, for example, the appropriate national association which provides information and help may well have information on the best policy for you. For children with cancer, consult (among others) the **Christian Lewis Trust,** The Child Care Centre, 62 Walter Road, Swansea, West Glamorgan SA1 4PT *website:* www.christianlewistrust.org.uk *Tel:* 01792-480500 *Fax:* 01792-480600.

Fish Insurance, 3-4 Riversway Business Village, Navigation Way, Preston PR2 2YP *Tel:* 01772-724442 has been in the business of providing insurance for people with disabilities and their families and companions for a considerable time. Cover can include the cost of a replacement personal assistant if someone fulfilling that role is ill or injured while you are abroad.

Europ Assistance, Sussex House, Perrymount Road, Haywards Heath, West Sussex RH16 1DN *Tel:* 01444-442038 provide a wide range of travel insurance. Like other insurers, they require that all and any medical condition is revealed, since, even if it has been stable for ages, it can be regarded as a pre-existing disability in the event of a claim. They may simply need a note from your doctor saying that there is no reason why you shouldn't travel. This would seem to be a sensible precaution before travelling anyway, to ensure that any insurance is valid.

Travelcare, 68 High Street, Chislehurst, Kent BR7 5AQ *see:* www.travelcare.co.uk *e-mail:* travelcare@compuserve.com *Tel:* 020 8295-1234 *Fax:* 020 8295-1345, offers an excellent and flexible policy. There is no age limit or loading, and you can exclude personal possessions cover if these are already covered under your household policy. They have a Medical Line on *Tel:* 0345-020303 (charged at local call rates) to consult if you have a medical condition diagnosed or treated within the last two years; if you have ever been treated for a heart or breathing condition; or if you have been diagnosed with cancer or a psychiatric disorder. A call giving details will enable them to detail what cover can be given, and for many situations you will be fully covered.

In making our enquiries, we got some basic quotations from different companies. What we paid ourselves, taking out what seemed to be an adequate policy for the disabled members of our group, was about £20 per person for insurance for two weeks in Israel. The policy was that of **STA Travel**, 86 Old Brompton Road, London SW7 *Tel:* 020 7361-6161, and covered medical expenses except for any condition that had been treated during the previous year, and excluded travel against the advice of a doctor. Travelcare quoted a basic cost of £42, and Europe Assistance quoted £64. The policies undoubtedly differ in many respects. Each may be good value for the cover given, but remember that IF you needed emergency repatriation on a stretcher for Israel for some reason, and you discovered that you weren't covered because of some undeclared pre-existing condition, you would look pretty silly.

It is not an issue to sweep under the carpet, nor to rely on a travel agent to deal with. The agent may know less than you do. The best thing to do is to make enquiries of three different companies, such as the ones we have mentioned, and possibly of a 'standard' supplier. You can then ensure by declaration, doctor's note or whatever method, that you are adequately covered.

RADAR at 12 City Forum, 250 City Road, London EC1 see p20, or **Tripscope** on the same page, will be able to advise about the latest position and of any new companies offering competitive policies.

In the US we can suggest various avenues of inquiry, in particular SATH (Society for the Advancement of Travel for the Handicapped) 347 Fifth Avenue, Suite 610, New York 10016 see p29, and look at the websites we mentioned on the same page.

American legislation is much stronger than Britain with anti-discriminatory clauses about areas like insurance. However, it is still as well to be careful. Insurance in the US seems to operate on a somewhat different basis from that in Britain. Certain aspects of your car insurance may cover you when driving a hire car abroad. Your household policy with 'all risks' clauses may cover your possessions when abroad, but many American insurers exclude theft of your belongings from their travel policies.

One major American player is **Travel Guard**, 1145 Clark Street, Stevens Point, WI 54481, USA *website:* www.noelgroup.com *Tel:* (1-800) 826-1300, and the cover they offer specifically includes pre-existing disability. The premium however is calculated in relation to the total estimated cost of your trip. From their published table, a trip costing $2000, cover costs about $150, while for one costing $3000, cover is $240 (at 1999 prices). Those figures seem high by British standards, but one has to take into account that the US is much further away, so repatriation costs would be much higher.

Other American insurance companies are listed in the RG.

It is essential to consider carefully the whole question of insurance. Although the chances of anything happening to you or your property aren't much greater than at any other time, the cost to you may be much, much more. It is worth shopping around to get adequate cover, since the cost of illness abroad or of emergency repatriation can be very considerable, and we would advise taking the maximum cover possible. It's important not to accept your travel agents advice without checking the small print relating to health insurance.

Local customs

There is a great deal we could say, but most of it doesn't really fall within the scope of an access guide, so we'd advise you to read elsewhere as well. However, we include a few basic points.

It is clearly important not to offend others in either Moslem, Christian or Jewish Holy Shrines by going "improperly dressed". In most places men should wear long trousers and women should cover their arms and possibly their heads and wear a reasonably long dress. Skull caps are worn by men in Jewish holy places, and these are normally available at the door. In mosques, and possibly some other places, you may be asked to remove your shoes. Not all holy shrines are open to the public. This applies to churches, mosques and synagogues. If you want to visit some of the places that are not part of the main tourist/visitor itineraries, then you may have to get permission from the appropriate authorities.

We came across a complete ban on the entry of chair-users into the main mosques when we first researched this guidebook some twenty years ago. This is because people normally take off their shoes, thus leaving the 'dust on their feet' outside the sacred building. For a chair-user this isn't quite so simple. We suspect that the Islamic authorities hadn't ever been asked about wheelchair access before. In correspondence, then, with the Awqaf authorities in both Amman and Jerusalem, we negotiated entry for chair-users into mosques. We know, however, that the guards at the door to the mosques often do not know about this discussion. In 1999 we got a new letter from the Awqaf Administration in Jerusalem, as those in charge are anxious to welcome disabled people see p21. This gives permission for wheelchairs and their users to enter the mosques on Haram al-Sharif, which are the most important ones for visitors.

We understand very well that mosques are primarily places of prayer, but they are appreciated also by those of other faiths, and by some with little or no faith. We were pleased to see an 'accessible' mosque while we were in Gaza City. We happened to be passing, and saw a man in an electric wheelchair outside this mosque. As we passed, the door opened, and a temporary wooden ramp, in two parts, was put down for the two steps at the entrance, and the wheelchair-user was able to go directly inside on to the carpets. We suspect that he may have been injured in the intifada, and that this may have forced a local rethink of the implications of Islamic law.

Only Kosher food is served in many, if not most, Jewish hotels and restaurants and this involves following the Jewish dietary rules. Basically it means that no butter or milk is served either with, or after, meat. In practice, and to the unknowledgeable outsider, it seems to make relatively little difference to the food served. It is important to respect Jewish custom by, for example, not smoking in dining rooms or public rooms on the Sabbath. Depending on where you're staying or where you're planning to go it's worth checking on what might give offence. In one or two ultra-orthodox areas (Mea Shearim in Jerusalem for example) pushing a button on an electric wheelchair on the Sabbath is normally considered to be work which breaks the Law. We would advise both care and sensitivity. Oddly enough, we were told that pushing a manual chair is not considered to be work. Pushing a button is.

Some people, particularly some Arab women and ultra-orthodox Jews, don't want to be photographed. To them, a photograph represents a "graven image", which is offensive. The sign language employed in such a situation is usually pretty clear!

There are a number of key festivals and public holidays, including:

- the Jewish and Israeli ones of Purim (March); Passover (April); Independence Day (April); Shevuot (May); New Year (Sept); Yom Kippur, Atonement Day (Sept); Succot (Oct); and Hannukah (Dec). Some of these involve the same kind of strictures as the sabbath, while Purim and Hannukah are more light hearted, and are not associated with the same discipline;

- the Muslim ones of Eid al-Adha (currently in March); Al-Hijra, New Year (Mar/April); Moulid al-Nabi (generally in June); Ramadan (starts in Nov or Dec) and Eid al-Fitr (Dec or Jan), but as explained in the section on calendars in use, the Muslim calendar steadily regresses against the Gregorian one by about eleven days a year;

- there are several Palestinian national days, such as Fatah Day (1 Jan); Jerusalem Day (22 Feb); Land Day (30 Mar); Black September (18 Sept); Independence Day (15 Nov); Palestine Day, declared by the UN as a day of solidarity with the Palestinian peoples (29 Nov);
- the main Christian festivals of Christmas and Easter take place according to the three different calendars already discussed. The main western celebration of Christmas is on December 25th while Easter falls either in April or towards the end of March.

Maps and guides

There are an enormous number of straightforward guide-books and also books about the "Palestine/Israel" situation. We shall concentrate here on the ones you should be able to get through British or American bookshops, and which will complement the information given in this book.

There's a scarcity of good maps and many of the street plans of towns leave much to be desired. Most are either slightly, or considerably out-of-date, and compared to the town plans commonly available in Britain, are of relatively poor quality. There is also the problem that different names are frequently used for the same streets, and the name on the map may not correspond to the nameplate in the street itself.

MAP – Mapping and Publishing Ltd, POB 56024, 18 Tschernikhovski Street, Tel Aviv 61560 *website:* www.mapa.co.il *e-mail:* info@mapa.co.il *Tel:* 03 620-3252 *Fax:* 03 525-7725 publish road maps of the whole country in different formats, and **the one we found to be most useful was the ringbound version using A4 size paper and a scale of 1:100,000**. The whole area is covered in eighteen double pages, and the maps are very detailed although not always completely up-to-date. They similarly publish a ring-bound A4 street map of Jerusalem as well as a single sheet fold out version which is less easy to handle, but can be helpful when you are driving and trying to follow a route across much of the city. Jerusalem is difficult, because the maps do not show the hills. The other major map publisher is **Carta** POB 2500, Ha'uman Street Jerusalem 91024 *website:* www.holyland-jerusalem.com *e-mail:* cartaben@netvision.net.il *Tel:* 02 678-3355 *Fax:* 02 678-2373. They produce a range of maps and books about the Holy Land, and whether or not the style and presentation appeals to you is largely a matter of personal taste. Carta are about to publish *Carta's Guide to Country Lodging 2000* which will list places with facilities for disabled visitors. This information will almost certainly be no better than that supplied by the kibbutz country lodging heqadquarters. Much more important is the updating of both maps and guides, and both Carta and MAP seem to be making efforts to update their main publications.

With the guide-books it's difficult to know where to start, as there are so many – and they all have different styles. Our favourites are the **Lonely Planet** and the **Rough Guide**, both called *Israel and the Palestinian Territories*, and the **Footprint Handbooks** *Israel Handbook with the Palestinian Authority areas*. All three are based firmly on the practical experience of travellers. None has much to say about access, but some of the maps and diagrams do give some access information, rather by accident. In this guide we have crossreferred to the Lonely Planet guide (1999 edition), referred to as LP, the Rough Guide (1998 edition), referred to as RG, and to the Handbook (1999 edition), referred to as IH. The Israel Handbook in particular has a large number of diagrams of the sites it is describing, although it also uses quite a small and not very strong typeface, which some will find difficult. The best maps and street plans are in the RG (in our view), the next best in the LP. Unfortunately in the new (1999) edition of the IH the maps are completely 'washed out' and difficult to interpret, although there are still some strong clear diagrams relating to various sites.

There are many other excellent guides, and these include:

- the **AA Baedeker** Israel guide with some good diagrams and maps as well as descriptions of the sites. It uses a small but strong typeface;

- the **AA Explorer**, and the **Insight Guide**, both with some spectacular photographs, giving a really good idea of the feel of many of the most important sights;

- the **Bazak** guide to Israel and Jordan, written primarily for Jewish visitors;

- the **Fodor** guide, perhaps particularly aimed at visitors from the US;

- the **Frommer** guides, including one entitled *Israel on $45 a day;*

- **Let's Go Israel and Egypt,** aimed mainly at the budget student-age traveller;

- the **Tzofit Guide for Touring Israel,** with extensive and detailed hotel listings, but less detailed information on the sights than other guides;

- *Easy Walks in Israel* by Aviva Bar-Am highlights a series of easy and attractive walks, some of which are wheelchair accessible. It is an enthusiastic little book where the needs of disabled people have been well integrated into the presentation, although unfortunately the reality of some of the access problems has been glossed over; and,

- *Bethlehem 2000* (a guide to Bethlehem and its surroundings) by Sawsan & Qustandi Shomali, published by Flamm Druck Waegner, Waldbröl, Germany, which is one of the few such guides originating from within the PNA areas.

In London, one of the best selections of guides we've come across is available from Stanfords Bookshop, 12 Long Acre, London WC2 *e-mail:* sales@stanfords.co.uk *Tel:* 020 7836-1321 *Fax:* 020 7836-0189. It stocks a variety of Israel maps, including street plans of Jerusalem and Tel Aviv. The shop is near the Leicester Square end of Long Acre, entrance +1 step and then +2 to the area with the maps. In Israel, we recommend the Steimatsky Bookshops, with branches in most large centres. **If you have time, it is well worth getting your maps and guides in advance as the local bookstores in Israel may not have what you want in stock.**

If you are planning to drive extensively, then there is no question (in our view) that the MAP *Israel The New Road Atlas*, the A4 size edition is the best. There is also quite a good road map of Israel published by Lonely Planet. After the overall map, street plans of both Jerusalem and Tel Aviv are essential, assuming that you are including both in your itinerary. Local street plans to smaller towns are included in some of the guidebooks, and you can also contact the local tourist office who will almost certainly have something.

One of the snags with the road maps is that most do not mark the new bypass roads in the West Bank areas. These are new roads which link the various Israeli settlements, bypassing Palestinian towns. On these new roads the signs are almost exclusively to Israeli settlements whose names may be known to local Jewish settlers, but not to foreign visitors, and so they can cause some considerable confusion.

Medicalert

The Medicalert Foundation provides an indispensable service for those with medical problems which could be compounded by treatment after an accident when the patient is unable to make known his or her particular condition. It is of special importance to those suffering from epilepsy, haemophilia, diabetes, allergies and many other conditions, or to those who need regular dosage of a particular drug. Life membership is available to anyone, for a nominal fee. Members wear a metal emblem engraved on one side with the name Medicalert, and bearing the phone number of the Emergency Service on the reverse side, where the immediate medical problems of the wearer are also noted, for example, "Allergic to Penicillin", "Taking Anti-coagulants", "Wearing Contact Lenses", "Under Steroid Treatment", "Diabetes". Additional medical information is filed at the Emergency Headquarters, where the telephone is manned 24 hours a day. There are further details on their www.medicalert.co.uk website.

Medicalert operate in a number of countries, and their main contact addresses are:

12 Bridge Wharf, 156 Caledonian Road, London N1 9UU *e-mail:* info@medicalert.co.uk *Tel:* 020 7833-3034.

2323 Colarado Avenue, Turlock, CA 95382-2018, USA *e-mail:* glazebrook-tanya@medicalert.org *Tel:* (209) 668-3333

Medical requirements

Obviously the first thing to do is to check with your doctor and ask whether there are any special precautions you should take, either in connection with travelling or with staying in Israel. There is good advice in the guidebooks, and we have borrowed here, some of the points made in the *Rough Guide* and in *How to stay healthy abroad* by Dr Richard Dawood (OUP) where the write- ups are particularly good.

There is a difference between jabs and inoculations that may be required for entry into a country and those that may be advised, and the regulations and advice changes from time to time. It is wise to check that you're up-to-date with polio and tetanus boosters, and protection against Hepatitis A is no bad thing, even if it is not an entry requirement.

If you have a longstanding medical condition such as diabetes, heart problems, high blood pressure, hay fever, or asthma, then get advice from your doctor before travelling. Even if you have been stable for a long time, it is almost certainly worth getting a doctor's note saying that you are fit to travel – principally for insurance purposes. Doctors these days are much less restrictive than they once were, and usually give good advice about the possible risk/benefit involved in travelling. If you need anything, carry enough medication to last the full duration of your trip, and a little to spare as well. If you split that, and carry it in two different places, then your chance of losing all of it is halved. Make sure that you know the pharmacological names of any medicines and the reason for taking them, and, if it might be useful, carry your doctor's phone number. If you have an occasional problem, such as asthma or hay fever, remember that you might just bump into the conditions that sparks it off, so take the necessary antidotes with you.

For minor complaints, if you feel you need help, it's probably best to go first to a pharmacy (*mirkahat* in Hebrew, and *saydaliya* in Arabic). For more serious complaints, it may be easiest to go to the hospital. Most larger towns have one and the standard of care and advice is generally good, although it is probably better in Israel than in the PNA areas. Your hotel/hostel desk will be able to advise, or will know of a local doctor if that is your preferred option, particularly if you cannot easily get to a hospital.

The most common holiday problem is stomach upsets and diarrhoea, and if you are only on a short holiday, this can be a particular nuisance. Mild diarrhoea usually lasts only for a day or two, and the general advice is broadly to 'do nothing' except to drink plenty and use rehydration solutions such as Dioralyte after an attack. These contain a mixture of salts and glucose.

If there is any sign of blood with the diarrhoea, then seek immediate medical advice, and if it lasts more than two or three days, the same applies. The various anti-diarrhoea medicines such as Lomotil, Imodium and Arret, should only be used if, for example, you have to go on a long journey where reaching the toilet may be difficult, or to permit attendance at important meetings. These medicines may bring a measure of relief, but they can also prolong any infection causing the problem. This is because they hold back the body's natural and appropriate response – which is, literally, to flush out any infection.

The best general advice we can give is the same as that for visiting all hot countries, and includes:

- don't eat unwashed fruit;
- don't eat food from roadside stalls;
- where the water is doubtful drink bottled drinks only, and don't use ice;
- in the summer, drink a lot (not alcohol);
- cover up in the sun and, especially, wear a hat.

A first-aid kit is invaluable for dealing with travel sickness, stomach upsets, sore throats, cuts, bruises, headaches and stings, and it's much better to take brands of drugs and medicines that you're used to, rather than have to experiment with local ones. You may want to take some insect repellant.

If you don't normally use a wheelchair, but tire because you can't walk too far, consider bringing a chair with you. You can rent or borrow one at home, and the airline will carry it free of charge. It's much easier to take one with you than it is to find and rent one in Israel.

Newspapers, radio and TV

There are two papers printed in English, the *Jerusalem Post*, a long-standing Jewish newspaper published daily, and the *Jerusalem Times*, which has a Palestinian viewpoint, published weekly. It is really interesting to see the different perspectives of the two communities. The *International Herald Tribune* is also widely available. Papers from abroad may he bought in the big cities and at Ben Gurion airport. There are English language broadcasts on the Voice of Israel five or six times a day. Reception of the Voice of America on 1260 kHz (medium wave) and of BBC Overseas Service broadcasts on 1323 kHz medium wave, and on short wave, is reasonably good. On TV there's a mixture of Hebrew, Arabic and English programmes. Multi-channel cable TV is increasingly available in hotels, hostels and in many homes, with BBC World, CNN and Sky.

Package tours

> Organised tours of one kind or another offer an economical combination of travel and accommodation. There's an enormous variety available and it's a market which is changing due to alterations in the fare structure and the competition from new companies operating charters.

The best thing to do is get a list of tour operators from your nearest IGTO and look at the adverts in the major national papers and the *Jewish Chronicle*.

You can also consult local travel agents. These will be only too willing to take your business, and it can be a considerable advantage to be able to talk directly to someone who is willing to help and find out all kinds of details. They will have all sorts of discount arrangements with suppliers (hotel chains, car hire firms, insurance companies etc) but remember that they will generally only offer services involving their particular suppliers. For the disabled customer, whose requirements are more specific than others, this can be a disadvantage and you may need to make enquiries of more than one agent. On the other hand, the assistance of one concerned and understanding agent who takes the trouble to get hold of the necessary detail to make things possible is worth losing one or two minor discounts.

We mention here a few of the largest agents in the UK, but we have no grounds for saying that one is better than another, since we've only used a tiny number ourselves. What we can do is indicate the range of packages available an then leave you to decide what sort of deal you want and to make your own inquiries.

One possibility of key interest to disabled visitors is the kibbutz fly/drive package. We list below the UK operators who were offering this, together with a range of other options such as tailor-made tours, Eilat wintersun packages, standard hotel-based tours, etc.

Abacus Travel	003531 670-9070
All Abroad	020 8458-2666
AMG Travel	020 8958-3188
Israel Travel Service	0161 839-1111
Longwood Travel	020 8551-4494
Peltours	020 8343-0590
Project 67	020 7831-7626
Pullman Holidays	020 7630-5111
Superstar Holidays	020 7957-4300
West End Travel	020 7409-0630
WST Holidays	020 8202-0800

The IGTO office in London produces a full list of companies operating in the UK which contains some forty to fifty names. There's a similar list available from the New York, Los Angeles and other US and Canadian offices.

Organised tours for groups are run by very big companies for whom Israel is one place among a couple of hundred others included in their brochure. There are also large companies whose main market is Israel and who will have a considerable number of local couriers and representatives, who can more easily check out necessary details for you. There are medium size firms, and then small ones where the owner may even travel with the tour parties and will have plenty of local knowledge. Some firms specialise in pilgrimages, visiting all the religious sites; some specialise in coach tours, where you stay in a different place each night; and some organise 'centre' holidays in which you are based in only one or two places and are left to arrange your own programme and transport from those bases. Individual companies will have block bookings or special discount arrangements with particular hotels, and you may have to shop around until you find one using a particular hotel you know to be accessible. If you want more freedom, we would particularly recommend some of the fly-drive packages using kibbutz inns.

There are some specialist operators (see p31) who are clued up and knowledgeable about the needs of disabled travellers. The level of service you can expect is high, but their charges may be somewhat higher. Because of their special local knowledge they may enable a disabled visitor to see a great deal more in a shorter time, thus, effectively, reducing the overall cost of a visit. They can put together itineraries for small groups. They could also offer day trips or a three/four day package which is tailor made to supplement your own independent plans. There may be some visits where you would appreciate avoiding the hassle of organisation and providing transport.

There are numerous local travel agents who can organise particular trips (for example to see the sunrise at Masada, or to go to Petra in Jordan). Almost wherever you stay the front desk can give advice about what is available locally, but nearly all these tours will use a conventional coach for transportation. If you are interested in visiting Palestinian areas, see the write-ups on p157.

Passports and documentation

Citizens from most countries automatically get an entry visa valid for three months on arrival. What you need is a passport which is itself valid for more than six months from your arrival date. The main problem over passports is the question of stamping. Once you've an Israel stamp on your passport you can't use it to visit some Arab countries, so you have to get a second one, which can be quite complicated. You can ask not to have your passport stamped, but this becomes slightly more complicated if, for any reason, you part with your passport at the airport, for example if you're in a wheelchair or part of a group. When you give your passport to a courier or official make sure they know if you don't want to have it stamped.

Part of the procedure it that you get am immigration permit with duplicate sections. One part they keep at the check point. The second part is a small piece of paper which you have to keep with your passport. This is easy to lose at hotels or when cashing travellers cheques. If you do lose it, it may delay you going through the exit procedures when leaving.

The regulations over visas and passports from various places are always subject to change, so make appropriate enquiries before leaving. It will be interesting to see what happens when a Palestinian state is established, and this may bring about some new requirements and red tape.

Place names and street names

When reading different guides, and certainly when in the country, you'll find different names in use for the same towns and places as well as for streets, people and everything else. This is because both the Hebrew and Arabic alphabets are different from the English one, and translations can he somewhat variable. Generally, if it sounds the same it's probably the same place. By way of example:

- Safed, Zefat and Tsefat are all the same place, as are
- Eilat, Elat or Elath,
- Jaffa and Yafo
- Caesarea and Qesariyya;
- Herzlia and Herzlliyya, and note that
- Mitzpe and Mezuqe are the same.

It's all a bit hairy and takes a bit of getting used to, but you get the hang of it after a while! Where it can become a real hassle and confusion is with street names. **When you are trying to look them up in an A/Z listing you may not find the spelling that you have been given which makes using street maps considerably more difficult.** There may be letters missing, or even more difficult, different letters used – so if you try the alphabetical listing you may simply not find it. Also, when you arrive at or near the street you want, the street name on the sign may be spelled differently both from the map and possibly from the original spelling you were given.

It's a recipe for difficulty and confusion, and sometimes that is what results. If you have to find a particular address, allow some extra time!

Sympathetic hearing scheme

Everyone with a degree of hearing loss is at a disadvantage, especially when travelling. It's a disability that attracts little sympathy and is something that can be both difficult and embarrassing. The Sympathetic Hearing Scheme aims to help where possible. You may find that some people at information desks and ticket offices are trained to he thoughtful and helpful.

What may help when travelling is the little plastic card they issue. It's just like a credit card, and it's an easy way of saying "I can't hear very well, please speak clearly". The international hard of hearing symbol is becoming increasingly well known, although you will certainly find people in Israel who haven't come across it. The card has some simple instructions and hints on the back for the person you're talking to. It certainly won't solve all your problems, but it may help. It's also a good thing to get people used to recognising the needs of the hearing impaired.

If you think the card would help, then contact:
The Sympathetic Hearing Scheme,
7/11, Armstrong Road, Acton, London W3 7JL
website: www.ukonline.co.uk/ hearing.concern
e- mail: hearing.concern@ukonline.co.uk
Tel: 020 8740-4447 *Fax:* 020 8742-9043 *Minicom:* 020 8742-9151.

Travelling

> This chapter covers:
> - **travel by sea, land and air**, and includes information on the principal airports in the UK and USA, as well as in Israel;
> - **getting around** in both Israel and the Palestinian Areas.

Most people travelling to Israel will fly there and consequently this part of the guide has concentrated on air travel. We have looked in more detail about facilities in Britain and in North America, but the same principles apply if you are starting from other places.

In Britain the best information source for disabled people is **Tripscope**, Alexander House, 247 High Street, Brentford, Middlesex TW8 0NE *Tel:* 08457-585641 *website:* www.justmobility.co.uk/tripscope *e-mail:* tripscope@cableinet.co.uk. The phone number offers a local call rate from anywhere in the UK. Tripscope have a wealth of practical information on travelling, and the aspects that disabled people need to consider. If you are flying and need special services, such as oxygen, or if you have incontinence problems, discuss it with them.

By sea

It is possible to go to Israel by sea, from Greece, and even to take your own car with you, but there will almost certainly be access problems on the ship. The route is not really recommended if you have mobility problems, unless you particularly want to include some Mediterranean cruising. If you need information, we suggest that you contact the IGTO to find out about the current operators of passenger ships in and out of Haifa. Our information is that there are two companies, one Greek owned, **Poseidon Lines**, and the other Cypriot owned, **Salamis Lines**. Sailing times vary at different times of the year, and the ferries may make stops in Rhodes, Crete and/or Limassol. The travelling time from Haifa to Piraeus (near Athens, in Greece) is nearly 60 hours.

Details

Poseidon Lines, *website*: www.greekislands.gr/greece.htm

Salamis Lines, *website*: www.viamare.com/salamis/salprc.htm

and both companies can be contacted via: **Viamare Travel Ltd**, 2 Sumatra Road, London NW6 1PU *website*: www.viamare.com *e-mail:* ferries@viamare.com *Tel:* 020 7431-4560 *Fax:* 020 7431-5456.

Viamare advised us that the ferries operating in the Mediterranean had somewhat variable access, most of it not good news for a wheelchair user. Only the newest ships are equipped with lifts, and the ones operating on the Piraeus to Haifa route are not the most modern in the fleet. Be warned!

By land

It is also possible to cross the border to and from Egypt and Jordan on land, but you need to check out the regulations carefully before trying it. Some private cars can cross the frontier, but you will almost certainly not be able to take your hire car across the border, and you may have to change/exchange taxis. You may need a special visa, possibly one obtained in advance. **As the rules will be subject to change, we simply suggest that you make the necessary enquiries just before travelling.**

By air

There are a wide range of direct flights into Ben Gurion Airport just outside Tel Aviv, and an increasing number into Ovda Airport some 60km north of Eilat. In 1999 the new airport in Gaza was opened, with flights to Cairo and Amman, although the number of destinations linked directly to Gaza is likely to be quite limited for a while. El Al and British Airways have scheduled services between Ben Gurion and several UK airports. Charter flights to Ben Gurion or Ovda airport, near Eilat, tend to leave from Gatwick Airport or Stansted. A number of carriers offer direct flights from airports in North America. The main El Al enquiry number in Britain is 020 7957-4100 and in the USA is (800) 223-6700.

Ticket prices go up significantly around the times of the main Jewish and Christian festivals, and it is often necessary to book well in advance at these times. Charter planes have the disadvantage of extremely restricted legroom, but we found that they gave good value from London. There's a particularly clear explanation of the various fares offered by travel agents and airlines, and details of some of the conditions and restrictions which apply to particular tickets in the LP p100/101. It is worth taking seriously the injunction to reconfirm your flight at least 72 hours before departure, as for part of the time flights are slightly overbooked.

Security on flights into and out of Israel is extremely tight, and you may be asked to arrive at the airport as much as three hours before the flight time. You will probably be questioned thoroughly, and one key thing that they are looking out for is whether anyone has given you something to carry.

There is good advice in *Door to Door* published by RADAR and written by Tripscope. It has a couple of chapters covering the necessary preparations for travelling by air, and on holidays generally. Airports and airline operators are generally used to dealing with chair users and other travellers with special needs, but the procedures adopted vary from airline to airline. Ultimately, what happens depends on who is on duty. If you need help to get on or off the plane, you may have to wait awhile. This aspect of 'handling' is normally the responsibility of the airport, and not the airline staff. **In recent years it has all become much easier and more routine**. As with anyone else, if you have a medical condition which might be a problem when flying, then consult your doctor. Get a brief note saying that you are fit to fly as this may be useful/necessary, and is a good insurance in the event of a hassle.

If you cannot get to the toilet, and the flight time is likely to be a problem, again, talk to your doctor. You will be in the aircraft for at least an hour to an hour and a half more than the advertised flight time to allow for getting on and off. Flight times are about four and a half hours from London and nine to eleven hours from destinations in the USA. There are simple precautions like not drinking anything before or during the journey, but your doctor may suggest the use of incontinence aids or medical inhibitors. It is essential to get proper medical advice.

The International Air Travel Association (IATA) has produced a standard medical information form (MEDIF) on which to define the help required. In some situations, for example if you have a chest condition, or if you're recovering from an operation, medical clearance is required, and your doctor will need to complete the necessary form. The forms should be available from either your travel agent or directly from the airline. Some airlines issue a standard Frequent Travellers Medical Card (FREMEC) to people with a stable condition who travel by air. This reduces administrative hassle, but you must still inform the airline of your needs when you book.

The volume of air traffic is now so great that many airports cannot really cope and places like Heathrow and Gatwick get very congested during peak periods. Any hiccup in the system causes disproportionate disruption. But, in spite of all that, you'll probably have a smooth flight. Take a good book with you!

Advice for air travellers

- when you book your flight, tell your travel agent any relevant facts about your disability and say what help you need;
- get hold of the tickets in good time, and check them;
- make sure that the airline has been notified that it is carrying a passenger with special needs, and preferably have something in writing with you either from your travel agent or the airline. Remember that there are special procedures for carrying an electric chair, and that is best checked directly with the airline. Airlines may be unable to carry some batteries,

and if that is the case you may need to organise a replacement to be available at your destination. Consult Yad Sarah about this if necessary;

- if there is any doubt, carry a doctor's note saying that you are fit to fly;
- travel light, and take an absolute minimum of hand luggage;
- if you have a wheelchair put a label and luggage tab on it before you travel, and remove anything that will come off, such as arms, footplates and cushions. Bring a soft empty bag to put these in;
- arrive in good time, and make your needs known at the check-in desk. Ask what the procedure will be;
- use a toilet at the airport before you leave, and make sure that the staff give you time to do this. Unisex toilets are available at most airports, so that your spouse or companion can help if necessary;
- on arrival check your wheelchair for any damage in the luggage handling system – and if there is, make sure it is reported and recorded at the airport. Keep a copy of the record and relevant reference number.

At most airports there are long distances, and disabled walkers are advised to make use of the special motorised buggies available at most airports.

Brief details of the main airports in Canada, Israel, the UK, and the USA

Canadian airports

Montreal: Dorval Airport, 975 Boulevard René Vachon, Montreal, Quebec *Tel:* (514) 394-7377 or 1-800 465-1213.

A fairly small airport, from where Air Canada and El Al fly to Ben Gurion. There are 45 parking spaces reserved for disabled people: 9 in the short term CP, 32 in the multi-level CP and 4 in the exterior CP. Apparently there are also "several" accessible taxis!

Toronto: Lester B Pearson International Airport, 3111 Convair Drive, PO Box 6031 Toronto AMF, Ontario L5P 1B2 *website:* www.lbpia.toronto.on.ca *Tel:* (905) 676-3580. Three fairly small terminals: Air Canada use Terminal 2, El Al Terminal 3. The **Travellers Aid** *telephone numbers* are: Terminal 1 (905) 676-2868; Terminal 2 (905) 676-2869; Terminal 3 (905) 612-5890. The interterminal shuttle bus between the terminals is wheelchair accessible. Parking for disabled people is in the garage in terminal 3 with lift access. The website has terminal maps.

Israeli airports

Ben Gurion Airport, Lod (Tel Aviv) *website:* www.ben-gurion-airport.co.il *Tel:* 03 971-0000/0478. The airport is well signed just off the route 1 motorway between Jerusalem and Tel Aviv. The current facilities have disabled persons' toilets adjacent to most of the main passenger areas, both before and after passport control. Getting on and off the aircraft involves steps to and from the tarmac, and a brief ride on an airport bus. Once inside the terminal there are step-free routes. Disabled passengers are loaded and unloaded from the plane using a special vehicle. This lifts a 'capsule' which can take about ten people up to the side of the aircraft, so that the transfer is essentially step-free. The whole procedure takes a little while, and disabled passengers normally board the aircraft first and leave last (which increases the time between possible toilet visits by as much as an hour). The rental car return parking areas are some way from the terminals, and the transport to and from is in conventional minibuses. If this is a hassle for you then make appropriate arrangements with your rental car company to leave it outside the terminal. If you need an accessible minibus to get to and from your hotel contact Yad Sarah see p31. There are plans for a new terminal to open at the end of 2002, and this is likely to include improved facilities for disabled passengers.

UK airports

Heathrow Airport, 234 Bath Road, Harlington, Hayes UB3 5AP *Tel:* 020 8759-4321 *Minicom:* 020 8745-7565 for general enquiries. There are four terminals, three of which (1, 2 & 3) are linked by underground passages with step-free access. There are several hundred metres between them. Terminal 4 is on a separate site. El Al flights use Terminal 1: BA flights to Tel Aviv use Terminal 4. Both sites have London Underground stations on the Piccadilly line where the only step involved is on and off the train, although it is a considerable distance along moving walkways between terminals 1, 2 and 3 to the station. There are also very few step-free Piccadilly line stations and none in central London. There is, however, an accessible underground link at Green Park to get on the Jubilee Line, and all the stations towards Waterloo and Stratford are fully accessible. Access to underground stations, or lack of it, is described more fully in *Access in London* (another guide in the same series).

A new express train service runs from Paddington station to stations at the central area and at Terminal 4. There is flat access onto the trains at either end and a facility for checking in at Paddington for certain flights, which may make the train a viable proposition for chair users. The refurbished and fully accessible station at Feltham (between Waterloo and Reading) has a wheelchair accessible bus link to all the Heathrow terminals. The Airbus route A2 from Euston station can also accommodate wheelchairs. If you are driving to the airport, there are disabled persons' parking spaces in the short stay CPs, close to the terminals. The long stay CPs are further away so if you are using a long stay CP, contact reception on arrival to get an accessible mini-bus to take you to your terminal. There are dropping-off points outside the terminals, although you can't park there. To connect between the terminals there are low floor buses.

Heathrow has a service called **Travel-care** *Tel:* 020 8745-7495 *Minicom:* 020 8745-7565 *Fax:* 020 8745-4161. They provide a useful booklet called *Travellers' Information – Special Needs Edition* which has practical advice and includes a plan of every terminal showing the location of the main facilities, including wheelchair toilets. It is also available as a talking book. For a copy, telephone the Brochure Line *Tel:* 01233-211207 *Fax:* 01233-500900. Not all wheelchair toilets are unisex, so if you need this facility, make sure you locate an appropriate one. If you have difficulty in going between terminals, there is a *Help bus* available (*Tel:* 020 8745-5185) which has a lift and wheelchair spaces. Free porters can be summoned from the green phones: just explain your requirements. Minicom phones should be available at all the information desks. Many black taxi cabs are now accessible to wheelchair users, although some disabled walkers can find them tricky as the main seat is set well back from the door. Alternatively Vic Hughes Accessible Taxis (*Tel:* 020 8831-0770/9393) offer vehicles with tail-lifts.

Gatwick Airport, Gatwick, West Sussex RH6 0NP *Tel:* 01293-535535 *Minicom*: 01293-513179. There are two terminals with a short train link between them with step-free access. BA flights use the North Terminal, and El Al charter flights use the South Terminal. There are accessible train services from London Victoria and other destinations to Gatwick station, which is beneath the South Terminal and linked to it by large lifts. Disabled drivers with orange badges can park in the short stay CPs for either short or long stays, and in the long stay CPs, although they are a bus ride away. Car/ taxi dropping off points are in front of the terminals The booklet *Gatwick Direct* includes some information for passengers with disabilities and terminal plans marking the location of wheelchair toilets. Minicom phones are available in both terminals. **Travel-care** (*Tel:* 01293-504283) offer help to anyone who has a problem; an alternative source of assistance may be your airline's handling agent, whose numbers are listed in *Gatwick Direct*. Accessible taxis are available from Gatwick Airport Cars (*Tel:* 01293-562291) or Barkers Taxis (*Tel:* 01293-527171) if you book in advance. Their normal taxis are ordinary cars, but they can get hold of accessible black cabs given notice.

Stansted Airport, Stansted, Essex CM24 1QW *Tel:* 01279-680500 *Minicom:* 01279-663725. A modern and relatively small terminal, used by El Al among others. There are accessible train services to Liverpool Street Station in London and other destinations: the station is underneath the terminal and linked to it by lifts and ramps. The bus service to the long term CPs is accessible, with lifts. A *Passenger Information Guide* is published, including some information for disabled passengers and a clear plan of the terminal. This shows the location of wheelchair toilets. A wheelchair accessible vehicle is available if booked in advance, from Stansted Airport Cars (*Tel:* 01279-662444).

Manchester airport, Manchester M90 1QX. *Tel:* 0161 489-3000. There are three terminals. Terminal 1 (used by El Al) is in the same building as Terminal 3 and is linked to Terminal 2 by a system of overhead moving walkways, via the railway station. There are spaces for orange badge holders in the short stay CPs by the lifts and in the long stay CPs, which are served by coaches with wheelchair lifts. There is some information in the *Timetable* published by the airport, and they are considering producing a guide for disabled people.

US Airports

New York, John F Kennedy Airport (JFK), New York *website:* www.panynj.gov/aviation/jadaovermain *Tel:* (718) 244-4444. A number of airlines fly to Israel, including El Al, TWA and Tower Air. There are nine separate terminal buildings, grouped around a huge circle which is probably about 1 km round, while the Tower Air terminal is about 1km away. Red white and blue accessible buses connect the central terminals, whilst yellow white and blue buses (also accessible) connect the central terminal area to the Tower Air terminal, long stay CP and Howard Beach station on the New York subway. A train link between the terminals and to the existing network is planned. Parking spaces for disabled travellers are reserved in the short stay CPs near each terminal, with stays charged at the long term CP rate: there are spaces within 70m of each terminal. Disabled passengers can get assistance from Travellers Aid *Tel:* (718) 656-4870. Information on public transport for disabled people into New York is available on *Tel:* (718) 330-1234. Detailed access information on the airport can be found at the JFK website.

Chicago O'Hare Airport, I 190 West, Chicago Illinois 60666 *website:* www.cityofchicago.org/aviation/ohare *Tel:* (773) 686-2200 *Teletypewriter number:* (773) 601-8333. There are four terminals, of which 1,2 and 3 are for domestic flights. The International terminal for Israel departures is number five. A wheelchair accessible train links all the terminals and also parking lot E. There are designated parking places for disabled passengers. Disabled passengers can get assistance and information from Travellers Aid on *Tel:* (773) 894-2427. The Blue Line train service into the city is fully accessible at the airport. It does not, however seem to be directly linked to the airport train system. Some stations in the city have lift access and are said to be fully accessible. You may be able to get more details from *Tel:* (312) 836-7000 *Teletypewriter number:* (312) 836-4949. The airport website was a model of absolute uselessness on access issues, but we got a more useful printed guide by writing to the Customer Services Department at the airport.

Los Angeles Airport, 1 World Way, Los Angeles, CA 90045 *website:* www.lawa.org/lax/welcome.htm *Tel:* (310) 646-5252. There are nine terminals. El Al use the Tom Bradley International Terminal. The FlyAway Bus service to and from the San Fernando Valley uses buses with wheelchair lifts. There are parking spaces for disabled people in all short term CPs and in Lots C and B, which are linked to the terminals by buses with wheelchair lifts. There is also a standby bus which serves Lot C; *Tel:* (310) 646-6402/8021 for a pickup. LAX shuttle "A" buses between the terminals are accessible: else you can 'phone the standby bus. Travelers Aid *Tel:* (310) 646-2270 is available to help disabled passengers: they have booths by the baggage conveyors in the arrivals hall of each terminal.

Newark Airport, Building 10, Tower Road, Newark, NJ 07114 *website:* www.panynj.gov/aviation/eadaoverframe *Tel:* (888) 397-4636 *Teletypewriter number:* (877) 438-7889. There are three terminals in a semicircle. El Al use Terminal B, and Continental fly to Tel Aviv from Terminal C. There are disabled persons spaces in the appropriate parking lots. A fully accessible monorail links all three terminals and long-stay CPs D and E. There does not appear to be an accessible transport route leaving the airport.

Getting around

One of the biggest difficulties for disabled people in Israel and in the Palestinian Territories is getting around to see and visit the sights. Choice is limited. The main public transport system is based on buses (with steps) together with taxis which are conventional cars. Tour operators mainly use coaches, again with steps.

The method that we used for getting around was that of hiring cars, which gave us the maximum amount of flexibility. In the two big cities of Jerusalem and Tel Aviv we also used taxis from time to time, since it solved parking problems, and meant that we didn't always have to navigate.

Your choice of transport will have a huge impact on what you can do. In particular places, it needs to be integrated with the location of your accommodation. In Jerusalem, for example, it might be possible to stay in Beit Shmuel, and walk and wheel to a range of the major sights, taking a taxi to a few that are a long way away. In Tel Aviv, you might want to use the Center Hotel which is right by Dizengoff Square. In Bethlehem and Nazareth, there is a lot to be said for staying overnight near the main sights (in the Bethlehem Hotel or Casa Nova Guest House in Bethlehem – or the Galilee Hotel in Nazareth).

One of the basic assessments you need to make is whether using cars most of the time is in fact practicable. One thing it depends on is whether there is one (and preferably two) reasonably confident and competent drivers in the group.

There are a few companies offering adapted transport of one kind or another (see p33), and this is what is used by some of the operators running special tours for disabled people. The adapted transport can be quite expensive to hire, and many of the companies involve insist on providing a driver – for which the passengers also pay. Some will not go into PNA areas.

By car

For many independent travellers, particularly those who cannot use the buses, travelling around by car is the only practicable way. There is information about car hire on pp35/39, and for a small group of people travelling together it can both provide good value, and enable you to visit many of the key sites before (or after) most of those who rely on tour buses to get them around.

Driving is not for the faint-hearted, although outside the two big cities (Jerusalem and Tel Aviv) there's not much too it, provided you are sensibly cautious and defensive. The driving style in Israel can be pretty aggressive, with some horn blowing and impatience. This is particularly bad on the route 1 linking Jerusalem with Tel Aviv, and also to an extent on the coast road up to Haifa. As we have clearly pointed out, in Jerusalem and Tel Aviv you may prefer to choose your accommodation in a location from which you can either walk or wheel to many of the sights, or use a taxi. Up in the Galilee, down by the Dead Sea, in the Negev and in Eilat, driving is pretty easy and relaxed, and the freedom which a car can give you is invaluable.

Some of the signposting on the biggest roads is quite good, but most of it in the towns and on smaller roads is dreadful. One of the problems with the signs in the towns is that they are too small to be read while driving a car in strange and sometimes slightly chaotic conditions. Having a reliable navigator to map read and look out for signs makes an enormous difference. Street names are also put up in small print, not even filling the area of the sign. Even accepting the difficulty in many places of needing signs in Arabic, English and Hebrew, the final result often isn't adequate for the visitor.

In towns, you have to get used to looking out for the blue discs with arrows which indicate which turn/s you can make at junctions and from what lane. British drivers will not be used to this system, and often you can only see and interpret these signs when you are quite close to the traffic lights (and you are probably in totally the wrong lane!). Note that a kerb marked with red and white stripes is a no parking area while one marked with blue and white means that parking is permitted. In many places parking seems to be totally anarchic, but as in many other countries, the enforcement of the regulations will become stronger as the number of cars increases. There is adequate parking at a great many of the main tourist sites, and also at most hotels and hostels. Even Jerusalem and Tel Aviv have MSCPs or UGCPs in the city centre areas, and you don't have to walk or wheel too far to get to the shops or restaurants.

By bus or sherut (service taxi)

The main public transport system is based on a combination of buses and of shared taxis called sheruts. These provide an economical and effective method of getting around, but they can hardly be described as 'accessible'. The buses are crowded, and it is a fairly competitive business getting on board. There are steps up to get into a bus, and most sheruts these days are mini-buses with two big steps to get in. It is not a method of transport that most disabled people will be able to use. The service taxis are usually either stretched Mercedes cars carrying six or seven passengers, or minivans carrying about a dozen people. They go, generally from recognised ranks and operate with fixed fares which are a little above those on the bus. Service taxis leave when they are full, and on the more popular inter-city routes they fill up quite quickly. If you can manage the access and negotiate the language difficulties they can provide a really good way of getting around.

By taxi

This is where the Middle Eastern character of the country is displayed. Taxis are normally large Mercedes cars, and provided you can get in OK are potentially very useful. However overcharging (particularly of unwary tourists) is almost the norm. If you use taxis, do not believe the 'my meter isn't working' story, nor the one which says 'for you, my friend, a special price' – which is probably twice as much as it should be.

Getting value and fair play is difficult, and yet you don't want to be spending all your time thinking that you've been 'done'. There are honest drivers around, and the best thing is to get one or two rides where the driver has agreed to use the meter. You can then reward that by giving a reasonably generous tip, **and** you have a good yardstick for comparing other fares which are demanded or requested later. Your hotel or hostel may well be able to order a cab that will operate fairly – in that the driver will want to keep his reputation and get repeat business.

Overcharging is not something to worry about unduly. You are on holiday in unfamiliar surroundings, and what you are there for is to enjoy yourself, and see and experience many new things. If you get 'taken for a ride' once or twice, put it down to experience, and think of it as being part of that. Once you know the form you can protect yourself against most of the excesses. More serious is that some taxi drivers are unwilling to stop for (or carry) chair users. Although we haven't found this to be a major problem, be aware that it does exist. You just have to be patient and persistent – and you'll get a cab eventually.

The railway system

Running down the side of Ayalon in Tel Aviv is a brand **new railway system**. When we discovered that Hashalom station was fully wheelchair accessible, down to the platforms, we got quite excited, as we thought that this might be a really useful facility. Unfortunately, while we did not survey the whole system, the only other accessible stations which we found were the Central station, a little way north of Hashalom, and the one at Nahariya in the north. Also, while the two platforms were accessible (by ramp and lift) without steps, it was a bit of a challenge getting on and off a train! There were +3 steps to get into the carriage with the lowest one starting from just below platform level. Our chair users were helped on board by staff, but it is clearly not a good design. We checked out some other parts of the rail system, but did not find any other places with step-free access. It may be that one or two of the terminus stations are accessible (though we looked at Haifa, which was not). Our view is that so little of the railway is accessible that it is of little help or value to disabled visitors. Apparently trains no longer go to Jerusalem.

Accommodation

> This chapter covers:
> - **accommodation in hotels, hostels, kibbutz hotels and inns**.
> - Listings are presented in the same geographical order as the guide contents, with Jerusalem first, followed by: the Dead Sea; the PNA areas, including Bethlehem and Gaza; Tel Aviv; and the Mediterranean coast; Galilee; the Negev and Eilat. There is finally a section on kibbutz hotel fly-drive packages.

After the question of accessible/practical transport, finding suitable and adequate accommodation at a reasonable price is the most difficult thing for the disabled visitor. Unfortunately, many travel agents, tour operators and even hotel managers, do not understand the necessary details which make a difference to access and are unable to describe their facilities accurately. A few, of course, do understand, and will give good advice and reliable information, and it is a joy to come across people who know what they are talking about. **The IGTO/Israel Hotel Association listings of hotels are a nonsense.** They include a category represented by 'DIS', which means that the hotel purports to have facilities for disabled visitors. Some do, and some don't, and it seems that **there are no standards or guidelines to validate the information**.

> **What 'dis' OUGHT to mean** is that there are reserved parking spaces near the hotel or guest house for disabled visitors, and step-free access to reception. There should then be step-free access to all of the main facilities, including the lounge, bar and dining room, as well as to any adapted rooms. The bedrooms should include enough space for a chair user to turn round, and in particular, have a bathroom with a door wider than 70cm and opening outwards, and side transfer space alongside the toilet of over 70cm. The bathroom should have either:
>
> - a wheel-in shower with a fold-down seat, easy lever controls and an adjustable height and a flexible shower head (see the chapter on *Design advice*); or
>
> - a bath with support rails and a transfer board, plus a flexible shower head with a long connector and easy lever controls, and a drain in the main floor which will take the flow without causing a flood. This would enable someone who cannot use the bath to take a shower sitting on a plastic chair.

> **Hotels and hostels should have a minimum of four adapted rooms**, two of which should have wheel-in showers. In addition to the physical provisions, staff should all have disability awareness training so that they can both understand and meet their customers needs. **Accurate information about these facilities, including details of distances and slopes should be available to the intending visitor.**

Unfortunately, many so-called adapted facilities do not meet these criteria, and some which we saw were simply 'standard' cramped hotel bathrooms where the hotelier has reversed the inward opening door and made it open out, calling this an adapted facility for disabled guests. We are very much in favour of starting with changes which constructively use the 'best practicable means'. This is a well known principle in engineering circles in Britain, and simply means looking for action which brings maximum benefit for minimum cost. Making a door open outwards instead of inwards, may be a good first step. If this is accompanied by the use of a transfer board over the bath (see the chapter on *Design advice*), a flexible shower head, and lever taps and controls, then it can make even a small room much more disability-friendly. Providing a well-fixed wooden ramp for the two or three steps at an entrance, and a handrail, can make getting in much easier. What is needed is accurate and factual information from the hotel or hostel about the provisions for disabled travellers, and this is not usually available. Managers and staff often do not know or understand what is important to a disabled person about the facilities they have, and the advantages and limitations of the facilities.

Carol Randall who runs the Accessible Travel Source website in the US gave us some excellent tips for finding out whether the information about a room was accurate. She said "ask if the person you are talking to has actually been IN the room themselves, and if they say no, treat the information with some care". A good ploy is to ask to speak to the person in charge of housekeeping and room cleaning, because these are members of staff who do go into the rooms and get to know the geography in a way that other staff do not.

A number of hotel chains claim to have a policy of providing adapted rooms for disabled guests, but the standards applied are highly variable.

One possibility is to use a kibbutz hotel fly-drive package, and this has several possible advantages. The packages are described at the end of the chapter.

ACCOMMODATION MAP 73

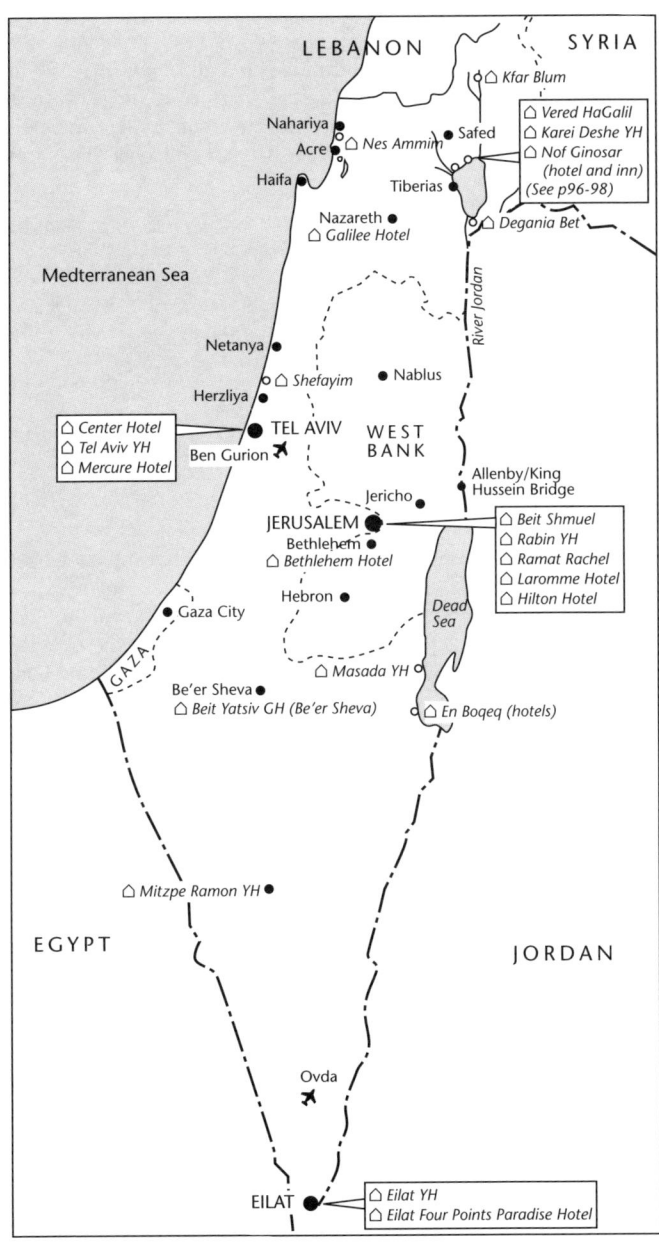

Recommended accommodation

Price indications are taken from a number of sources, and identify only broad ranges – ie bottom end, mid-range and top end. **Prices vary considerably depending on the time of year and on how many people are sharing a room.** You can find more up-to-date indicative prices in the IGTO/IHA listings, and also from websites. The broad brackets we have adopted are that:

- **bottom end** costs less than $60/night for two people including breakfast;
- **mid-price** costs less than $120;
- **mid-price to top end** costs less than $200/night; and
- **top end** costs more than $200/night for two people, including breakfast.

Jerusalem

There are only a tiny number of affordable and accessible hotel/hostel rooms in or around Jerusalem. The two in Beit Shmuel are superb with step-free access and a spacious bathroom with wheel-in shower, but the six bed arrangement will not appeal to all. The three rooms at the new Rabin Youth Hostel are also excellent. The one adapted room in Christ Church Guest House, and the one at St George's are both worth considering. After that, there are a number of expensive hotels including the Hilton and the Laromme with adapted rooms; then there's the new Eldan Hotel (see write-up), which is less expensive; and there are places like Notre Dame where the bathroom doors are about 60 cm wide. If you can cope with that they offer good value. There is also the Ramat Rachel Kibbutz Inn about 5km from the centre, and the Bethlehem Hotel about 10km away.

Beit Shmuel, 6 Shamma Street, Jerusalem 94101 *Tel:* 02 620-3473/3465 *Fax:* 02 620-3467. Situated off David Street, with the only approach by car via Emil Botta. There's a petrol station on the corner. Go down Emil Botta and turn left into Shamma. It's in the area of what was 'no mans land' between 1948 and 1967, and is now being extensively rebuilt. The guest house operates as a place of dialogue for Jews of all religious movements and for visitors of all faiths, promoting religious pluralism, mutual respect and tolerance. Street parking. From street level, there are two large metal electric doors that lead to the UGCP. An entry button (H100) will alert security staff of your presence. **Entrance via the UGCP**. Go to the left to find the lift, over two 5cm lips and D80. This bypasses +3+9+5+3 steps (outside) up to reception. The lift (D110 W130 L200) goes to all floors. Step-free to dinning room, small café, courtyard, conference room and roof garden. **Two well adapted rooms, numbers 217 (D94) and 317 (D97),**

which both have six beds. BathroomD80, and each has a wheel-in shower and ST100+. **Wheelchair cubicles** in the toilets on the GF.

It is a relatively easy walk/wheel into either the Old City (Jaffa Gate) or into the Ben Yehuda Street area of west Jerusalem. The 'relatively easy' routes still involve going up and down long, steepish slopes to both destinations. To get to the Jaffa Gate, you can go down Metiv Nagen Street in David's Village, just up the road from Beit Shmuel. The fairly gentle ramp down about 100 steps is bizarrely designed, with split ramps in some places and a lethal −1 step right at the bottom. The builders hadn't appreciated the reason for the ramps! Go across Ha-Emek, with the large UGCP, and then there's a ramped route up to the Gate, bypassing another ~100 steps (so it's quite a long route).

Bottom end for a group sharing.

Caesar, 208 Jaffa Road, Jerusalem *e-mail:* caesarjm@netvision.net.il *Tel:* 02 500-5656 *Fax:* 02 538-2802. Situated north of the museums, up Ha Nasi Ben Zvi Road, turning right on to the Jaffa Road. Steepish ramp into the foyer. Lifts (D80 W130 L130). Bar and restaurant step-free. They said that they had seven adapted bedrooms, but we were not able to see any of them. **Adapted toilet (D80 ST80, partially obstructed by a basin, reducing it to 55)** off the foyer, on the right.

Mid price to top end.

Christ Church Guest House, Jaffa Gate, Old City, Jerusalem *e-mail:* christch@netvision.net.il *Tel:* 02 627-7727 *Fax:* 02 627-7730. Located some 150m from the Jaffa Gate opposite David's Citadel. Old and atmospheric buildings. Pedestrian entrance has +1 step, up a slight slope. CP in courtyard. Somewhat bumpy. Dining room step-free from the end nearest the gate, there are −2 via the main way in. Lounge −1−1. **One well adapted bedroom** (Room 15) separate from the main accommodation via +1 [6cm]; D70+, bathroomD76, ST130 and a wheel-in shower. Two other bedrooms on the GF via just a few steps with standard facilities. **Brilliant location inside the Old City.**

Bottom end to mid-price.

P △ A ⌖✗ ◯R1

Crowne Plaza (Holiday Inn), Ha Aliya Road, Givat Ram, Jerusalem *Tel:* 02 658-8888 *Fax:* 02 651-4555. The hotel is something of a landmark being on top of the hill with twenty floors. CP outside with disabled persons' spaces. The ramped kerb was obstructed when we visited. Flat entrance, with restaurant and bar on the GF. Lifts (D120 W200 L140). **Four adapted bedrooms**. Room 834 seen, with D75, bathroomD75, no ST

to toilet and a low bath H40.
Top end

R4

Eldan Hotel, 24 King David Street, Jerusalem *website*: www.eldan.co.il *Tel:* 02 567-9777 *Fax:* 02 624-9525. Situated next to the YMCA with its distinctive tower, and very well placed for visiting either the Old City or west Jerusalem. CP outside. Step-free to the main facilities, restaurant and bar. It is a modern hotel with lift access to all floors. **Two adapted rooms** (numbers 101/102) on the GF, with bathroomD75, ST70, but there is only a gap of W35 between the toilet and the basin which would prove something of a challenge to a chair user who wants to take a bath! We have suggested a redesign, to move the basin and have a wheel-in shower.
Mid price to top end.

R2

Hilton Hotel, 7 King David Street, Jerusalem *e-mail:* fom–jerusalem@hilton.com *Tel:* 02 621-2121 *Fax:* 02 621-1000. Centrally placed and within easy walking distance both of the Old City and the centre in west Jerusalem. Two disabled persons parking places with ramped kerbs nearby. Step-free to all main facilities, including the lounge, bar, café (on the first floor) and restaurant (on the fourth floor). They have **five adapted**

rooms, four of them on the first floor with bathroomD80, ST120 and both a wheel-in shower and a bath. There is one on the ninth floor with bathroomD85, ST65 and a wheel-in shower.
Top end.

 R5

Laromme Hotel, 3 Jabotinsky Street, Jerusalem *e-mail:* managmnt@laromme-hotel.co.il *Tel:* 02 675-6666 *Fax:* 02 675-6777. On the edge of the Ha'Pa'amon Garden, and near the junction with David Street. It is almost within walking/wheeling distance of the Old City, although there is a valley in between. The information we have comes from the hotel management, but their description indicated that they understood access requirements and criteria. There is parking, and step-free access at the entrance, and to the bar, lounge, dining room and lifts. In a hotel like the Laromme, the lifts are likely to be very adequately sized. There are **eight adapted rooms** for disabled visitors, some with a connecting door to a second room. BathroomD85, and has both a bath with support rails and a wheel-in shower with flexible shower-head. Although we have not seen the Laromme, we were impressed by the quality of the information the management provided.
Top end.

 8

Notre Dame Guest House, POB 20531, Paratroopers Road (opposite New Gate), Jerusalem 91204 *Tel:* 02 627-9111 *Fax:* 02 627-1995. The guest house has been extensively modernised, but not yet to the stage of providing any adapted rooms. CP outside, but there's a steep slope up outside of about 25m to the entrance. You can drive up and drop-off, but there's no guarantee that a car can be left there (although when we stayed there, our driver, who used a wheelchair, was able to park outside). Whichever way you go out from the guest house it is hilly (as is much of Jerusalem), but you are very close to the Old City, and the New Gate. Step-free access to GF café and restaurant, and to the lifts (D80 W120 L110). The chapel is on the first floor and there's a bar on the fourth floor, all step-free. There are 150 rooms, and the ones we have stayed in all had bathroom doors D60 to 65. Notre Dame say that they now have about twenty rooms more or less fitted for guests using wheelchairs with bathroom doors D65 to D68.
Bottom end to mid-price

 20

Rabin YH and Guest House, POB 39100, Givat Ram, Jerusalem 91390 *Tel:* 02 678-0101 *Fax:* 02 676-6566. Situated near the Israel Museum on the junction between Yehuda Bourla and Nahman Avigad, and opposite a

petrol station. It is a superb facility, and construction was nearly complete when we visited. It was due to open late in 1999. UGCP with lift access (D80) to all floors. The two lifts had not been commissioned when we saw them, but are almost certainly of adequate size. On the main floor with the reception, there is an atrium, suitable for socialising and for some small performances. Lift to the dining room where there are **wheelchair cubicles (D70 ST70)** in both men's and women's toilets. There are **three well adapted rooms** with a separate wheelchair toilet (D80 ST70) and wheel-in shower (D80, sliding) attached to each room. Outside there is a small ampitheatre for performances with step-free access to the front via the lift and CP. **A remarkably well designed facility**.
Bottom end.

St George's Guest House, POB 19018, 20 Nablus Road, East Jerusalem 91190 *e-mail:* sghostel@netvision.net.il *Tel:* 02 628-3302 *Fax:* 02 628-2253 is situated by the cathedral, some 800m from the Damascus Gate. CP outside. **The rooms are mainly on the GF.** Ramp to reception, bypassing +2 steps. There are odd steps around the place, and some of the bathroom/s would be a bit of a challenge for a chair user. We stayed in **room 10** on the GF, which was step-free from reception, and then to the dining room. It had a wheel-in shower in the bathroom, and the shower tray was only slightly recessed into the floor by about 3 cm. It was surrounded by a movable curtain. **They have promised to widen the door by moving the surround and making it open outwards**. When that is done it should be D70, just wide enough for most chair users, and while ST is a bit restricted, front transfer should be fairly straightforward. The guest house is also an excellent place for disabled walkers. Dining room and lounge on the GF, bar –15.
Bottom end to mid-price.

There are other top end hotels listed as having adapted rooms and facilities for disabled people, including the Hyatt (*e-mail:* hyattjrs@trendline.co.il), and Renaissance (*e-mail:* renjhot@netvision.net.il). The Renaissance e-mailed us to say that they were putting in two adapted rooms to be available from March 2000, but gave no details.

Outside Jerusalem

Mitzpeh Ramat Rachel Hotel, Kibbutz Ramat Rachel, DN Tsfon Yehuda, Jerusalem 90900 *website:* www.ramatrachel.co.il *e-mail:* resv@ramatrachel.co.il *Tel:* 02 670-2555 *Fax:* 02 673-3155 is on the southern outskirts of Jerusalem off the Derech Hebron at Arnona. It is best approached either via Khanokh Albek running into Leeb Yafe or by turning into the area at Ein Gedi. It is more than 0.5km south of the main built-up area, down Goud Ha-Avoda. The hotel is quite spread out, and it's nearly 100m from the CP to reception, another 50m to the lifts and 50m to some rooms.

Large CP; step-free to reception and to the two lifts (D100 W140 L165). A ramp avoids the +3 steps to the lifts, restaurant and gift shop. Reception and the hotel lobby are on floor 2 as indicated by the lift buttons. **Seven adapted bedrooms**, two with just a wheel-in shower, and five with both shower and bath. All had card operated locks, which are generally easier than using a key. One seen (room 474) with D85, bathroomD80, ST110, it has a wheel-in shower as well as a bath. In spite of the fact that the door opened in there was plenty of room.

To get to the swimming pool is over 300m from reception, going up the hill and then down again. The route for a chair user is somewhat tortuous, going down in zig-zags inside the kibbutz, to avoid steps. The pool is covered with a pressurised tent during the winter, making it slightly more difficult to get in the building because of the air-locks involved. Stepped access into the shallow end of a large pool.
Mid-price to top end.

Kibbutz Hotel Maale Hachamisha, Judean Hills, 90835 *e-mail:* maale5@netvision.net.il *Tel:* 02 533-1331 *Fax:* 02 534-2144. Located off route 1 from Jerusalem to Tel Aviv near Abu Ghosh approximately 15km outside the City. Abu Ghosh is well signed. New hotel built on the side of the hill with long ramps in place of steps. CP with four disabled persons spaces and ramped kerb. Reception, lounge, bar and dining room are step-free. **Six adapted bedrooms**, one seen: D70+, bathroomD70, ST 110, with a wheel-in shower. **Two adapted toilets (D100 ST55)** on the GF to the left of reception.
Mid-price.

[P] [H] [M] [&wc] [&X] [●]R6

Dead Sea

In the Dead Sea area there are a good number of accessible places to stay. The only 'bottom end' one is the Masada Youth Hostel where there is one 'accessible' room with a somewhat cramped bathroom. At the south end of the Dead Sea there are a number of spa hotels, which are mainly up-market and quite expensive.

> The hotels are listed starting at the north end of the Sea and finishing in the south

Kibbutz Almog Guest House, MP Aravot Hayarden, 90665, Northern Dead Sea *Tel:* 02 994-5201/5 *Fax:* 02 994-2447. Almog is signed from the Jerusalem-Jericho road, route 90. The guest house is inside the guarded area of the kibbutz, and is a small vacation village with chalets and a swimming pool. Step-free to reception. The site is quite large, but the paths are mainly paved and flat. It is about 100m to the dining room, which is step-free and has a **disabled persons toilet (D70+ ST70+)** attached. We were told that there is **one adapted room** number 50 with wide doors and a wheel-in shower, but we did not see it. In their brochure they advertise that three rooms (out of the fifty) are suitable for disabled guests.
Mid-price.

Kalia Guest House, MP Kikar Hayarden 90666, Kibbutz Kalia, Northern Dead Sea *e-mail:* kayliagh@mishkei.org.il *Tel:* 02 994-2833 *Fax:* 02 994-2710. Located 1.5km north of Qumran off route 90. It has over forty chalets, with another thirty under construction. There is a water park, swimming pool, solarium and a zoo featuring farm animals, all nearby. Spacious CP. Reception has +4 steps with a ramped bypass. Self-service restaurant with movable furniture and step-free access. **One adapted room** (number 24) with no steps and D80, bathroomD80, ST180, wheel-in shower with a [4cm] step for drainage purposes. It interconnects with room 23, so that a small group could share the bathroom facilities.
Mid-price.

Metzoke Dragot, Kibbutz Mizpe Shalem, 86983 Dead Sea *e-mail:* metzoke@netvision.net.il *Tel:* 02 994-4222 *Fax:* 02 994-4333. The hostel/guest house is well signed from route 90 as Metsuqe Deragot. Take the right fork at the entrance to the complex, which consists of several buildings, see write-up on p151. There are several rooms with big bathrooms which are better than many 'adapted' rooms we have seen elsewhere. We saw room 51 at the top end of the complex. Parking outside, step-free entrance with D80, bathroomD70, ST250 and a sunken shower cubicle [–8cm]. From this room it was about 100m down a steep slope to the dining room, which has step-free access, but you could drive to within about 20m.

Ein Gedi

Ein Gedi Guesthouse Resort Hotel, MP 86980, Kibbutz Ein Gedi, Dead Sea *Tel:* 07 659- 4222 *Fax:* 07 658-4328. Situated about 500m off route 90, a few km south of the Nahal David Nature Reserve. Reception +1 step, bypassed by ramps about 5m on either side. There are over 100 chalets, and the dining room is about 75m from the main complex. It is up a slope from the adapted rooms with +5 bypassed by a ramp on the left. There are **five adapted rooms** with parking outside and ramped entrances. We were told that the ensuite shower and toilet were not adapted, and that the only difference in the rooms was the wider entrance door.

Mid-price to top end.

Ein Gedi YH, MP 86980, Dead Sea *Tel:* 07 658-4165 *Fax:* 07 658-4445. Up the first turn to the right at Ein Gedi as you approach from the north, at the entrance to the nature reserve. It is built on the side of a hill. Steep ramp at the front bypasses +26 steps, and another ramp bypasses +3. It is possible to park for a short time just by the +3. Step-free to reception and café. Rooms 6-9 on the GF are step-free. We saw room 7 with bathroomD60. Other rooms have just 2/3 steps from the upper CP, but doors to showers and toilets can be as narrow as W56. There are no adapted rooms.

Bottom end.

Masada

Masada YH, MP 86935, Dead Sea *Tel:* 07 658-4349 *Fax:* 07 658-4650. Follow the Masada turn from the route 90, and the YH is on the far left of the roundabout. CP at the front. 40m steepish ramp to reception and dining room. **One adapted room** near reception, (number 2) with a wheel-in shower, bathroomD70, ST40 (and generally quite cramped).

Bottom end.

En Boqeq

Crowne Plaza, MP 86930, En Boqeq, Dead Sea *Tel:* 07 659-1919 *Fax:* 07 659-1911. CP outside with five disabled persons spaces and ramped kerb. Flat to reception and lifts (D90 W135 L150). Two restaurants on the lower GF. The main one is 50% step-free, while the rest has −4 steps. In the Giraffe Restaurant there is a gentle ramp bypassing +4. **Nine adapted bedrooms**. Number 624 seen, with bathroomD85, bath and ST80. **Wheelchair toilet (D80 ST75)** near the restaurants. Also on the lower GF are the Health Spa facilities. Flat access to the majority of pools and treatment areas. The sauna had D65 and +1 [10cm]. There is access down a shallow ramp to the large outdoor swimming pool, and then it is some 50m to the beach and a further 20m to get to the sea. +1 to the shower. The

spa and beach facilities are available to the public (presumably for an appropriate fee), but this would seem to be one of the easier and more pleasant places to go if you want to have a "swim".
Top end.

R9

Hod Hotel, En Boqeq, Dead Sea. *Tel:* 07 658-4644 *Fax:* 07 658-4606. A slightly smaller and more friendly-size hotel than some others in En Boqeq. CP outside with two disabled persons spaces. Step-free to reception, bar, lounge and restaurant. Three lifts (D85 W130 L140). **Two adapted rooms** (numbers 319/321) with a sliding bathroom door D70, but no ST. What they had done was to replace the inward opening door with a sliding door on two standard bathrooms, and then called them adapted rooms. We were told that they have a special chair to put in/on the bath if required.

To get to the sea, there is a paved ramp to within 20m, and a gently sloping sandy approach. They have provided an interesting floating wooden platform with HRs to help people to get into deeper water. A new pool for Dead Sea water was under construction.
Top end.

P M ↑↓ ♿✕ ⬤R2

Hyatt Regency Resort and Spa, MP 89680, En Boqeq, Dead Sea, *Tel:* 07 659-1234 *Fax:* 07 659-1235. With 600 rooms, this claims to be the largest hotel in Israel, and is enormous. CP outside with disabled persons spaces some 40m from reception. There is flat or ramped access almost everywhere, but the place is big, so there are some quite long distances. Lifts (D100 W200 L200+) to all floors. We were told that there are **eight adapted rooms**, but we did not see one. We also did not find any wheelchair toilets in the 'public' areas.
Top end.

⌈P⌉ /D\ M ↑↓ ♿✕ ⬤ /R\ 8

Lot Hotel, MP 86930, En Boqeq, Dead Sea, *Tel:* 07 668-9200 *Fax:* 07 658-4623. CP outside with disabled persons spaces and a ramped kerb. A ramp bypasses +3 steps at the entrance. Lift (D95 W125 L200), plus a smaller one. Bar and restaurant on the GF. Step-free almost everywhere. **Five adapted rooms**, one on each floor. We saw room 836 with D70, bathroomD70, ST60, and a bath with HRs. Spa on lower floor with **wheelchair toilet and shower (D75 ST200+)**. To get to the sea there is a ramped path to within 10m of the sea, and then a sandy stretch.
Mid price to top end.

R5

Park Inn, En Boqeq, Dead Sea, *e-mail:* via yamith@netvision.net.il *Tel:* 07 659-1666 *Fax:* 07 658-4162. CP outside with two disabled persons spaces. Kerb [14cm] then it is step-free to reception, bar, restaurant (on the first floor), swimming pool and garden. Lift (D80 W150 L80). Two adapted bedrooms, but with inward opening bathroom D70, and some quite restricted gaps. ST to the toilet is obstructed by the basin. The shower door means that there is a gap of only W38 into the shower, even though it is flat. Removal of that door (and of the bathroom door) would improve things considerably.
Mid price to top end.

Tsell Harim Hotel, MP 96930, En Boqeq, Dead Sea, *website:* www.tsell-harim.co.il *Tel:* 07 658-4121 *Fax:* 07 658-4666. The hotel has an unusual design in that it is built as a recreational village. CP outside. It is a relatively low building with four floors, including the swimming pool, restaurant and bar. There is ramped access to all of these from outside, although the solarium on the top floor can only be reached via about 15 steps. The bedrooms are in eight separate bungalow blocks between the main building and the sea, and there is only **one adapted room** with bathroomD75, bath with HR but ST0. **Adapted cubicles (D68 ST100 men's; D60 ST100 inward opening door, women's)** in the toilets on the reception floor of the main building. The ramp to the sea stops about 10m short. There is a sandy stretch, then there is a ramp with HRs to a depth of about 0.8m.
Mid price to top end.

Newe Zohar

There are several hotels at Newe Zohar and more are under construction. They provide complete package on-site holidays, often including a 'kids club' or some such, as there is nothing else to do or see outside the hotel, unless you go off on a tour.

Grand Nirvana Hotel, MP 84960, Newe Zohar, Dead Sea, *e-mail:* info@nirvana.co.il *Tel:* 07 668-9444 *Fax:* 07 668-9400. A huge spa/resort hotel alongside the Dead Sea with nearly 400 rooms. CP outside. There's a small lip [2cm] at the entrance followed by step-free access almost everywhere to the lounge, bars, restaurant and swimming pool. The pool has ordinary water, and stepped entry. Lifts to all ten floors (D80 W130 L130). **Five superb adapted bedrooms.** We saw number 141 with D80, bathroomD80, and ST70 to the toilet. It had both a wheel-in shower and a bath with rails and a movable bench seat. These were amongst the best we saw anywhere. **Wheelchair cubicles (D70 ST70)** in the men's and women's toilets in the basement, near the lift.

Access is possible into the Dead Sea with some minor difficulties. After the paved path there is about 20-30m of gently sloping sand, and then in the water, there's a wooden ramp with handrails. The sea itself is pretty shallow.
Top end.

R5

PNA areas

There are relatively few places to stay in the PNA areas, and sadly, in some of the new buildings going up, access has not been considered. Bethlehem, Gaza, Jericho and Ramallah all have hotels, but we found few that were remotely accessible without problems.

Bethlehem

For accessibility, the Bethlehem Hotel is outstanding, although for location the Casa Nova Guest House is also worth considering. In Bethlehem you will get a much better feel for the place if you stay there, and wander around before and after the main tour groups have invaded.

Bethlehem Hotel, POB 1069, Manger Street, Bethlehem *website:* www.bethlehem-hotel.com *e-mail:* bhotel@p-ol.com *Tel:* 02 277-0702 *Fax:* 02 277-0706. A large hotel with 180 rooms built into the side of the hill. It is some 500m from Manger Square, which is further up the hillside, and so there's a bit of a climb near the square. Entrance +1 [20cm] step which can be avoided if you use the CP on the first floor. Lifts (D75 W120 L140) give step-free access to all the main facilities including the dining rooms, lounge and meeting rooms. **Six adapted rooms**, on different floors. We saw room 521 with D72, bathroomD85, a wheel-in shower and ST200+. The toilets near the dining room had **adapted cubicles (D80 ST100 but with inward opening doors)** in both men's and women's.
Mid-price to top end.

R6

Casa Nova Guest House, POB 996, Manger Square, Bethlehem *Tel:* 02 274-3981 *Fax:* 02 274-3540. In an ideal location, almost next door to the Church of the Nativity, and right at the top of the hill. Well worth battling with a few internal access problems for the benefit of being right on the edge of the Square. Entrance +2 steps from Manger Square, or step-free from the CP underneath via the lifts (D75 W110 L110). There is a small step [11cm] from the CP which can be bypassed. The lifts give step-free access to the restaurant and bar, and to some rooms. We were told that all the bathrooms were the same, and the one we saw in Room 407 (+3 from reception) had D70, bathroomD63 and an inward opening door to a shower

with a conventional tray. Removing the door would make it slightly better, but it was still somewhat cramped. In the men's toilets by the dining room there was a cubicle with D63 ST73.
Bottom end

Grand Hotel, POB 591, Paul VI Street, Bethlehem *e-mail:* Bandaks@pol.com *Tel:* 02 274-1440 *Fax:* 02 274-1604. Situated some 500m from Manger Square, and slightly further up the hill. Small UGCP. Entrance +8 steps, but we were told that these could be bypassed from the parking place. Flat to dining room. Two lifts (D70 W100 L100). Most bedrooms have a bathroomD60 (though easily capable of enlargement). There are some apartments with bathroomD70.
Mid price.

Paradise Hotel, POB 96, Manger Street, Bethlehem *e-mail:*paradise@pol.com *Tel:* 02 274-3769 *Fax:* 02 274-4542. 180 rooms and some 800m from Manger Square. CP across the road. Entrance +2+3 steps, but a portable ramp is available. Step-free to bar and dining room on the GF. Lift (D75 W100 L110). No specially adapted rooms, but we saw room 315 with D75 bathroom D60, and flat to a shower which was recessed/sunk by 4cm, allowing possible ST to the toilet. No wheelchair toilet elsewhere.
Mid price.

During 1999 when we visited, two large new hotel complexes were being built. These were the Jacer Palace Inerconinental on Manger Street, near Rachel's Tomb, and the Meridian, on a hilltop some way south of the town. Both will have top end prices.

Ramallah

Ramallah Hotel, POB 843, El Masoun Street, Ramallah, West Bank *website:* www.ramallahhotel.com *e-mail:* kaoud@bigfoot.com *Tel:* 02 295-3544 *Fax:* 02 295-5029. Apparently 'El Masoun Street' refers to all the streets in one of the suburbs, so it is not, perhaps, a very precise address. From the main street, go past the police station, and turn off down the slope. The third on the right has a sign to the Ramallah Motel, and you continue downhill to the hotel. Entrance +8 steps, GF restaurant, no lift and +21 to unadapted bedrooms. They claimed that there would be a lift and a swimming pool by 2000 as major renovations were planned.
Mid price.

Jericho

We looked at two new hotels in Jericho, but neither had made any provision for disabled guests, and accessibility had not been considered in the design.

Jericho Resort Hotel, Qasr Hisham, Jericho *Tel:* 02 232-1255 *Fax:* 02 232-2189 is just outside Jericho, near Hisham's Palace. A brand new hotel and bungalow complex, where, unfortunately, accessibility has not been considered in the design. CP outside. High kerb [20cm] leads to a ramp bypassing +5 steps. Lounge and dining room on the GF, and lifts (D75 W100 W130), but no adapted rooms/bungalows. We saw one room with D70, bathroomD65 and an inwards opening door, and virtually no ST space.
Mid-price.

Gaza

There are quite a number of new hotels, but, as yet, accessibility has not, generally been a design feature. The Beach Hotel had no lift and no GFBs.

The **Adam Hotel**, Al Rasheed Street, Al Meena *Tel/fax:* 07 286-6976; 07 282-3521. Parking outside. Entrance +6 steps. Then step-free to reception, lounge and restaurant with super views out over the Med. Lift (D68 W85 L180) to the five floors with bedrooms. There are many adapted rooms, but the adaptations vary considerably. One idea used by the management which makes the bathrooms much more accessible is the use of plastic folding concertina-type doors. These are a very neat way of minimising the intrusion of the door into the bathroom area. We saw several rooms, of which the 'best' were room 664 with bathroomD70, ST70+, impeded only by a slightly recessed shower tray (about 5cm down), and room 656 with bathroomD68, ST60 and level access to the shower.
Bottom end to mid-price.

[P] [◾] E6 [↕] [♿✗] [⌂] R5

Palestine Hotel, Ahmed O'Rabi Street, Gaza Beach *Tel/fax:* 07 282-3355; 07 282-3356. Parking outside. Entrance +1 [9cm] step. Then step-free to lift (D75 W110 L120) which goes to the bedrooms, but the dining room is via −26. Perversely there is an **adapted cubicle (D70 ST66)** in the men's toilets on the lower floor (down the 26 steps!), and this cubicle includes a bath with low sides [17cm], and a shower and floor drain. We were told that there were some adapted bedrooms, but we were unable to see them.
Mid price.

Tel Aviv

There is only a limited amount of reasonably priced and accessible accommodation. The youth hostel in the north has two adapted rooms, and there is the Center Hotel just by Dizengoff. Other accessible places are in the four and five star class and price-range. The Mercure is worth considering for value/accessibility. We have also included the Moss Hotel which we have used several times as it is well sited and reasonably priced. There are access problems detailed in the write-up.

Center Hotel, 2 Zamenhoff Street, Tel Aviv *Tel:* 03 629-6181 *Fax:* 03 629-6751. Ideally situated just off Dizengoff Square, so parking could be a problem. They have an arrangement with the CP for the Dizengoff Shopping Mall for overnight parking, but it will cost money. Parking hassles may be worth it for the very central location. Alternatively, don't bother with the hire car while you're there. Entrance +3 steps, bypassed by a ramp. Lift (D75 W125 L75) step-free from reception. Lounge area −3, and −15+2 from the 1st floor to the breakfast room. The management are happy, however, to bring your breakfast to your room, and eating out in the evening is no problem because of the central location. **Three adapted rooms** (105, 205, 305). Room 205 seen, D85, bathroomD85 and although ST0 because of the basin, there is adequate space in front of the toilet. All the rooms have a bath, with only minimal handrails, but the management plan to purchase a special chair to fit over the bath to facilitate showering for some.
Mid price.

Crowne Plaza, 145 Hayarkon Street, Tel Aviv 63453 *e-mail:* hicpta@netvision.net.il *Tel:* 03 520-1111 *Fax:* 03 520-1122, just north of the Sheraton, with seventeen floors (and therefore something of a landmark). Parking outside, and the concierge will park your car for you. Lifts (D80 W120 L145) provide step-free access to most facilities, although one of the two restaurants involves +8 steps. **Three adapted rooms**, number 115 seen, with D75, bathroomD75 and a wheel-in shower. ST was slightly obstructed by the basin, and there are no grab handles. Balcony with a 14cm threshold. To get to the beach, and bypass the −17, use a staff lift (D70 W150 L120) and then there's less than 100m across the sand to get to the sea.
Top end.

P M ↕ ♿ ✗ ⬤R3

Hilton Hotel, Independence Park, Tel Aviv 63405 *Tel:* 03 520-2222 *Fax:* 03 527-2711. A large hotel with seventeen floors which is easy to spot. Drive in through Independence Park to the CP around the main entrance. A ramp bypasses +1 step at the entrance. There are several bars and

restaurants on the GF, and access is step-free to all main facilities. Lifts (D105 W195 L130). **Four adapted rooms**, but we were unable to see any of them. We were told that they had both a bath and a floor drain, so it would be possible to use the flexible shower head outside the bath.
Top end.

HI Tel Aviv YH, POB 22078, 36 Bnei Dan, Tel Aviv 62260 *Tel:* 03 544-1748 *Fax:* 03 544-1030. Located in the north near the Yarkon River and near the junction with Brandeis. Street parking is relatively easy. A ramp at the front bypasses +5 steps. Flat to reception and dining room. There are steps to most of the bedrooms, but there are **two adapted rooms** (nos 5 and 6) which are off a courtyard with ramped access from reception. No 5 seen, D85 bathroomD85 ST100+ and a wheel-in shower. The room had four beds (two bunk beds). Contrary to some reports, there's café life and shops about 500m away in Yehuda HaMakabi.
Bottom end.

Lusky Suites, 84 Hayarkon Street, Tel Aviv 63432 *Tel:* 03 516-3030 *Fax:* 03 517-1047. Just south of the Sheraton and on the opposite side of the road from the sea. Therefore considerably cheaper! UGCP and step-free to lift (D80 W105 L150), or flat from the street. Café and bar on the GF with no steps, and **wheelchair toilet (D85 ST85)**. One adapted suite, No 102 with D75, bathroomD75, ST80 and a wheel-in shower with a 2cm lip. –1 [5cm] to get out on the balcony.
Mid-price to top end.

Mercure Marina Hotel, POB 3282, 167 Hayarkon Street, Tel Aviv *e-mail:* marina@mercure.co.il *Tel:* 03 521-1777 *Fax:* 03 521-1770. Towards the northern end of Hayarkon Street. No hotel parking, but there's a UGCP under the shopping mall with spaces near the basement level of the hotel, and with lift access to reception. The main hotel entrance on the beach side was being rebuilt when we visited, and our team found their way in from the shopping arcade. Flat access to reception. Lifts (D75 W135 L115). Bar and dining room on the first floor. **Two adapted rooms,** number 354 seen: D95 bathroomD75 ST85 with a wheel-in shower.
Mid-price to top end.

Moss Hotel, 6 Nes Ziona Street, Tel Aviv 63904 *Tel/fax:* 03 517-1655. A friendly and inexpensive hotel with a small CP on-site. Virtually the only way of approaching it by car is to come down Herbert Samuel from the north and turn left just past Planet Hollywood where Pizza Hut is. You then go across Hayarkon and turn left and left again. Entrance +7 steps. Small lift (D68 W144 L100) can take some chairs with footplates removed. The rooms have different bathroom designs, and some have direct access in from the bedroom, albeit through a narrow door. Room 315, for example, had D75, bathroomD58 and a bath with a seat at the back. Restaurant in the basement via −16. While the hotel is *not* accessible by most standards, it is centrally situated, good value, and if you can cope with the bathroom, quite practical for some. Our survey team used it.

Bottom end to mid-price.

Near the Mediterranean, going north

The main places of interest from an accessibility viewpoint are the Kibbutz Hotels at Shefayim, and Nes Ammim, just past Acre/Akko.

Kibbutz Hotel Shefayim, Kibbutz Shefayim (Shfayim), 60990 *e-mail:* shefayim@kibbutz.co.il *Tel:* 09 959-5595 *Fax:* 09 959-5555. Located 15 minutes drive from Tel Aviv and 35 minutes from Ben Gurion Airport. Approximately 200m from route 2, well sign-posted roughly 5km north of Kfar Shemaryahu, It is a substantial site with a conference centre and the adjoining Shefayim Water Park. It also has a popular private beach, which can make car parking difficult in the afternoons.

Step-free to the main facilities. There are **seventeen adapted rooms**. We saw room 135, with D80, bathroomD80, but ST only 38. It had a bath with an inflexible shower head.

Top end.

Netanya

Arches Hotel (Park Inn Suites), 4 Remez Street, Netanya 42271 *e-mail:* dalia.shaked@arches.co.il *Tel:* 09 860-9860 *Fax:* 09 860-9866. CP at the back of the hotel. Entrance +6 steps, bypassed by a side entrance to the left, en route to the CP. Step-free access to the room where breakfast is served. Lifts (D75 W110 L130). **Seven adapted suites**, and we saw numbers 821 and 841. The accommodation we saw consisted of a twin bedroom, sitting room and kitchen. It would be perfectly possible to put extra beds in the sitting room which would reduce the cost per person. BathroomD70, and although it opens inwards, there is reasonable space inside. Wheel-in shower and ST150+.

Mid-price to top end.

 R7

Haifa

Beth-Shalom Hotel, POB 6208, 110 Hanassi Avenue, Haifa 31061 *e-mail:* mail@beth-shalom.co.il *Tel:* 04 837-7481/2 *Fax:* 04 837-2443. Located opposite the large Nof Hotel in Central Carmel, this small but friendly hotel only has thirty rooms but **ten are GFBs**. Parking space outside and +1 step at the entrance. There is a lift (D75 W110 L114) to the restaurant in the basement. TV lounge +2–3. Room 101 seen, with D69, bathroomD70 and a bath but no ST.

Bottom end to mid-price.

Haifa Bayview Holiday Inn, 111 Yefe Nof Street, Haifa 34454 *Tel*: 04 835-0835, *Fax:* 04 835- 0836. This luxury hotel is set on the hillside of Mount Carmel with stunning views. CP with two disabled persons spaces. Entrance step-free. Restaurant on the GF with a view right over Haifa. The lobby area in front of reception is –2 but there are portable ramps. There are a hundred rooms over five floors served by two lifts (D88, W110, L150). Room 811 seen: D85, bathroomD85 with a 3cm lip, ST80. Bath with a fixed handrail. **Wheelchair toilet (D80 ST75)** on the GF.

Top end.

 R1

Nof Hotel, 101 Hanassi Avenue, Haifa 34642 *e-mail:* sl@actcom.co.il *Tel:* 04 835-4311, *Fax:* 04 838-8810. Set in the hills overlooking Haifa, The Nof Hotel is located on a main road almost adjacent to the Panorama Hotel/Shopping Centre Complex. Entrance +5 steps, bypassed by a steep ramp. Lounge and bar +3. Dining room is step-free. Three lifts. We saw room 104 with D70, bathroomD55. The hotel could be suitable for disabled walkers but would be difficult for a chair user.

Mid-price to top end.

Near Acre

Nes Ammim Mobile Post Western Galilee 25225 *e-mail:* ghmanager@nesammim.com *Tel:* 04 995-0000 *Fax:* 04 995-0098. Situated approximately 10km north of Akko off Route 4 and well signed. CP about 100m and step-free to reception, bar and shop. The +8 steps to the dining room can be bypassed by going up a slope outside and tapping on the window to attract attention.

There are **twenty-four adapted rooms** (nos 101-112; 301-312) all on the GF, in two separate buildings. We suspect that they weren't designed with access in mind but nonetheless they provide a valuable facility. Room 101 seen: D80, bathroomD75, but opens in, and past the toilet the maximum width is W68. ST is blocked by the basin but because the basin and toilet are down one side of the room, most chair users will be able to cope, though possibly with the door open. The bath has a handrail. The flexible shower head over the bath can probably be used over the floor space as there is a floor drain, and a 1cm lip by the door to prevent flooding the bedroom carpet. There are **wheelchair cubicles (D80 ST80)** in both the men's and women's toilets by reception.

There is a lovely big swimming pool about 100m from reception. It is reached via –1 [5cm] +1 [5cm] through a foot-cleaning bath, and has stepped access into the pool itself.

Nes Ammim is one of the few accessible hotels in the region, and particularly with three beds in a room provides good value. It may be worth booking dinner in advance, as there's nowhere nearby to go out and eat. The kibbutz to which the hotel is attached is working for reconciliation between Christians and Jews. If you're interested, they will tell you about this, and take you for a kibbutz tour (which is virtually step-free).

Mid-price.

 R24

Lohamei Hageta'ot Country Lodging, Kibbutz Lohamei Hageta'ot, Bait Vakait, Western Galilee 25220, *Tel:* 04 993-3271, *Fax:* 04 993-3218. The Kibbutz is well sign posted from route 4, just north of Akko. Enter through the gates, turn immediately left and follow the signs. The CP is outside on rough ground; there is then a 60m walk along a concrete path to the office, which has +1 [5cm] step then ±1 [15cm] threshold. There is cabin-type accommodation (in separate buildings), with no adapted rooms at the time of our visit but we were told that there will be two, possibly during 2000, although plans had yet to be finalised.

Bottom end to mid-price.

Nahariya

Carlton Hotel, POB 124, 23 Haga'aton Street, Nahariya *Tel:* 04 992-2211 *Fax:* 04 982- 3771. About 50m from junction with Golomb Street, with some on street parking. The entrance is ramped, bypassing +4 steps. Step-free to the bar and restaurant. Lift (D80 W110 L140). Room no 323 seen with D78, bathroomD69 inward opening; no side transfer because of the bidet is in the way. Our surveyors didn't think this was one of the adapted

rooms offered by the hotel.
Mid-price to top end.

Erna Hotel, 29 Jabotinsky Street, Nahariya *Tel:* 04 992-0170 *Fax:* 04 992-8917. The hotel is 150m from Steinmete Street, there is on street parking outside with a dropped kerb [5cm]. The entrance is flat. The lift (D80 W115 L105) is –6 steps from reception, on the dining room/bar level. Room 101 seen which is a GFB, step-free from reception, D70, bathroomD60, ST85 with a bath. Other rooms are reached via the –6 and the lift. **Unisex wheelchair toilet (D80 ST120)** on the left hand side on this level.
Bottom end to mid-price.

Hotel Frank (Days Inn), 4 Haaliyah Street, Nahariya *Tel:* 04 992-0278 *Fax:* 04 992-5535. Located 20m from David Ela'Zar Street. There is on street parking with a 10cm "dropped" kerb. Entrance ramp (80cm wide) bypassing +6 steps. There are a further +6 (not ramped) to the bar and restaurant. The hotel has two GFBs step-free from reception. We were told that one of these was adapted, but we were unable to see it. The swimming pool is across the road via two kerbs.
Mid-price.

[P][A][◾]N6

Sol Marine Hotel, Haaliyah Street, Nahariya *Tel:* 04 995-0555, *Fax:* 04 995-0556. The last building on this street at the far northern end of town. CP outside, and a +1 [15cm] kerb, unramped. Entrance with +8 steps which are ramped. Step-free to the bar. Lifts (D90 W130 L160) to the dining room and bedrooms. There are **two adapted rooms**. Room 202 seen with D75, bathroomD90 and ST65, with a 3cm lip into the shower. There is a ±1 [9cm] threshold to the balcony.

The pool is –8 from the lobby, but it can be reached step-free from the street by going through the gate just to the left of the main entrance. The gate also gives step-free access to the beach, but it was locked when surveyed. **Adapted toilet (D85 ST55)** with a fixed handrail by the pool, reached via a ramp behind the water slide.
Mid-price to top end.

[P][A][↑↓][&X][●]R2

North of Nahariya

Kibbutz Gesher Haziv Country Lodging, Western Galilee 22815 *Tel:* 04 995-8568 *Fax:* 04 982-5971. Just 4km north of Nahariyia off route 4 and clearly signed to the right. The site consists of a number of chalets built onto a hill, and consequently there are some steepish paths. CP by the tennis court. The office was not clearly signed but is to the left of the path as you leave the CP. **One adapted room** (number 16) with step-free access, and a big bathroom with a wheel-in shower: D85 bathroom D85 ST100. From the main part of the site there are +25 steps to the dining room. An alternative way of getting there is to use the 'top' road. It involves leaving the CP, turning right and right again at the roundabout, then follow the road round to the large green fuel tanks, it is then the fifth turning on the right. It's about 1.4km, but gives you step-free access for breakfast! Bed and breakfast only.

Bottom end to mid-price.

Shlomi YH and Guest House, Shlomi, Northern Israel *Tel:* 04 980-8975 *Fax:* 04 980-9163 is only a few km from Rosh Hanikra in northern Israel. Off the 899, take the turn to Harita (north), and then turn right through a new housing estate. The redbrick hostel stands out overlooking the valley. CP outside. Flat to reception, and to the dining room via a lift (D70 W95 L110). **There are three so-called adapted rooms** with a cramped and badly designed bathroom. D75, bathroomD75, ST0. There's a narrow gap about W80 past the basin to the wheel-in shower D70 with a 90° turn. There is no way that a chair user could turn around in the space, and the provision is disappointing in such a relatively new building. Level with the dining room on floor −1 there are **adapted cubicles (D80 ST50)** in the men's and women's toilets.

Bottom end.

Galilee and around the Sea of Galilee

The write-ups start in Nazareth and the surrounding area. This is followed by accommodation on or near the Sea of Galilee (Lake Kinneret) starting at the northern end, then Tiberias, the southern end, and the holiday villages on the eastern side. Finally, it covers Western Galilee towards the Mediterranean, and the northern part of Israel, towards the Lebanese border.

There is quite a wide range of places with 'accessible' rooms with various degrees of adaptation made. The ones that we would highlight beacuse of particular access/value features are the Karei Deshe Youth Hostel; the Nof Ginossar Kibbutz Hotel and Inn; Ma'aleh Gamla Country Lodging; the Galilee Hotel in Nazareth and Kibbutz Lavi. Many other places are described with their various advantages and disadvantages. We did not manage to find any remotely accessible accommodation in Zefat (which is a difficult place for access because it is built on a steep hillside) although the youth hostel is said to have two adapted rooms.

Nazareth

Galilee Hotel, 65 Paul VI Street, Nazareth *Tel:* 06 657-1311 *Fax:* 06 655-6627. It claims to be the oldest hotel in the Middle East, and Winston Churchill (among other famous people) slept there. About 500m from the Basilica, down the hill, and at the other end of Paul VI Street from Mary's Well. On street parking. Entrance +1 step [18cm]. Three lifts (D80 W110 L140). **Six adapted rooms**. Room 231 seen: D75, bathroomD75 but opens in; ST40. There's a good shelf at the back of the bath for transfer. Meeting room and restaurant on first floor: step-free. **Adapted cubicle (D75 ST53)** in the men's toilets in the restaurant.

The arrangement of the hotel souvenir shop and bar is interesting. You get there, following the signs from the first floor, via ±1 [25cm] and –20 steps. It is in fact a shop just to the side of the main hotel entrance, so the easiest way to get there is via –1 to the street and +1 into the shop and small bar. The shop offers substantial discounts to hotel guests, much as it does to other customers we suspect.

They are building another floor on top of the existing hotel, and we left them with the outline design for an accessible bathroom with a wheel-in shower. The management said that they were planning to include at least three such rooms in the new development.
Bottom end to mid price.

Sisters of Nazareth Convent (Religieuse de Nazareth), POB 274, No 3 Street 306, Nazareth *Tel:* 06 655-4304 *Fax:* 06 646-0741. There is a guest house as part of the convent. It is some 100m from the main entrance to the basilica, and level with the main entrance. Go up Casa Nova Street and turn left opposite the basilica entrance. Flat through the car entrance. Small CP for three cars. Small lift (D75 W100 L90) to the dining room (with +1 [10cm] step), and bedroom +1–1 with bathroomD60. There is one small dormitory –6, with showers and toilets with D55. The guest house is friendly and atmospheric, and an ideal location for visiting the basilica and souq. Some chair users might cope (at a pinch, and with some help), but it is better suited to disabled walkers.
Bottom end.

St Margaret's Guest House, Orfaneg, Nazareth *Tel:*06 657-3507 *Fax:* 06 656-7166. A really nice place with a superb view over the town, but the

whole area is extremely hilly, and you will need transport to get in and out of town. A steep slope down off Salesian Street up near the St Gabriel Monastery, leads to a large CP. Ramped bypass through the main entrance leads to a lovely courtyard with quite rough flagstones. Entrance +2 steps to reception, with seven bedrooms then step-free. Although the bathrooms are quite small, by the main entrance there are two **adapted toilets/showers (D67 ST90, although the door opens in there is room for most chairs)**.
Bottom end to mid price.

There are a number of other hotels, some of them quite expensive, like the Marriott, but none are within walking/wheeling distance of the Basilica or of the town centre.

Near Nazareth

Kibbutz Hasolelim, D.N.Hamovril, near Nazareth. *Tel:* 06 640-6506 *Fax:* 06 646-3060. Well signposted off route 79, just south of the junction with route 77. A track runs round the outside the site so it is possible to park within 10m of everything. When we visited, reception was in a Portacabin, but the manager uses an electric scooter, and so is well aware of access issues. Restaurant 100m from rooms down a gently sloping, smooth path: flat access, with movable tables and chairs. **Three adapted rooms**, about 50m from reception down a gently sloping, smooth path. Room 41 seen: bathroomD80, ST80 and a wheel-in shower. There are plastic chairs in the room which could be used in the shower. The beds can be varied in height. Shops nearby.

Mid-price.

En Route to the Sea of Galilee

Kibbutz Lavi Hotel, Lower Galilee 15267 *website:* www.lavi.co.il *e-mail:* lavi@lavi.co.il *Tel:* 06 679-9450 *Fax:* 06 679-9399. It is the only Orthodox Jewish kibbutz hotel in the Lower Galilee. It offers programmes and seminars for groups interested in understanding Judaism and the kibbutz way of life, and brings groups of Christians and Jews together to study. CP outside. Entrance 30m from CP and +4 steps, bypassed by a ramp. From reception there are +3, bypassed by a ramp to the lift (D75 W100 L125). **Twelve adapted rooms**. Room 302 seen: D80, bathroomD75 (inward opening but lots of room), ST80. Bath with a movable shower head. Restaurant +3 (ramped) from the lift and slightly congested. **Wheelchair**

cubicles (D88 ST85) in both men's and women's toilets on the GF. A new block is planned and will include more adapted rooms.
Mid-price.

R12

Around and near the Sea of Galilee

The listing in this section is arranged in geographical order, starting to the north of the lake, and going southwards on the west side first, and then back northwards on the east side.

Amiad Kibbutz Country Lodging, Galilee *Tel:* 06 693-3829 *Fax:* 06 690-9307. The kibbutz is well signed off route 90 just north of the Amiad junction with route 85. The lodging is signed to the left, inside the kibbutz entrance. Gravelled CP. Reception +1 [17cm] step, but it is not always staffed, and there is a phone inside to contact the duty manager. There are twenty-four simple chalets, and guests use the kibbutz facilities. **Three adapted rooms/chalets**, numbers 22-24 near reception. We saw no 23: D80, bathroomD75 ST90+ and a wheel-in shower with a slightly recessed shower tray [3cm] in the ST space. The whole site is fairly flat and well paved. The shop is about 200m away with a ramped bypass to +3. The dining room is a further 100m, and step-free. Another 100m and you find the swimming pool with a step-free entrance on the far side, furthest away from the dining room. You come first to the children's pool and then to a steep narrow (W60) ramp bypassing +5 to the main pool. There's an alternative gate with just −1 giving access to the grass by the main pool, nearer the dining room. Stepped access and a handrail for getting into the pool.
Mid-price.

R3

Vered HaGalil Guest Farm, Korazim Junction, Galilee 12340 *website:* www.virtual.co.il/travel/travel/vered or www.veredhagalil.co.il *e-mail:* avni@canaan.co.il or vered@veredhagalil.co.il *Tel:* 06 693-5785 *Fax:* 06 693-4964. On the road towards Korazim, just off route 90 and well signposted. From the signposted CP there are +4 steps to the main building, but there is a step-free route from an adjacent parking space (take the turning just before the one marked CP, if you are coming from route 90). It is 30m over crazy paving to reception with +2 steps. Step-free to restaurant. **Rooms 11 and 12 are described as accessible** with wheel-in showers, good ST and parking outside. Both are "cabin style" like all the others. They are across the road from the main building. From the main building you can walk around the farm step-free. To the pool, there is a steep slope and −4, but you can also drive round. At the top of the slope (about 60m from reception across the lawn) is a toilet block which has a **wheelchair**

toilet (D85 ST80) and a wheel-in shower (entrance 75cm) Mid-price.

Karei Deshe YH, MP Korazim 12365, Galilee *Tel:* 06 672-0601 *Fax:* 06 672-4818. Situated approximately 12km north of Tiberias on route 90, well signed. It is a big new youth hostel that does not (yet) have any adapted rooms. Large CP outside. A steepish ramp bypasses the +6 steps up to reception. The hostel has a wonderful feeling of space, and is built close to the edge of the Sea of Galilee. Step-free to the self service dining room. There is also a substantial bar built overlooking the lake. A grassy slope leads down to the shoreline.

There are **two unisex wheelchair toilets**, one **(D90 ST120)** is to the left of reception on the GF, the other is on the 1st floor **(D70 ST100)**, reached via the lift (D80 W105 L140).

GFBs numbers 7,8,9,16,17 and 18 can be reached via ramps. Room 18 has an open area to sink with separate toilet and shower adjacent to each other. Door to walk in shower 60cm, door to toilet 60cm, access to sinks, toilet and shower 95cm. First floor has flat access to rooms 37-46. **They say that they are going to adapt two of the GF rooms to improve access to the toilet and shower. The changes mean making the door to the toilet/shower wider and removing the dividing wall, thus making enough space for a chair user to move around. This would make the hostel really good for access, and we hope that this will have been done by the time we publish.**
Bottom end.

[P][A][↕][♿wc][♿✗](▲)R2 (planned)

Nof Ginosar Hotel, Kibbutz Ginosar, Galilee 14980 *e-mail:* ginosar@netvision.net.il *Tel:* 06 679-2161 *Fax*: 06 679-2170. Situated on the edge of the Sea of Galilee some 10 km north of Tiberias, and a good centre for touring. CP outside. Ramped kerb and flat entrance. Step-free via the lifts (D75 W110 L135) to all major facilities. **Wheelchair toilet (D80 ST100)** on the first floor near the restaurant. **Eight well-adapted bedrooms** with D75+ and bathroomD75+, ST90+. The bathroom has a bath with a movable wooden bench: really helpful for people getting in and out. Wheel-in shower as well. Swimming pool outside: step-free. Water about 25cm below the edge, and stepped access with a handrail, into the water. It is possible to swim in the sea, but only after crossing more than 80m of rough gravelly sand.
Mid-price to top end.

Nof Ginosar Inn, Kibbutz Ginosar, Galilee 14980 *e-mail:* ginosar@netvision.net.il *Tel:* 06 679-8762 *Fax:* 06 672-2991. Close to the hotel, the inn offers simpler and less expensive accommodation. The inn has +1 step [9cm] to reception. The buildings are spread around the site. Paths are generally flat, with smooth, but slightly variable surfaces. **There are many GFBs and six adapted rooms**. We saw room 28 which had a ramped entrance, D70, bathroomD85, ST70 and a wheel-in shower. Others were being built to similar criteria. All rooms have self-catering facilities. You may have to take breakfast in the hotel 100m away.
Mid-price.

Tiberias

Caesar Resort Hotel, 103 The Promenade, Tiberias 14202 *Tel:* 06 672-7272 *Fax:* 06 679-1013. On the right, through the public CP, as you go down Hayarden Street towards the Lake. Eight disabled persons parking spaces by the drop-off point at the front. Entrance +4 steps, bypassed by a ramp. Reception area flat with three lifts (D80 W140 L125). Bar and restaurant +3, bypassed by ramp to right of lifts. No adapted rooms. Room 718 seen: D78, bathroomD57, ST0, due to bath and inward opening door.
Top end.

Gai Beach Hotel, Hamerchazaot Road, Tiberias *Tel:* 06 670-0700 *Fax:* 06 679-2776. On the left as you leave Tiberias on route 90 to the south. CP directly outside. Entrance up a kerb [13cm], then step-free to reception. From reception there is ramped access to lobby and lift (D100 W130 L140) to all floors, including the restaurant. One GF room seen: D85 bathroomD80 and inward opening, ST130, bath with movable shower head. The small balcony with wonderful view of the lake has a 2cm lip.
Top end.

Holiday Inn, PO Box 22, Tiberias 14100 *Tel:* 06 672-8555 *Fax:* 06 672-4443. 1.5km south of Tiberias on route 90. Fifteen disabled persons parking spaces outside the main entrance (chained off when we visited). Step-free to reception, ramped to lifts (D85 W105 L140). Flat access to restaurant by the lifts. **Seven adapted rooms**. Room 461 seen: fairly spacious with bathroomD80, ST60.
Top end.

Jordan River Hotel, HaBanim Street, Tiberias 14201 *Tel:* 06 671-4444 *Fax:* 06 672-2111. In the town centre, 100m from the promenade. CP by the side of the hotel, with three disabled persons spaces 20m from the entrance. There's quite a steep ramp up from the road, and reception is effectively up at 1st floor level. Entrance +5 steps, bypassed by a ramp. Flat to reception, with plenty of seating, and to two restaurants. Lifts (D75 W170 L100) to rooms. **Eleven adapted rooms**. Room 208 seen: bathroomD70, ST0. **Adapted cubicles (D67 ST85)** in both men's and women's toilets on the level below the lobby, from where there is also ramped access to the pool. To get to the toilets from outside, go up the ramp, into the main lobby. The lifts are straight in front of you, past the hotel reception desk on your right. Take either the one on the left or the one on the right, and NOT either of the central ones. Go to level −1, and the restrooms are well signed.

Mid-price to top end.

R11

Radisson Moriah Plaza Hotel, PO Box 375, HaBanim Street, Tiberias 14103 *Tel:* 06 671-3333. *Fax:* 06 679-2320. In the town centre 100m from the promenade. Three disabled persons parking spaces by the main entrance (chained off). Step-free to lobby and lifts (D80 W140 L120). Restaurant and bar −3 steps, bypassed by a ramp. **Four adapted rooms claimed**. Room 524 seen: bathroom D66, ST0. There is a tight 90° turn into the bathroom. A chair will be provided to go into the bath if requested. Top end.

R4

At the southern end of the Sea of Galilee and on the eastern side

Alumot Kibbutz Country Lodging, Alumot, Sea of Galilee *Tel:* 06 665-3494 *Fax:* 06 670-9790. Situated some 3km from the Sea of Galilee off route 767, the kibbutz has built some thirty small family units. They are just above sea level with superb views over the (sunken) Jordan Valley and Lake Kinneret. CP outside. Reception is +5 steps from the CP and is at the end of the parking area. There is flat access to reception if you come down the path behind the dining room. The dining room is an old kibbutz building with +4. There are **ten adapted units**. No 406 seen with +1 [5cm] at the entrance, D70 and bathroomD66 opening inwards. Access for a chair user is complicated by the use of two hinged shower doors. With a little determination and flapping of doors, transfer, washing and showering are possible, much of it with the door open. If they had used shower curtains and made the door open out the provision would have been much better.

The bungalow units have twin beds and a sitting room with two settees which can turn into temporary beds. To get to the swimming pool, go right past the pool, some 400m from the CP, and down a sloping tarmac path to a gate which you may have to get opened specially. If you ignore the 'no passing cars' notice, you can park off the path and just by the gate, making the whole exercise rather easier.
Mid-price.

[P] [H] [A] [⌂]R10

Degania Bet Country Lodging, MP Jordan Valley, Kibbutz Degania Bet, 15130. *Tel:* 06 675-5758/5660 *Fax:* 06 675-5877. Degania Bet was the first kibbutz, established in 1909 and now in the silicon business. Follow the signs for "First Kibbutz" or "Tank". The lodging is in converted kibbutz buildings spread out for about 150m. Drive past the tank on your right and follow signs for reception. **Three adapted rooms**. Room 21 seen: entrance +1 [14cm] step, D75+, bathroomD85, ST90, with a wheel-in shower. Room 6 also seen: with +1 [8cm], bathroomD85 ST70. The dining room is 150m from reception on the flat. Ramped entrance, bypassing +2 and an **adapted toilet (D75 opening in, ST70).**
Mid-price.

[P] [D] [♿WC] [♿X] [●]R3

Maagan Holiday Village, Jordan Valley 15160 *website:* www.inisrael.com/maagan *e-mail:* maaganhv@netvision.net.il *Tel:* 06 665-4400/11 *Fax:* 06 665-4455. Just to the east of the junction of routes 90 and 92 and well signed. CP outside. Ramped kerb and flat to reception. It is about 30m to the back entrance of the restaurant, which is flat. The resort isn't yet finished, but there are presently **two adapted rooms**, nos 108 and 109. D85, bathroomD73, ST110 with both a wheel-in shower and low bath with a seat. Steep ramp from bedrooms to beach and pool, soon to be bypassed by a lift.
Mid-price.

[P] [D] [H] [●]R2

Ha'on Holiday Village, Ha'on, Sea of Galilee *Tel:* 06 665-6555 *Fax:* 06 665-6557. A simple lakeside holiday village, just off route 92, with about forty chalets and a restaurant. As elsewhere, swimming in the sea isn't easy. There are +4 steps to the restaurant, bypassed by a ramp. **Ten of the chalets are adapted for disabled guests**, with a (temporary) ramp for the +2 at the entrance. We were told that the bathroom had an outward opening door D70+ with a wheel-in shower with a curtain. The shower space provides ST for the toilet. There was a group of disabled people using the facilities when we visited, and that was why we were unable to see a room. There is accommodation for up to four people in each chalet. **Wheelchair cubicles**

(**D70 ST70**) in both men's and women's toilets by the restaurant. Mid-price.

 10

Golan Rooms, Sagi Farm, Moshav Ramot, Sea of Galilee 12948. *Tel/Fax:* 06 673-1814. Inside the Moshav, about 2km from the green gates at the entrance, which is 2km from route 92. It is well signed from the green gates: follow the arrows on the Hebrew signs over the "Golan Rooms" signs. CP outside the farmhouse/reception: 20m walk and +2 steps. Breakfast is served upstairs, and there is no lift. **Two adapted cabins** (numbers 7 and 8) with ramped entrance, D85, bathroomD80, ST120, and a wheel-in shower. Flat to pool and **wheelchair toilet** (not seen). Self-catering.
Mid-price.

Ma'aleh Gamla Country Lodging, Golan, Northern Israel *Tel/Fax:* 06 673-2430. Described by Arik Vamosh, who is a wheelchair user, as a 'jewel of a country lodging that specialises in accommodating disabled guests'. There are two cottages, and plans for two additional units. **The rooms, bathrooms, showers and other facilities are all designed for special needs visitors.** The addition of a heated swimming pool, jacuzzi, sauna and treatment room is planned during 1999. It sounds really good, although our survey team failed to find it and so we didn't visit.
Bottom end to mid-price.

Western Galilee and towards the Lebanese border

Peki'in YH and Guest House, Peki'in, Northern Israel *Tel:* 04 957-4111 *Fax:* 04 957-4116. The village is on the 864 and also called Bukei'a. It is not the village a little way north called Peki'in Khadasha. The village is predominantly inhabited by Druze, but according to tradition, there was a Jewish community there who had never been exiled, right up to 1936. The hostel was opened in 1998.

If you come from the north along the 864, the hostel is remarkably well signed at every junction. Small CP outside with a ramped kerb. The hostel is built on a hillside. Access has been considered, and there are ramped bypasses to steps. The lift (D85 W110 L140) leads to other floors. The dining room is reached via an open lift (W80 L90) to bypass –10 steps, but it is tested only twice a year (see comments about small lifts in the *Design*

advice chapter). There are **three adapted rooms**, but the bathroom layout was very poor considering the space allocated – which was generous. BathroomD75 opens inwards and there is ST30. No attempt had been made to provide ST because of a large horizontal shelf into which the basin was recessed. The wheel-in shower had D70 and a 90° turn. It's all usable, but could have been so much better at no extra cost. Disappointing in a brand new building.
Bottom end.

Sde Nehemya Country Village, Galil Elion, Northern Israel 12145 *Tel:* 06 694-6010 *Fax:* 06 694-7449. A group of just ten chalets located 5km off route 918 in the Hula Valley near the Lebanon border. No adapted rooms, but all the rooms are on the GF, as they are in bungalows, and the bathrooms seem to be generously sized. Reception is just past the restaurant, 100m from the main entrance. Uneven grass stretch to get to bungalows. Room 2 seen: +1+1 steps at the entrance, bedroom with double bed and bunkbed. BathroomD77, ST 90. Step-free to restaurant. Uneven path from restaurant to the bar with –2.
Mid-price.

Kfar Blum Kibbutz Guest House, Upper Galilee 12150 *Tel:* 06 694-3666/695-9441 *Fax*: 06 694-8555. Located off route 90 to Kiryat Shmona, turn right at Gomeh Junction onto route 977, then first left to Kfar Blum on Route 9778. Two disabled persons spaces in the CP. Step-free access to reception, shop, bar and restaurant. **Six adapted rooms** out of the twenty-one GFBs. Room 61 seen with D83, bathroomD83 ST160; a wheel-in shower and a bath. Unisex **adapted toilet (D90 ST60)** just past reception. The management seemed both aware and helpful about the requirements of disabled travellers, and can possibly borrow extra equipment if guests have special requirements.
Mid-price.

Kfar Giladi Kibbutz Guest House, Upper Galilee 12210 *Tel:* 06 690-0000 *Fax:* 06 690-0069. Situated halfway between Kiryat Shmona and Metula in the far north. This information is based on our 1988 visit, confirmed by telephone. The area is hilly, and there is a CP outside. Facilities in the main building are on two floors. Entrance flat. Reception, bar and dining room on the GF. **Two adapted rooms** (numbers 80 and 85) with spacious bathrooms; bathroomD75 and ST75+. These are in chalets a little way from the main building, but step-free. There is a wheelchair cubicle in the women's toilets near reception. The place was generally very

wheelchair friendly when we visited, and the manager at the time was a chair user himself.
Mid-price.

Hagoshrim Kibbutz Hotel, Hagoshrim, Upper Galilee *e-mail:* hotel-hg2@hagoshrim.org.il *Tel:* 06 681-6000 *Fax:* 06 681-6013. Off route 99 between Kiryat Shmona and Hermon, about 5km from the junction with route 90. Gently ramped from CP to entrance, from where there is step-free access to the bar and restaurants. **Unisex adapted toilet (D75 ST50)** at the back of the lobby by the reception desk. **Five adapted rooms**, of which four are in the new block, including 2 GFBs. Room 1315 (GF) seen: D80, bathroom D80 but inward opening (a chair user in our team only just got in) ST95. There was a wheel-in shower and a low sided bath (H40).

The hotel swimming pool is about 200m downhill from the main hotel reception area. It is down a path which is steep in places, though there is car access to it. The **wheelchair toilet (D90 ST120)** by the pool is used as a store cupboard.
Mid-price.

The Negev and Eilat

Be'er Sheva

Beit Yatsiv YH and Guest House, 70 Ha'atzamut, Be'er Sheva *Tel:* 07 627-7444 *Fax:* 07 627-5735. There is only a tiny sign outside, and Ha'atzamut is one way. To reach the CP, go on around the British Military Cemetery, going left, left and left again, and you come past the back of the hostel. It is not at all obvious! From the CP there is ramped access throughout the site. It is about 50m to reception. The youth hostel is in one group of buildings (and it cheaper to stay in) while the guest house is in other buildings, and is somewhat more expensive.

The **Youth Hostel** has some GFBs, with no steps, which might be suitable for a disabled walker.

The **Guest House** is some 80m from reception, and has **nine adapted rooms**. The adaptations vary. Room 309 had a sliding bathoomD75, a wheel-in shower, a toilet with ST100+. Another adapted room had a shower cabinet in it restricting wheelchair access, and ST to the toilet. It is step-free to the dining room which is behind reception.
Bottom end to mid-price.

Desert Inn, POB 247, Sederot Tuvyahu, Be'er Sheva *website:* www.desertinn.hotel.com *Tel:* 07 642-4922 *Fax:* 07 641-2772. When we came to Israel for the first time in 1978, the Desert Inn was the only hotel which we found in Israel with adapted rooms. These are now being modernised and improved, and **we were told that there will be four adapted rooms when renovations are completed**. CP outside, and also parking outside the adapted rooms which have a ramped entrance. Step-free to reception, bar and restaurant – and also to the swimming pool. The pool has a stepped entry, with HR, and there is a nearby large changing cubicle and a **wheelchair toilet (D100 ST150+)**.
Mid-price.

Mitzpe Ramon

Mitzpe Ramon YH, Nahal Ela Street, Mitzpe Ramon *Tel:* 07 658-8443 *Fax:* 07 658-8074. CP outside, with ramps to bypass +8 steps. Small lip [3cm] at the main entrance. Step-free to dining room. About ten GFBs including **one well adapted bedroom (no 104).** It has D75, bathroomD70, and a huge area inside including a toilet (ST200), wheel-in shower and a basin.
Bottom end.

Eilat

In Eilat, the hotels are split into three areas. The largest group are on the North Beach, but their address in the IHA listing disguises the fact that some are on the seafront, some are in the next row back, and a further line are in a row further back again. The second group of hotels is on the far side of the airport runway, and the third (including the youth hostel) is on the road running south towards the Coral Beach.

Crowne Plaza Hotel, North Beach, Eilat *Tel:* 07 636-7777 *Fax:* 07 633-0821. The hotel backs on to the marina, and there is a steep slope up from the road (Kamen Street) to the main entrance, but one disabled persons parking space near the door. Step-free access to all the main facilities, including the bar, dining room, lounge and pool. **They claim to have four adapted rooms**, but we were not able to see one.
Top end.

Eilat YH, Hahandassa, Mitzrayim Road (next to the Club Hotel), *Tel:* 07 637-0088/637- 2358 *Fax:* 07 637-5835. The hostel is on the right as you go

south towards the coastal road from the Tourist Information Office. There is a CP outside. At the main entrance there are +19 steps to the lift (D75 W90 L150) which takes you up to reception. The hostel is, however, built into the side of a hill, and **there is a way round the back giving step-free access to reception**. You have to go further down the road towards Taba (south), past the Dortel Sol Hotel. Take the first road to the right, then first right again. Where the tarmac road turns left, go straight on, and you will find the back of the hostel – where it is possible to park – just past the rear wall of a small open-air amphitheatre. You have to go up a steep rough track to get there, just before two pylons carrying high-voltage electricity. Once at the back of the hostel (to walk, it would be over 500m from the front entrance), there are two step-free entrances to reception and to the TV room area. **Two rooms near reception are adapted (nos 11/12) with D78 and a 1cm lip. They have bathroomD78, ST80, and a wheel-in shower.** There are ten other rooms on the same level with no steps. The lift mentioned above goes down to the dining room.
Bottom end.

[P][A][&x][⌂]R2

Eilat Four Points Paradise Hotel, Kamen Street, North Beach, Eilat *Tel:* 07 630-4444 *Fax:* 07 633-2348. Street level parking with disabled persons spaces 40m from the hotel entrance which is up a slope. The hotel is compact, and is in the second row of hotels behind the north beach. The bar, dining room and pool can be reached step-free. There are **eight adapted GFBs** close to the main facilities. Five have wheel-in showers. We saw room 1101 which had a sliding bathroom door (D90), and was spacious inside, although strictly ST was 0 as the toilet was partially recessed. There are many other GFBs.
Mid-price to top end.

[P][/H][M][&x][●]R8

Holiday Inn Patio, 3 Shfifon Alley, Eilat, 88000 *Tel:* 07 636-4364 *Fax:* 07 634-0118. On the west side of town. One disabled persons parking space by the main entrance. Step-free via lifts (D90 W120 L200) to all the main facilities, including the bar, dining room and pool. **One adapted room**, number 102: D80, bathroomD80 and ST70. **Wheelchair toilet (D70+ ST70+)** but the basin in the ST space means you can't a chair get right back to the wall.
Mid-price to top end.

Mercure Mirage Hotel, 3 Hativat Hanegev Street, Eilat 88000 *e-mail:* Mirage@mercure.co.il *Tel:* 07 638-2333 *Fax:* 07 638-2301. On the west side of town. UGCP with three disabled persons spaces and step-free via

two heavy doors to lifts (D80 W120 L160). Step-free at the main entrance, and to all main facilities, including the pool. This has the water level almost up to the edge, and wide steps into it for children and others. **Four adapted rooms** near the lifts. One seen: D80, bathroomD80 but limited ST space. It had a bath and overhead shower, but no support or grab rails. On level –1 there are **adapted cubicles (D65 ST60)** in both men's and women's toilets.
Mid-price to top end.

Nova Hotel, 6 Hativat Hanegev Street, Eilat 88000 *Tel:* 07 638-2444 *Fax:* 07 638-2455. On the west side of town. It is an 'all-suite' hotel which can be somewhat expensive for just one or two people staying, but the suites can sleep four or even five people, it can be good value on a per head basis for that number. Main entrance +2 steps, but with a ramped bypass to the right. UGCP with step-free access to the lifts (D80 W120 L180). Step-free to the main facilities, including the bar, dining room and pool. The pool has water up to the lip, and stepped access for children and others. **Three adapted suites**. Room 540 seen, with D80 bathroomD80 ST60, and good rails on the bath. If needed, and with some hassle, there are step-free wheel-in showers in the employees' washrooms on level –1.
Mid-price to top end.

Palmira Hotel, Kamen Street, North Beach, Eilat 88000 *Tel:* 07 636-6000 *Fax:* 07 633-7279. In the second row of hotels behind the North beach, and opposite the Crowne Plaza. Step-free access to all the main facilities, including the bar, dining room and pool. **We were told that there are four adapted rooms**, accessed by lift (D80 W120 L200).
Top end.

Radisson Moriah Plaza Hotel, North Beach, Eilat *Tel:* 07 636-1111 *Fax:* 07 633-4158. Steepish slope up to the hotel entrance. CP outside, but about 80m away. One disabled persons space near the entrance, but with a very steep kerb ramp to negotiate. Step-free access to the main facilities with the ramped route to the main pool at the east end, bypassing –9 steps. **There are said to be two adapted rooms** on the first floor, but we were unable to see one. **Wheelchair cubicles (D80 ST70)** in both the ladies and the gents in the east wing, to the left of reception, but ST is slightly obstructed by projections.
Top end.

Red Sea Four Points Paradise Hotel, Kampen Street, North Beach, Eilat *Tel:* 07 636-3636 *Fax:* 07 636-3630. Step-free at the entrance, and to the main bar and dining room. +3 to a small central coffee bar. There is a gentle slope down to the pool. **One adapted bedroom** number 188: with D70, bathroomD75, ST60.
Top end.

Kibbutz fly-drive packages

Many of the larger tour operators provide fly-drive packages using kibbutz hotels which can be particularly appropriate for small groups of people where one or more member is disabled. Those offering fly-drive are listed on p55. Prices depend on when you go, on the size of car you choose and the level of the accommodation you use. Consequently you need to put together some sort of plan, and the travel operators will quote you a price. Be particularly careful if you want to go to places like Bethlehem and Jericho (and other parts of the PNA areas) as several of the hire companies do not provide insurance cover for this. Eldan and Petra certainly do provide cover, but they are not fly-drive package partners – so you may even be better off, if you want flexibility and freedom, making your own bookings directly.

We got the brochures from most of the operators, and this revealed quite a variety of provision. They use different car hire companies, and offer a narrow or a wider choice of kibbutz hotels that you can stay at. Some of the operators do put indicative prices in their brochures. Of the ones we got, Pullman have prices and outline the car hire restrictions. They do not use all the hotels, and in particular do not use Ramat Rachel near Jerusalem. Longwood have prices for two, three or four people sharing, and use a wide range of hotels. Peltours offer small hire cars to those aged 21+, and larger ones to those over 24. The Israel Travel Service sent us the best map and probably the widest choice of kibbutz accommodation. They did not include any prices nor details of insurance restrictions for car drivers.

There are a good number of kibbutz hotels and country inns that have adapted rooms, and we have described many of them earlier in the chapter. The number of adapted rooms is quite limited, so you'd probably be advised to book before setting out. Information is available from **Kibbutz Hotels Chain Ltd**, 1 Smolanskin Street, POB 3193, Tel Aviv 61031 *website:* www.kibbutz.co.il *e-mail:* yael@kibbutz.co.il *Tel:* 03 527-8085 *Fax:* 03 523-0527 (reservations *Tel:* 03 524-6161 *Fax:* 03 527-8088).

Key locations with good adapted rooms (in our view) are Ramat Rachel for Jerusalem, Nof Ginosar (hotel and country inn) for Galilee,

Nes Ammim for Acre and the coast, Shefayim for Tel Aviv and Ein Gedi for the Dead Sea. Most are quite expensive, and if your budget is tight you might consider booking youth hostels and hiring the car independently.

The Kibbutz Hotels map is excellent, and has a local street plan for finding each hotel/inn, which can be invaluable. To get one you may have to ask specifically. It is called *'The Map of the Israel Kibbutz Hotels Chain – The 30 Location Vacation'*. We got one from the Israel Travel Service, but no-one else sent us one. The information which we were given by the Kibbutz Hotels Chain Ltd towards the end of 1999 was as follows:

Kibbutz hotel	Rooms for chair users
Kfar Giladi*	2
Hagoshrim*	5
Kfar Blum*	6
Ha'on Holiday Village*	10
Maagan Holiday Village*	2 + adjoining rooms
Nof Ginosar*	8
Nes Ammim*	24
Nir Etzion	6
Nasholim	5
Shefayim*	17
Neve Shalom	2
Maale Hachamisha*	3
Ramat Rachel*	2
Almog*	3
Kalia*	1
Ein Gedi*	6
Hafetz Haim	1

* full description earlier in the chapter

The difficulty with this information, useful though it is, is that the listing does not depend on any kind of criteria relating to the design of the 'rooms for chair users'. On the basis of what we have seen – and we have visited about two-thirds of the Kibbutz hotels listed – the standards really are quite variable. If your requirements are not too exacting, then the list is a good starting point.

Kibbutz Country Lodging

Afik	1
Marom Golan	2
Ortal	2
Amiad*	3
Kfar Sold	2
Manara	4
Parod	2

Alumot*	10
Ashdod Yaacov Ichud	1
Degania Bet*	1 + 1
Sagi Farm – Moshav Ramot*	3
Gesher Haziv*	1
Harel	6
Mashabei Sade	5

* full description earlier in the chapter

In addition there is the kibbutz country inn at Nof Ginosar*, considerably less expensive than the hotel.

Youth hostels

The information we were given by the Youth Hostels Association in September 1999 is that there are at least two rooms for disabled persons at the following Youth hostels:

Tel Hai, Galalee	*Tel:* 06 694-0043 *Fax:* 06 694-1743
Safed/Zefat, Galilee	*Tel:* 06 692-1086 *Fax:* 06 697-3514
Shlomi, Galilee*	*Tel:* 04 980-8975 *Fax:* 04 980-9163
Karei Deshe, Galilee*	*Tel:* 06 672-0601 *Fax:* 06 672-4818
Peki'in, Galilee*	*Tel:* 04 957-4111 *Fax:* 04 957-4116
Tel Aviv*	*Tel:* 03 544-1748 *Fax:* 03 544-1030
HaDavidka, Jerusalem	*Tel:* 02 538-4555 *Fax:* 02 538-8790
Masada*	*Tel:* 07 658-4349 *Fax:* 07 658-4650
Be'er Sheva*	*Tel:* 07 627-7444 *Fax:* 07 627-5735
Mitzpe Ramon*	*Tel:* 07 658-8443 *Fax:* 07 658-8704
Eilat*	*Tel:* 07 637-0088 *Fax:* 07 637-5835

On the basis of our visits (and those marked with a * have a full description earlier in the chapter), we would add the following:

- in Jerusalem in particular, the information is misleading. HaDavidka is not accessible without steps (there are +6 to get to the lift), and no adapted rooms. Better options are Beit Shmuel and the new Rabin YH. The Louise Waterman Wise YH on Mount Herzl is potentially suitable for disabled walkers as it has a good number of bedrooms which can be reached step-free. The bathroom doors are all too narrow for a chair user, with W55-60;

- both Masada and Mitzpe Ramon hostels only have one adapted room;

- Karei Deshe had no adapted rooms when this list was put together, and will only have them if they follow up our suggestions made some months ago (see text on p97).

Jerusalem

> The chapter covers:
> - **The Old City** with its Moslem, Jewish, Christian and Armenian quarters
> - **Outside the City Walls**, including Mount Zion
> - **East Jerusalem**, including the Mount of Olives and Mount Scopus
> - **West Jerusalem**
>   the city centre, and area north of the Jaffa Road
>   western suburbs, including Givat Ram
>   southwestern suburbs, around George V, David Street and Keren Ha-Yesod
>   western outskirts, including Mount Herzl

Although its name means 'City of Peace', Jerusalem has probably been destroyed and invaded more often than any other city in the world. It has, however, been tenaciously restored and rebuilt after every conquest. **It is *the* Holy City, sacred to the followers of three major world religions, and a place of quite extraordinary diversity.** Its current status is the matter of continuing controversy and discussion between Israelis and Palestinians.

Many of the important shrines and places of interest are in the Old City. Here you will find the *Al Aqsa* mosque, and *Dome of the Rock*, sacred particularly to Moslems; the *Western Wall* of the Temple, sacred to Jews and the *Via Dolorosa* and *Church of the Holy Sepulchre* of special importance to Christians. There's the Arab souq (market) with its narrow passages and inviting shops. No visit is complete without a bit of bartering and bargaining. In addition, there's the extensively rebuilt Jewish Quarter.

There is also much to see outside the Old City, both in the western (Jewish) area and the eastern (Arab) part. If your time is limited, the Old City is the place to go first. In our view, no visit to Jerusalem is really complete without going to Yad Vashem, the Holocaust Museum, and to the Mount of Olives which played such an important part in Jesus' life, and from which there is a magnificent view over the Old City and the Dome of the Rock.

If you're worried about **driving in Jerusalem**, and about finding your way through the poorly signposted maze of streets, then the ideal time to arrive is on Friday evening or early on Saturday morning. Everything in the new city is shut, and there is very little traffic. You can learn to navigate the main boulevards and junctions in some peace, and you'll feel much happier doing it later in the week. When there's plenty of traffic, you do need to be quite sharp (and defensive). Signposting is not good, and the names are quite small and on green backgrounds. Watch out for the 'bus lane only' signs and 'no entries' which are not always easy to spot. As Jerusalem is quite small, and many of the places to visit are in the Old City which is almost entirely a pedestrian area, you may prefer simply to leave your car at the hotel and use taxis where necessary. The location of your accommodation then becomes particularly important.

Navigating in some of the outer suburbs can be a bit of a challenge, because the maps do not mark the hills. If you have a good navigator, you'll be fine. Note that the road past the Damascus Gate, Sultan Suleiman Street, is nearly always full of traffic and pedestrians. Just edge gently along, and keep smiling, and again, you'll be fine. If you want to drive around the walls of the Old City, remember that the section from the Dung Gate to Zion Gate is one way only, and in that direction. If you come the other way from the Jaffa gate, past Sultans Pools and up to the Zion Gate, then you'll get no further.

The street names used in this write-up are largely the same as those used on the Jerusalem City Map with a yellow cover, published by Map – Mapping and Publishing. This has a street directory and grid system for finding out where places are. As we have mentioned elsewhere, various different spellings are used for the same street/place, sometimes based on phonetics, and sometimes on a different language (generally Hebrew, Arabic or English).

Views of Jerusalem

The classic view over the Old City is that from the Mount of Olives. Go there early in the day if possible, when the sun shows off the white stone at its best. In the afternoon, the shadows make it look rather washed out. You can approach the viewpoint just below the Seven Arches Hotel, either by coming up the steep road from Gethsemane, or from Shmuel ben Adaya, turning right at the top along the ridge. In either case, when you reach the junction with the sign to the Carmelite Monastery (just past the Church of the Ascension, and by the Mount of Olives Bazaar) turn RIGHT to get to the viewing point. The view over the Jewish cemetery, and towards the Old City is stunning. When we visited early in 1999 the site was being enlarged and rebuilt in anticipation of the large numbers of visitors expected in 2000.

Another spectacular viewing spot is the **Hass Promenade**, East Talpiyot to the south of the city. It is near the UN Headquarters and at the junction between Alar Street and Razi'el Street. It views the Old City from a different angle, and looks straight across at Al Aqsa. The route is badly signed, and the way we found it was to go down past the Jaffa Gate underpass, and keep going straight over four sets of lights. There's an S bend at the bottom of the valley, and you follow the Hebron Road past the

Mount Zion Hotel. Carry on until you see a sign for Gilo at a set of traffic lights, then go straight on until you reach two sets of lights very close together. At the second set (just past no 42 on your right), go LEFT up the hill and past a new Israeli housing development. Then finally, LEFT again at the lights (currently a bit of a wilderness area), and it's then about 700m on your left. Large CP. We are reliably told that there is an adapted toilet at the western end of the promenade.

The **Promenade Restaurant** is immediately below the Hass Promenade, with ramped (and car) access to the right. You can have a snack or a meal while enjoying the view. We are reliably told that there is now an adapted toilet in the restaurant.

From the top of Mount Scopus there are fine views of the wilderness towards Jericho. There is a good observation point for both old and new Jerusalem, at the top of Gershom Scholem Street at the Wall of Life by the corner of the Hebrew University. Just 50m away is the Gerald Halbert Park and Observation Plaza looking towards Jericho. Although very recently built, access was not considered, and the ramps are covered with a coarse gravel which is particularly difficult for chair users. You can see quite a lot from the tarmac road.

Information

Tourist Office, Saffra Square, 17 Jaffa Street *Tel:* 02 625-8844. This is the only official tourist information office and is run by the Jerusalem Municipality. It is in City Hall at the end of Jaffa Street. UGCP accessed off Shivtei Yisra'el. This has several disabled persons spaces, and lift access from levels 2, 4 and 6. The Tourist Office is some 100m off Jaffa Street, and ramped access is possible by going almost up to the wall towards Kheshin. Go up the slope, and at the top, you have to bear to the right. The tourist office is further back from the road, and this route is about 150m long. All that they have is general tourist information and virtually no knowledge about access or access issues. The public toilets nearby in the new City Hall do not include adapted cubicles.

The **Christian Information Centre**, Omar Ibn el Khattab Square, Jaffa Gate, POB 14308, Jerusalem 91142 *e-mail:* cicinfo@cicts.org *website:* www.cicts.org *Tel:* 02 627-2692 *Fax:* 02 628-6417. It is just inside the Jaffa Gate, and opposite David's Citadel. As the name implies, this is the information centre of particular interest to Christian visitors. Good for opening times and events, and for contact details of those running particular shrines and churches. Entrance +2+9 steps, and a door W65cm. The **Franciscan Pilgrims Office** operates from the same office, and they can provide certificates relating to a completed pilgrimage, and are also the organisation to apply to for tickets for the Midnight Mass each Christmas in Bethlehem.

There are three useful post offices:

Post Office, 23 Jaffa Street, *Tel:* 02 624-4745, opposite City Hall, has two entrances +2 or +3 steps. One is ramped, with a 90° turn.

Post Office on the corner of Saladin Street and Sultan Suleiman Street, and opposite Herod's Gate. Entrance +8 steps.

Post Office, Omar Ibn el Khattab Square, Jaffa Gate, Old City. It is just past the Christian Information Centre and next to the entrance to Christ Church. Entrance +2 steps.

The Old City

Jerusalem covers over 100 sq km, and the walled city occupies less than 1% of this. The present walls, built in the 16thC enclose less than half of Jerusalem as it was before its destruction in 70CE, but it includes many places of vital importance to Jews, Christians and Moslems. **The City is divided into four 'Quarters'**, the largest of which is the Moslem Quarter. In addition, there is the newly rebuilt Jewish Quarter, the Christian Quarter and the Armenian Quarter.

The main problem in visiting the Old City is that it's built on the side of a hill, and unless you follow particular routes, there are steps everywhere. There are also some crowded passages, and a few spots where there are large drain gratings set in the paving. We have made a Step Map (see pp22/23), and if you start at the right gate/s, and know where to go, then access problems can be minimised and virtually all steps avoided.

Depending on where you want to go, a taxi to just inside the Dung Gate, St Stephen's Gate or the Zion Gate will put you on to what we have established as **the 'step-free route'** round the Old City. If you start at the Jaffa Gate, go along the road to the right, past the Citadel. It is fairly smooth and only up a gentle slope, leading round to the Zion Gate. The route/s for a chair user are clearly shown on the map, and are marked in colour. **The step-free route goes from the Dung Gate and up El Wad towards the**

Damascus Gate (with a spur to St Stephen's Gate). At the Damascus Gate it leads you back along Bet Ha-bad alongside the Souq to the Jewish Quarter, from which you can leave, or enter, via the Zion Gate. The area by the Western Wall is well paved, but El Wad has a more uneven surface, and is up a significant slope to the Damascus Gate. The route in from St Stephen's Gate also has some slopes. From the Damascus Gate, Bet Ha-bad is fairly level, but it is narrow, and can get very congested. A lot of patience may be needed. If it's busy, keep smiling, and keep cool. There are a few large sunken drainage grids on the route, particularly in El Wad, and these can be a hassle, as the groove width is much the same as that of the tyre on most wheels. Make sure that you approach the grooves at a 45° angle.

Note that the step-free route takes you past the inside of the Damascus Gate. To get in and out of the Old City at this point involves long steep slopes and some steps (see the Step Map).

Using this step-free route will enable you to visit virtually all the key sites/sights in the Old City. If you start at the top and work down (this means from the Zion Gate), you will first visit the rebuilt Jewish Quarter, and then go through part of the Arab Souq past the Church of the Holy Sepulchre. Carrying on through the Souq, you turn sharp right at the Damascus Gate, and El Wad will take you down to the Western Wall plaza, and to the gate that gives access on to Haram al-Sharif. Note, however, that if you want to go up on to the mount, the advice we give is to 'go early'. Depending on how many days you have in Jerusalem, you might want to go to the Dung Gate first, and visit the mosques on top of the Mount. You could then take a taxi round to the Zion Gate, and complete the rest of the tour going downhill most of the way, back either to the Dung Gate or to St Stephen's Gate.

Moslem Quarter

The Moslem Quarter comprises Haram al-Sharif/Temple Mount, most of the Souq and also the areas round Herod's Gate and the Damascus Gate which are residential and full of flights of steps. It can be entered from the Damascus Gate, Herod's Gate or St Stephen's Gate. At the Damascus Gate there is a substantial hill, and although there is a ramp outside, it is really quite a hassle getting down to the junction between El Wad and Bet Ha-Bad. There are steps and steep slopes. Via Herod's Gate there are a considerable number of steps, and again, you are going down a considerable hill.

One of the most interesting aspects of the Old City is the living community there with schools, clinics and other services. The **Moslem souq** is full of small shops selling the food and goods necessary to maintain that community, as well as the shops which cater for the tourist and visitor. Do take the time to eat in one of the small restaurants, and enjoy the atmosphere of the places selling spices and fruit.

Haram al-Sharif/Temple Mount (Har HaBayit) dominates the Old City. It is the site of both the Hebrew/Jewish Temples, the second of which was destroyed by the Romans in 70CE. The mount is a massive raised platform built on a low hill on the eastern side of the city. The only remaining part of Herod's Temple is the **Western Wall**, which is the holiest religious site for Jews, described in the section on the Jewish Quarter.

On top of Haram al-Sharif (the Noble Sanctuary to Muslims) are the **Dome of the Rock**, and the **Al-Aqsa Mosque**, the third and fourth most holy sites in the world for Muslims. Tradition links the hill on which the Temple was built with Mount Moriah on which Abraham offered his son Isaac as a sacrifice, although Muslims believe that it was Ishmael, not Isaac, who was offered for that sacrifice. The rock which is now under the Dome is traditionally the place from which Mohammed ascended at the end of his life, and is thought to be the rock of Abraham's sacrifice. It may therefore be the site of the Holy of Holies of the Second Temple, and orthodox Jews will not enter because they might inadvertently trespass on to that area.

One of the hassles in terms of visiting Haram al-Sharif is the seemingly slightly capricious visiting times. The principle is that the area is open to visitors, except during the hour/s of prayer, on Fridays (the Moslem holy day) and at festival times. **The principle 'go early' definitely applies** here, and the site is normally open from 08.00 until 15.00, apart from the time for midday prayers. During Ramadan it is only open from 07.30 to 10.00. It can be a problem if you arrive shortly before one of the chucking out times. As it is a large site it takes some while to clear everyone out, and you may have to leave through an exit with steps. Note that you need to have bought a ticket (from the kiosk near the entrance) to get into the mosques.

The walled temple mount area is huge, measuring some 300 by 500m. There are gates into the area on both the west and north sides, but **the official entry point for non- Moslems is Bab al-Magharibeh (the Morocco or Moors Gate)**. This is reached from the Dung Gate to the south of the Western Wall. It is up a smooth steepish slope of about 100m with 1+1+1+1+1+1 shallow steps [15cm] towards the top and a ±1 threshold. There is a security check en route. There is step-free access through Bab al-Asbat, by St Stephen's Gate on the opposite side of the site and you can leave through any of the gates, except just before the site is being closed to visitors.

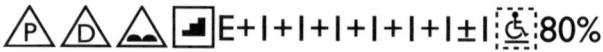

Once on Haram al-Sharif, and coming from the Moor's Gate, there are step-free routes all the way round. **A good plan is to visit Al-Aqsa and the Islamic Museum first, and then to go round and see the Dome of the Rock and some of the other smaller remains of Mamluk buildings on the site, finally leaving on the other side of the Mount, through Bab al-Asbat.**

The Dome of the Rock is built on a raised plinth, with several different flights of steps (around +20 or +25) leading up to it. There is, however, a ramped path on both sides of the plinth with a gentle slope, and if you go up to the northern side (the far side from Al-Aqsa), there is a ramp which bypasses these steps, providing a step-free route on to the raised platform. **The route/s are shown on the Step Map**.

One of the difficulties in the past relating to visits by disabled people to the mosques has been the question of wheelchair access. Most visitors to the mosques take their shoes off at the entrance, both as a mark of respect (it is common practice in many people's houses as well), and leaving outside the 'dust off their feet' when entering a holy place. As a result, there is a possible problem for both wheelchair users and for those with a prosthesis or artificial leg or foot. In discussion with the Islamic authorities, we found that they were very understanding of the difficulties, and that they in fact welcome those in wheelchairs. We include a copy of a letter written by Adnan Husseini who is the administrative head of Awqaf affairs in Jerusalem, saying that those in wheelchairs are welcome to visit the mosques. The letter is included in full on p21 while the main part and an English translation is shown below.

لمن يهمه الامر

يسمح للزوار اللذين بحاجة الى كراسي متحركة للتنقل داخل الحرم الشريف بالدخول مع الكراسي الخاصه بهم، وسوف تقدم لهم كل مساعدة من قبل العاملين في الحرم الشريف لتسهيل الزيارة.

10th October 1999/29 Jamadi El-Akhar 1420

To whom it may concern. Visitors who use wheelchairs are allowed to enter the mosques of Haram Al-Sharif with their wheelchairs, and move around inside. They will be given any necessary assistance to make their visit easier by the workers there.

Adnan Husseini, Director of Awqaf and Islamic Affairs, Jerusalem

Additionally, for those to whom it may be helpful, two wheelchairs are placed inside the mosques, for the use of someone with a prosthesis (for example) or anyone who would find them a help in getting around inside when in stockinged feet.

The **Al-Aqsa mosque** has −1 step at the entrance, although you can see quite a lot from the doorway. It is entirely step-free inside.

The **Islamic Museum** is in the south-western corner of the site, near the Moor's Gate entrance. +3 steps to the forecourt, then +3−3 at the entrance. Exhibits are around three split levels divided by −4 and −2.

To get into the **Dome of the Rock** there is +1 step, a ±1 [20cm] threshold, and −1, all of which are quite shallow. Inside there are thick carpets, and it is flat throughout apart from −16 to a small grotto, the 'Well of Souls'.

The whole area on Haram al-Sharif is wonderfully atmospheric, and photogenic, and it is really good to get away from the two main sights, and just sit down in the shade somewhere and admire the variety in the architecture and scenery. A few areas, such as Solomon's Stables and the parts around the Golden Gate are off-limits to non-Muslims, but don't worry, as there will be guards around to advise.

The Muslim quarter also includes much of the **Via Dolorosa** which is the traditional route along which Jesus carried his cross from the Roman fort to where he was crucified. It is where many pilgrims come, to pray and reflect, along the 'Way of the Cross'. As can be seen on the Step Map, this involves at least 75 steps, not counting those which are involved in getting into any of the chapels en route. The formal site of the last stations is inside the Church of the Holy Sepulchre, and the 12th and 13th, for example, involve 18 very difficult (large, steep) steps. However, for many of the larger processions, for example on Good Friday, the generality of the route is followed, but the remembrance is undertaken in places where a crowd can gather – thus making access easier. You will still encounter a good number of steps en route.

Just inside St Stephen's Gate is **St Anne's Church**, and the **Pools of Bethesda** *Tel:* 02 628-3285 *Fax:* 02 628-0764. You can get a taxi round to St Stephen's Gate, or get there from the Via Dolorosa (see the Step Map). The pools resulted from damming a stream, and between 150 BCE and 70

CE a popular healing centre developed nearby. The church is a place where pilgrims can be confronted by Jesus' question "Do you want to be well?".

Ramped entrance, and the –1+2 steps past the ticket office can be bypassed by keeping to the left. Inside there is a flat paved courtyard. **On the right is the church**, reached via –1+2 with a small ±1 threshold [+12cm–3cm]. We are told that this entrance has now been ramped.

A little further on are the excavations, with the remains of a Crusader church, some pagan baths, and the traditional site of Jesus' healing of the paralytic. There are good plans of the remains both in the leaflet you get at the ticket office, and near the site itself. About 80% can be seen from the step-free parts of the paths going around the compact site, and there's a special observation point with a ramped bypass to the +3. If you want to see more, there are +1–7 going one way round, or –8 going the other, and then, in either case, you will find that there are up to 30 steps down to the lower parts of the site. **We are told that there is now a disabled persons toilet on the site**, but this was added after we had visited.

Jewish Quarter

The Jewish Quarter is effectively on two different levels. The upper, residential part is approached from the Zion gate, while the central focus is the Western Wall of the Second Temple. This is much lower down, and approached from the Dung gate, or down nearly 80 steps from the upper residential area. The Wall is the last relic of Herod's Temple, destroyed by the Romans in 70CE, and is overlooked by towering and massively redeveloped buildings clinging to the hillside. There are six huge candles on one side commemorating the six million Jews who died in the Holocaust.

Lower part

Western Wall (Wailing Wall). This is *the* most important Jewish shrine, on the side of a large plaza, slightly sloping down from the Dung Gate and from the Jewish quarter side. There is a taxi drop-off point inside the Dung Gate entrance. Whichever way you approach the Wall, you pass through an airport-type security check There are no steps from the Dung Gate or coming down El Wad (see the Step Map p22/23). In front of the gently sloping wide-open square which faces the Wall, there are two clearly marked synagogue areas, one on the left for men, and the other for women. Around the back of the plaza there is a low wall, suitable for sitting on if you just want to watch. As there's a significant slope down towards the Wall itself, you can get a really good view, even if you're sitting. By the barrier separating the plaza from the synagogue area it can get pretty crowded, and there's an irritating +1 step just before the fence, so a chair user may have a poor view from there.

The Wall is an interesting place at sundown on Friday, the start of *Shabbat*, or on any of the major festival days. It is effectively a great open air synagogue, and to one side is the women's section of the prayer place, and to the other (the larger area) is the men's. There's something going on all the time, and men can go down to the wall, provided they put on a yarmulke/kippa (black skull cap). Women can go into the smaller section alongside. To the side of the men's prayer area is **Wilson's Arch**, and a tunnel running alongside more of the wall. The arch is inside a narrow room running some 30m alongside the wall. The room is lined with Jewish scripture books and prayer manuals. Halfway along, on the right is an illuminated shaft, protected by a grille which goes down about 10m. It is possible to get an idea of the full height of the original Western Wall. The area is step-free throughout.

On the far side of the plaza from the Dung Gate are **toilets with adapted cubicles (D70 ST60)** in both the men's and women's, which are on either side of the exit to El Wad and at the top of the ramp leading down to the men's side of the synagogue.

Western Wall Tunnels (Kotel Tunnels). These are run by the Western Wall Heritage Foundation, 2 HaOmer Street, Old City, Jerusalem 97500 *website:* www.hakotel.org *Tel:* 02 627-1333 *Fax:* 02 626-4828. **Visits to the tunnels have to be booked in advance**, and as there are some access problems, chair users may have to be quite insistent that arrangements are made. The problem is simply that tours go through every twenty minutes. Chair users can only go about half-way, and there is a perceived problem associated with the fact that, while leaving, they are going back to the entrance against the flow of the next batch of visitors. In our brush with the bureaucracy, we found that it was essential to have clearly made arrangements, preferably confirmed in writing.

The entrance to the tunnels is just to the left of the entrance to the Western Wall prayer area. The office where you collect your tickets is at the back of the plaza about 100m away through the door with a large red box outside.

The route through the tunnels is about 600m long, with some roughish surfaces. Most is fairly flat. As outlined above, chair users can only get about half-way as the last stages of the route are through an ancient and very narrow (W50) aqueduct.

From the entrance, after about 100m of rough ground, the tour uses a tiny 'theatre' with fixed seats overlooking a model of the Second Temple. The layout of the tunnels, and what you will see, are explained. The route then goes via –10 and –18 steps, both bypassed by platform stairlifts and then a further +5+7 also with stairlifts. This brings you to the closest point to the Holy of Holies in the old temple, and there is a prayer place similar in principle to that by the Wall outside, where Jews can leave prayers on a slip of paper, putting it in the gaps between the stones. From this point, chair users have to go back, since there is another 350m to go, with gaps of W50 en route and +18+9 and +40. You also go over some wet and slippery glass panels in the floor (they are there to help you see the lower parts of the wall) and finally meet a completely immovable two metre high turnstile near the end. The turnstile is a solid piece of engineering designed to stop people slipping in via the exit.

It's a fascinating visit, and you can see one single foundation stone for the walls which weighs well over 500 tonnes. How such stones were put precisely in place some 2500 years ago remains a mystery For wheelchair toilets, see the write-up above.

Upper part

The rest of the Jewish Quarter is some 25-30m higher than the Western Wall plaza, up the hill (see the LP p160, map 9). The upper part of the Quarter can be approached either from the Zion Gate, or by using the step-free route up El Wad from the Western Wall and back past the Souq, *see* the Step Map. **The Quarter has been largely rebuilt since 1967**, following substantial destruction during and after the 1948 war. It covers much of the area between the Zion Gate and the Dung Gate, and there is a CP just off the perimeter road inside the walls, with one disabled persons space. This CP gets extremely crowded, and the approach road from the Zion Gate is often blocked. As in the other Quarters, there is a living community there, with shops, schools and other supporting services. There's a lively atmosphere around the shops and cafés.

All the sights listed below can be reached step-free from Hurva Square, although many of them have steps inside. Surfaces can be a bit rough as some of the new streets have shallow drain channels in the middle and all have been surfaced with rough white stone blocks. Beyond Misgav Ladach Street there are nearly –80 steps to the Western Wall, and there is a stepped area towards David Street. The streets which can be reached step-free are shown on the Step Map p22/23.

There is a **unisex wheelchair toilet (D88 ST124)** in the public toilets on Plugat Ha-Kotel Street, about 10m from the Jewish Quarter Road and the Cardo going towards Hurva Square (marked in the LP map). Go through the unmarked door on the right-hand side as you enter. There is another **unisex wheelchair toilet (D80 ST70)** in the entrance to the women's section of the toilets opposite the Burnt House on Tiferet Yisrael Street.

If entering from the Muslim Quarter, there are three parallel step-free passageways. These are narrow and often crowded, and are in the covered area of the souq. The central one leads to the **Cardo,** the old Roman collonaded street. All shops along this involve at least +2 steps at the entrance, and there is no exit at the far end, so you'll have to come back to the David Street end. In the centre of the Quarter, **Hurva Square** is the main focus, and it has been restored in keeping with the traditional style.

A prominent feature is the arch of the **Hurva Synagogue,** which was destroyed in the 1948 war. To get inside the synagogue from Hurva Square there are +12+13 steps, and from the Jewish Quarter Road there are +7+4+2 +1+2. The arch is clearly visible from the square.

⬛ E25/16

Under the ruins, reached round the back, is the **Ramban Synagogue,** which was established c1400 and was used for many years as a workshop before being reinstated as a synagogue after 1967. Entrance –7+1. Inside is step-free, the narrowest gap being 70cm.

⬛ E8

Wohl Archaeological Museum, Ha-Karim *Tel:* 02 628-3448, contains excavations of several Roman and Herodian era houses. During the period 37 BCE to 70 CE, Jerusalem prospered, and this was an exclusive residential area, evidenced by some of the exhibits. Entrance +1 step to the ticket office, then –16–6 to the upper complex of the excavations. Then –8–8 to the shop and lecture room, and a further –3 to the middle complex, with more remains and finds. The southern buildings are a further –5 and the route leads down –4 rough steps, with an 80cm gap at the bottom. From here there are –2 to the House of Columns, and the exit is –4–4, or –1–1 via a ramp. You come out part-way down the hillside, and there are about +50 back to Ha-Karim in the upper/residential part of the Jewish quarter.

⬛ –50+50 ⚠

Temple Model, 79 Misgav Ladach *Tel:* 02 626-4466. Part of the Hechal Wohl Convocation Hall of Yeshivat HaKotel. Small exhibition of scale models of what the temple, tabernacle, temple vessels and religious items might have looked like. Entrance +1 [15cm] then flat throughout. Unadapted toilets (D49 ST0).

The Burnt House, 73 Tiferet Yisrael *Tel:* 02 628-7211. An excavated house belonging to a Jewish priestly family. The extensive signs of burning suggest that it was destroyed in the Roman Siege of 70CE. Entrance –26 steps, bypassed by a **platform stairlift (W80 L90)**. At the bottom, the archaeological remains are clearly visible, as is the audiovisual presentation in six languages: headphones are provided if you don't speak Hebrew.

War of Independence Memorial, corner of Jewish Quarter Street and Lohang Harova Bi Tashah Street. A small room, which you can see most of from outside. To get in, there are +1–7, steps, the +1 being particularly awkward as you go straight down afterwards.

Four Sephardi Synagogues. Alongside the CP by the perimeter road. Dating from the 16thC, they were built partially underground to comply with restrictions on worship at the time. They have been restored with items from various ruined European synagogues. Entrance –11–12 steps from the CP area, where there is one disabled persons space. Thereafter, there is step-free access to all four synagogues. An exhibition of photographs of the synagogues before 1967 is –5 and in a darkened area.

■E23N5

Jerusalem in the First Temple Period Exhibition, Rachel Ben-Zvi Centre, Shone HaLakhot Street, *Tel:* 02 628-6288. Opposite the Israelite Tower. The centrepiece is a 3D slideshow around a topographical model of Ancient Jerusalem. Entrance +2, then to the slideshow it is +1 [25cm] and down a narrow (W58) mock-up tunnel. **The easiest way in for a chair user is via the exit** about 20m to the right of the entrance. This route bypasses all steps, all narrow gaps and most uneven surfaces (except a 3cm lip). Chair users can see the screen and models clearly from the left-hand side of the screen. Unadapted toilets in the tunnel.

Israelite Tower, opposite the above. Entrance –10 steps, and there are a lot more before you see anything, We couldn't ascertain where to buy tickets: you can't get them on the door. If you fancy, you can have a row about it in French with the stroppy guy on the door. We did just that, but learned nothing.

There is a **'Wheelchair Friendly' trail around the Jewish Quarter**, which is signposted reasonably well. Information about it is available from the **Hymie Moross Community Center,** Misgav Ladach Street *Tel:* 02 628-3777 *Fax:* 02 626-0194. There is a booklet and map, but we were unsuccessful in getting them to send it to us, despite three telephone requests. We paid three visits to the Centre while in Jerusalem, but they were always closed, and we obtained a copy or the map by chance, from a friend who had managed to call in when they were open. Opening times are clearly dependent on Jewish holidays. The tour is said to take you as much as 2km. It starts in the CP and goes down the Jewish Quarter Street to the edge of the souq, and then back up the Cardo, which is a dead end. You then retrace your steps back to Plugat Hakotel Street, going along Bonei HaChoma and then Tiferet Yisrael Street. On Misgav Ladach Street, the Moross Center is to the left, and they almost certainly have adapted toilets. You go there and back, and the further on to Beit HaSoevah Street, a corner of the Rothschild Building via HaChatzoztrot to the CP. The trail is described on the Yad Sarah website.

Christian Quarter

The Christian Quarter is the second largest, and is dominated by the central shrine of Christendom, the **Church of the Holy Sepulchre**, which is revered as the scene of Christ's crucifixion and resurrection. Both the Jaffa Gate and New Gate lead into the quarter, but there are many steps between this upper part and the Holy Sepulchre Church. Note that the Via Dolorosa, which finishes at the Church of the Holy Sepulchre lies largely in the Moslem Quarter, and so is described in that section, see p118.

Church of the Holy Sepulchre, has its entrance off Bet Ha-Bad on the step-free route marked on the Step Map. It is best approached either up El Wad or from the Zion Gate via the Jewish Quarter. The secluded courtyard is approached through an archway, after passing numerous souq stalls. In the courtyard, **there are −4 steep steps, which are normally ramped by wooden boards**, although these are quite steep. The ramp is not always there, in our experience, but it is, most of the time. From the courtyard, there is −1 into the church and to the Stone of Anointing which is overhung by a lantern for each of the denominations running the church. From here, **a major part of the church is step-free**. You pass the tomb, which is a 19thC monstrosity, with +2+1 to the Chapel of the Angels, the outer bit. The inner tomb has a door W55 and H120, so a chair user may simply have to look inside. Don't worry if you hold up a slightly impatient queue, as it's quite cramped. In the centre of the church is the magnificent Greek choir, which was being restored and redecorated when we visited.

> If you want peace and quiet, wander on past here over the large rough flagstones, and there's the Fransciscan chapel, +2. You are in an area bounded by the Seven Arches of the Virgin, and the Prison of Christ, which seems to be in a different world from that of the clamour around the entrance and the tomb, and is often quiet and undisturbed. Further

round, there are −29 to the Chapel of Helena, and another −30 to the Chapel of the Finding of the Cross. Nearer the main church entrance there are +18 steep and awkward steps to four of the later Stations of the Cross.

A good way of experiencing some peace is to come early in the morning, as the church normally opens at 05.00, long before the tour groups arrive.

The adjacent mosque is dedicated to Caliph Omar, who took the city in 638 AD, and refused to pray in the (then) Church, as he thought that his fellow Muslims would want to turn it into a mosque if he did. He therefore prayed nearby, where the mosque now stands. An example of religious sensitivity many centuries ago, although it didn't quite have the outcome that he had hoped for.

Armenian Quarter

Armenian Christians are well represented in the Holy Land. The church broke away from Constantinople in 506 AD on the issue that Christ had "one nature of God the Word Incarnate" and not as declared at the Council of Chalcedon "two natures, divine and human, united in one person". The quarter runs from the Jaffa Gate round to the Zion Gate.

The **Jaffa Gate** is a lively spot, with numerous cafés, and the nearby Citadel where access has been greatly improved recently. We recommend two particularly good cafés, the **Samara**, +1 [17cm] step, and next door, **Cafeteria St Michel** +1 [3cm] step. The menu is simple and the prices are displayed outside. We ate there several times, and at that stage the Samara offered more choice. The **Christian Information Centre** is described on p113.

David's Citadel, Jaffa Gate, *e-mail:* tower@netvision.net.il *Tel:* 02 626-5333 (an automated enquiry line). The citadel and tower, also known as Herod's Citadel, is an imposing landmark alongside the Jaffa Gate. Its halls, rooms and cellars house an extensive museum, presenting Jerusalem's history from a largely Jewish perspective. The structure forms a five-sided enclosure around a large central archaeological site. Several routes are signed, including two for chair users which have ramps throughout. Most have quite a gentle gradient, and the site has been very sensitively adapted for disabled visitors.

Entrance some 150m from the Jaffa Gate. The room numbers used are those on the plan you are given at the ticket office. The +14 steps can be bypassed further up the hill where there is a ramp with uneven flagstones. There are portable metal ramps to get over the substantial threshold at the top. **You can get a good feel for this ancient building from the ramped routes**. The ramped trails, middle and lower, are clearly signed leading to many parts of the Citadel apart from the first few spots on the standard itinerary, numbered (1) to (5) on the plan.

The middle level route is about 150m long and takes you past rooms (4) and (5) which both have steps (33 and 14 respectively), to exhibits covering the time after 70 CE. From (6) onwards, with exhibitions covering the late Roman period right up to 1967, the rooms are step-free. Only room (10) with a 19thC model of Jerusalem involves steps, and there are more than 40. There are +3 to the shop, and a steep ramp into room (8).

To join the lower route you need to retrace your steps to the junction. It is about 100m long, past various excavations, and goes down to the café, from which you can exit (step-free) to outside the city walls, quite near the Jaffa Gate. There is a **wheelchair toilet (D80 ST75)** with the toilets which are below the café area but with ramped access. The wheelchair toilet is kept locked (grrrrr) although the key is available from the café.

To get to the first sections of the citadel, such as the Phasael Tower, and the room where the introductory film is shown involves more than 50 steps.

Christ Church, Jaffa Gate *e-mail:* christch@netvision.net.il *Tel:* 02 627-7727 *Fax:* 02 627-7730 is the oldest Protestant church in Jerusalem. Jewish text and symbols are incorporated within the church, acknowledging the Jewish origins of Christianity. The entrance to the site is opposite David's Citadel, and after the 50m slope, there are +6 steps into the church.

St James's Cathedral, Armenian Orthodox Patriarchate Road, is only open when there are services. It is richly decorated. Entrance is via a few (ancient) obstacles, in the form of steps and thresholds. The entrance is just past the junction with St James's Road, and it is about 25m to the cathedral over −1 [7cm] step, ±1 [10cm], +1 [5cm], +1 [20cm] and then +1–2 into the church. The floor is carpeted, and the only seats are some folding canvas stools.

▲ ◾E− 1 ± 1 + 1 + 1 −2

The **Armenian Museum**, Armenian Orthodox Patriarchate Road, *Tel:* 02 628-2331. There is a steep slope for 10m, followed by 30m of rough paved surface and −1 step to ticket office. There are +24–24 to see the exhibits, with two small thresholds into and out of the rooms. It is a quietly impressive presentation of the Armenian story.

 E I N24

Outside the City walls

It is possible to get up on the city walls at various points, but access is up 30 steps+ in every case. The pathways on the top are narrow, with further steps en route.

The area in front of the **Jaffa Gate** is being extensively rebuilt and redesigned. There is now a traffic underpass where the road used to go directly past the gate, and there's a large **UGCP** in Ha-Emek. **A wheelchair accessible (step-free) route from West Jerusalem to the Jaffa Gate was almost completed when we visited, although there are some substantial slopes**. Coming up from Ha-Emek there is a zig-zag ramp to bypass the 70 or so steps to the Gate.

New Gate is at the highest point on the hill in the Old City, and there is a steep slope down (outside), either to the Jaffa Gate, or to the Damascus Gate.

Outside the **Damascus Gate** there is always a busy scene. Just up the road there is an open air market (see Step Map). The Damascus Gate is a focus for the Moslem/Arabic community, and the main link from the Moslem Quarter of the Old City to East Jerusalem, with the Arab Bus Station, Nablus Road and Saladin Street. **Access into the Old City is down a long steep ramp and then, inside, down more steep ramps and some steps**.

Solomon's Quarries are ancient excavations which lie directly under the Old City. The entrance is near the Damascus Gate, and Zedekiah's Cave, under the outside of the city wall. There are seats outside. You might find parking up the Nablus Road. There are steps at the entrance, about –15 altogether, and inside a long steeply sloping path leads downwards into the caverns. Earthy surface, and slippery in parts. It's quite hard work getting back up again, and a chair user would need strong friends to make it possible. There are a further –3 and–6 steps at various points, but you can get a fair idea of what it is like after going down the steps at the top, although it is rather dark and gloomy.

Rockefeller Museum Suleiman Street, *Tel:* 02 628-2251 *Fax:* 02 620-4624, just past Herod's Gate. About 150m up a steepish slope from the main road. CP inside the compound. Don't be put off by the ferocious looking barrier at the entrance. Entrance +13 steps, then +3–3 at intervals.

It is attractively built round a courtyard lake, but with split levels. It you're not into archaeological remains it isn't worth the effort.

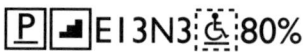 80%

Just outside the Dung Gate are the **City of David excavations**, Warren's Shaft, the Gihon Spring, Pool of Shiloah and Hezekiah's Tunnel. The area includes the remains of David's City, dating from some 600 BCE. It has to be said that access to all the sites is challenging. The excavations are on a steep hill. There are dozens and dozens of steps. To go through Hezekiah's Tunnel you have to go nearly 1km, in the dark (with a candle), through a W40cm gap, wading through water between shin and thigh height. Need we say more?

Mount Zion

Lying just south of the Old City next to the Zion Gate, the mount is of great significance to Jews, Christians and Moslems, and at various times has been inside the city walls. As well as being the traditional site of David's tomb, it is also thought to be where the Last Supper took place, see map IHp161, which unfortunately has tiny script. **The area is hilly**, and although the paths are mainly paved, there are slopes and some steps. There are two CPs: a lower one which is quite steeply sloped, and an upper one nearer the Zion Gate. This one is particularly useful for visiting the Old City.

The **Dormition Abbey** *Tel:* 02 671-9927, marks the site of Mary's death. From the Zion Gate, follow the pedestrian walkway and take the right fork. Entrance is via two small thresholds, then +4 steps into the church. Crypt –24. Flat to the shop and café, although there are –2 to the seating area.

P /H\ E4N24 & 70%

The **Cenacle of the Coenaculum** is the/a traditional site of the Last Supper. It is reached from the Zion Gate by taking the walkway, and forking left. It is just over 100m, and entered through a discreet door on the left. As it is an upstairs room, access is via steps, +22, and then –3±1. Not worth a huge amount of effort in the view of our surveyors.

P /H\ E27

David's Tomb is reached via +1+1+1+1 steps. The entrance is just past that for the Cenacle. Entrance to the tomb is via two thresholds [10cm], although one can be bypassed by using the exit arch.

 E4

Turning to the left from the tomb it is +2 to the **Museum**, which is in a series of small caves, each with +1. From here it is –3 to a small room in which you can light a candle in memory of the Holocaust victims, then –9 to the exit.

Opposite this exit is the **Chamber of the Holocaust**, the first Holocaust museum. This consists of four small rooms and three courtyards, mostly filled with plaques. Entrance –15, with a few steps between the courtyards.

St Peter in Galicantu Church *Tel:* 02 673-1739 *Fax:* 02 673-4837 is built on the side of Mount Zion, with extensive ruins underneath. These have been well restored, but there is only stepped access. Steep slope down to the CP from the perimeter road near Mount Zion. There is then about 100m down a steepish slope, and –22+1 steps into the upper part of a beautifully decorated modern church with an altar background showing Jesus' trial.

> We are told (by two reliable sources) that these steps can now be bypassed by a lift which is to be found in the new cafeteria, along with a disabled persons toilet.
>
> From the upper church there are –32 to the lower chapel and excavations, then –27 to some underground caves close to Caiaphas' palace, and a further +6–16 [W58cm] to the place where Jesus may have been imprisoned. You can see some of this through a glass panel without going down all the steps. Just below the CP is a good viewing point out over the valley reached via –11.

Sultans Pools are down in the valley from the Jaffa Gate, and also down from Mount Zion. It is where the Hebron Road starts. During the summer it is the venue for various concerts and open air performances. It can be approached by car from Emile Botta and Eli'el on the other side of the valley from the city walls.

On the site itself there is a tarmac path leading from Entrance 1 (labelled to the Merrill Hassenfeld Amphitheatre) across the site and then about 100m down the left side of the valley. The equivalent path on the right side is much rougher. As the seating was not set up when we visited, it was not quite clear what happens at the end of the tarmac, but you'd probably have a good view from there anyway.

East Jerusalem

The scene outside the Damascus Gate can be very lively. Some 300m up the Nablus Road (Shekem) is the Garden Tomb, not marked on the Jerusalem map.

Garden Tomb, PO Box 19462, Nablus Road, East Jerusalem, *Tel:* 02 627-2745 *Fax:* 02 627-2742. This is a quiet garden and shrine, discovered relatively recently. It contains a tomb of the type in which Jesus was buried, and is near a rock formation (behind the Arab bus station) which is remarkably skull-like. The English owners make no great claims about its authenticity, but suggest simply that it is a good place to come and pray. Parking in the Nablus Road outside if you're lucky, but it's a one way street, so if there's no slot you have quite a long way to go round the circuit again and it can be very slow because of congestion at the bottom of the Nablus Road. Probably the best thing is to park up past the small roundabout towards St George's Cathedral.

The entrance is about 100m up a tarmaced cul-de-sac, Conrad Schick, off the Nablus Road. There is a small ±1 threshold [+3cm–7cm] at the entrance. Inside, while the paths are slightly rough, there is a ramped route around the site of about 100m. A central part has split levels of +2 or –6 steps, but you can easily bypass these. There are several different worship areas for groups, most of which involve steps. There are –11 quite rough steps to get down to look at the tomb.

A part of the garden over towards the bus station and overlooking the skull-like formation in the rock is reached via +9 but there are plans to build a ramp to bypass these.

The shop has +2 to get into it, but a portable ramp is readily available. There's a **unisex wheelchair toilet (D70 ST70)** but with a very unusual system of support bars and some projections which interfere with transfer.

The easiest way to get out is via the entrance as the standard route is through the shop, and a further +2 into the pathway outside.

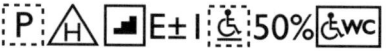

St George's Cathedral, Nablus Road, POB 19018, Jerusalem 91190 *Tel:* 02 628-3261 *Fax:* 02 627-6401. The centre of the Anglican presence in Jerusalem, the cathedral celebrated its centenary in 1998. It serves the Palestinian Christian community in east Jerusalem. CP in the cloister outside. Entrance +2 steps from the CP, or, to the right, a bumpy ramp and +1 [15cm]. Small threshold ±1 [3cm] into a beautifully restored Gothic nave where the white stone contrasts with the black marble pillars.

Mount of Olives

The slopes of the Mount of Olives house the graves of many Jews who died with the hope that the resurrection from the dead would start from the Mount. The viewpoint has already been described on p112. There are two sites on the ridge on top, and then several churches, including the ones in Gethsemane, towards the bottom of the hill. The main hillside down to the Kidron Valley is very steep. It links the Seven Arches Hotel and the viewpoint over the Old City with Gethsemane and Mary's Tomb at the bottom. The road from Gethsemane going up, past the Russian church and the Dominus Flevit, is usable only by the slightly more adventurous driver. Chair users may prefer to start at the top and come down, picking up a taxi at the bottom, but beware, as parts of the road are quite precipitous. It is easy to take a taxi either to the viewpoint, or to Gethsemane.

Along the top of the ridge

Pater Noster Church, El Sheik, *Tel:* 02 589-4904 is shown on the map IHp165. It is set in an enclosed garden and built over a cave. Crusader tradition associates it with the place where Jesus taught his disciples the Lord's Prayer. Entrance ±1–14, although if a gate to the right is opened, these can be bypassed. The normal route to the cloisters is then via –11 and +10. There are a further –3 into the chapel. If, however, you start in the shop to the left of the entrance, you can see most things by going down the –3 into the chapel and bypassing the –11+10. There are plaques with the Lords Prayer in various languages all round the cloisters.

The **Church/Mosque of the Ascension** is the traditional site of the Ascension of Jesus on Rub'a Al-Adawiya, about 0.5km along the ridge from the Mount of Olives viewpoint. It is complete with traditional footprint of rather dubious authenticity. Parking outside. Entrance +8 steps, and then a threshold ±1 [4cm] to get inside the walls. There's a second threshold –1 [3cm] into the small chapel, surrounded by the walls of an old mosque.

On the hillside

The **Tomb of the Prophets** is the first site going downhill from the viewpoint. It is traditionally the tomb of Haggai, Zechariah and Malachi. Reached either by –39 steps from the viewpoint, or on the steep road up/down to Gethsemane, then –19 uneven steps into the tomb. No HR. Not really worth much effort (we thought).

Dominus Flevit church was built in 1955 and resembles a teardrop. The view through the semicircular wrought iron grille, with a cross in the centre looking out over the Old City is stunning. It is possible to be dropped off outside from a car (although the road is steep). Access via a fairly flat path about 100m leads to the entrance.

St Mary Magdalene's Orthodox Church is further down the hill. It is magnificent from the outside with its Russian-style golden onion-shaped domes. It is only open twice a week. From the entrance, there are +52 shallow steps through the gardens, and +32 to the church itself with no HRs.

At the bottom of the hill

The Church of All Nations, Garden of Gethsemane, Jericho Road, Kidron Valley *Tel:* 02 628-3264. It was financed by twelve different countries in 1924, and is also called the Basilica of the Agony. It is one of the most important Christian sites in Jerusalem and beautifully decorated. Parking is possible by Mary's Tomb on the Jericho Road, but sometimes the area is very busy with tour groups. It is also possible to park in newly designated areas on the Jericho Road. The entrance is about 50m up the steep side of the Mount of Olives. Entrance −1 step, and then −5 and then the rough stone path takes you about 60m around the garden to the church, which is step-free throughout, although quite dark inside. It is worth having a look over the low stone rail (H90) around the altar to have a look at the motif around the rock in front of the altar, which comprises a crown of thorns with doves overlooking a cup. **There is a plan to ramp the −5, making access much easier, and this should be completed before the end of 1999.** That would leave only the −1 at the entrance. The normal exit via +14 shallow steps, but it's probably easier to go out the way you came in, although the paving is somewhat smoother on the exit route.

Opposite the church it is possible to get good views across the Kidron Valley, but there are −50 steps down to the path through the valley and about double that number up on the other side.

Mary's Tomb, also known as the Church of the Assumption, is a mix of Crusader and Byzantine architecture. It is a holy site both for Christians and Moslems and is on the Jericho Road, just opposite the Garden of Gethsemane. Parking is possible on the road. There are two staircases leading down from the road, one with −48 steps and the other with only

–24, to the courtyard. There are then –44 down the wide staircase with no HRs into the church. Because it's dark inside, it's really difficult to see anything from the top of the stairs.

The **Cave of Gethsemane** is reached from the courtyard of Mary's Tomb, and is a further +1–8 steps. It is a pre-Christian cave said to have been used by the disciples, and later by Byzantines and Crusaders. The grotto is now run by the Franciscans and includes a very small chapel.

Bethany/al-Azaria. The route 417 Jericho Road leads from the Kidron Valley, through Silwan to Bethany. The site is recognisable as there is a sharp right-hand bend about 6km outside Jerusalem with a clearly identifiable CP just below a church. The Franciscan church marks the site of the raising of Lazarus. It is one of many built in the 1950s and designed by Barluzzi. Access from the CP is up a steep slope for about 80m, followed by 20m which is flat and then –3 steps with a further +4 into the church itself.

In the courtyard there are several glass-covered mosaics from previous churches. Adjacent to the courtyard are the remains of a 5thC church, reached via +3+1–2, and there's a section of this chamber which has a rather narrow passage, W64, and a 90° turn. You can, however, go out the way you came in. There's a new toilet block at the top of the 80m slope leading to the Franciscan Church. Sadly, it has **badly designed adapted cubicles (D80, opening in ST40).** We did not get a good response when we suggested that at least the door could be made to open outwards without much trouble or expense.

A little further up the hill is a site which calls itself the **Tomb of Lazarus**. This has –26 very rough variable steps and W60 at one point. These lead to a chamber where it is still very difficult to see into the traditional tomb. Even though we always try to be positive, our survey team described it as accessible only to the extremely agile.

Mount Scopus

British Military Cemetery, Har Hetzofim, Mount Scopus, near the (Scopus) Hadassah Hospital. This is a quiet reminder of the hundreds of Allied soldiers who died in Palestine during the First World War. Their resting place is on a hillside overlooking the city, and you can see the whole site from the road outside. It is beautifully kept. Entrance +2 steps, and a gravelled slope to +9. A further gravelled slope to +15 leads to the Memorial Chapel, and the wall with the names of hundreds of soldiers who fell in Egypt and Palestine in the Great War, and have no known graves. **A sobering place.** It is some 100m from the entrance to the chapel, but you can get a good feel for the site by going along a flat grassy passage between the first lines of stones (the +2 at the entrance, then a slight slope followed by a level stretch for up to 50m).

The **Lutheran Church of the Ascension**, POB 14076, Jerusalem 91140 *Tel:* 02 628-7704 *Fax:* 02 627-3148 is in the grounds of the Auguste Victoria Hospital. It is on the south side of Mount Scopus, where Martin Buber joins Rub'a El-Adawiya going towards the Mount of Olives. It is right on the ridge, and has a prominent tower. Go through the hospital entrance gate, and there's a CP inside. Sloped kerb +1 [3cm]. There are two portable ramps for the +1–1 [13cm] at the entrance, and then it's step-free inside. +4 to the altar. The church is new and beautifully decorated. There are some fantastic mosaics in the roof and around the apse. **Unisex wheelchair toilet (D70 ST200)** just inside the entrance. There's a lift (D100 W250 L150) in the tower, but although there is a step-free route at the bottom, there are +37 at the top. Access to the café across the path at the entrance is via a sloped kerb +1 [7cm], a ramp, and then +1 [4cm].

West Jerusalem

City centre, and area around the Jaffa Road

West Jerusalem has a main shopping and commercial area centred on the Jaffa Road and on George V. The Jaffa Road (or Jaffa Street, the names seem to be completely interchangeable) goes right up to the Old City. Zion Square is the focus for secular Jerusalem with its nearby bars, shops, restaurants and cafés. **A considerable area around the junction between Ben Yehuda Street and the Jaffa Road has been pedestrianised**. It's a lively spot, particularly in the evenings when there's considerable competition for your custom at the different restaurants. If you want a good meal while avoiding some of the 'sales pressure', try the restaurants in **Yoel Moshe Salomon Street**, also off the Jaffa Road. Many restaurants have tables with step-free access from the pavement. In the winter months they use plastic curtains and elevated gas heaters to make it comfortable. We visited several while surveying in Jerusalem, and found them to be good value.

There is a **central UGCP off Akiva Street** with disabled persons spaces near the lift (D75 W100 L130) on levels –4/–5. Access to the lift is step-free at all levels, and at ground level. The lift is unsigned, and off a small courtyard, under a tower block and to the left of the Rose Café. Very convenient for Ben Yehuda Street. There's another **CP, both surface and UG, in the corner of Independence Park**.

Another parking possibility is the **UGCP under City Hall**, accessed off Shivtei Yisrael. This has several disabled persons spaces, and lift access from levels 2, 4 and 6. The CP exit, together with an alternative entrance, is on the Jaffa Road, near the Post Office.

The **Bell Centre** is by the junction between George V and Jaffa Street. It is a small shopping centre with lift access throughout and is step-free at two entrances, one on George V and the other from Ya'abetz Street off Jaffa Street. There are two lifts (D80 W120 L90) one at each end of the centre. One, past Shannel on the GF, goes to 'Doctors' on the fourth floor, but only when the surgeries are open. There is an **adapted toilet (D80 ST60)** on this floor. There is a second **adapted toilet (D80 ST60)** in the basement adjacent to the bomb shelter. You will need to ask security staff for access to the basement toilet.

The **Mahane Yehuda Market** is situated between the Jaffa Road and Aggripas Street, well up the road from the smart area around Zion Square. CP on Israel Alliance Street some 50m away. Our surveyors commented that the market was 'louder than London's east end', and it's a great way to experience modern Jerusalem. It is in the middle of a Sephardi Orthodox neighbourhood, and consists of three parallel pedestrianised streets, over an area perhaps 150 by 150m. It is flat and Mahane Yehuda is step-free. The +2 or +3 steps in side streets can be avoided by using interconnecting routes

Mea She'arim is an ultra-orthodox Jewish area north of the Jaffa Road where the residents wear the traditional clothes of East European Jewry from the 18thC. The name means '100 gates', which were originally for defensive purposes. It is a surprisingly poor area, with dilapidated shops, dingy houses and torn religious posters, almost giving it the appearance of a shanty town. It is essential to wear modest dress, and to remember that public displays of affection (like holding hands) are not tolerated. Photography is forbidden, especially during *shabbat*. The residents take themselves and their faith extremely seriously, and do not regard themselves as a 'tourist attraction'. If you offend, you're quite likely to be spat at and/or thrown out. Road surfaces are sloping and somewhat uneven, and there are a few steps around. **There is a good step-free route** off Mea

She'arim Street, down Ha-Rav Shmu'el Salant. Turn right immediately into a passage underneath a yellow sign proclaiming 'no entry for the immodestly dressed'. This passage opens out into En Ya'akov Street which is about 150m long and contains a number of old-fashioned shops. A right turn at the end will take you back into Mea She'arim Street. We are not quite sure what view would be taken if someone pushed a friend in a wheelchair through the area on *shabbat*, as this could constitute 'work'. The advice we have been given is interesting. We are told that pushing a wheelchair is not a problem, but that someone driving an electric chair, where they need to push a button to make it go and stop might run into problems. It's a touchy and very technical subject.

Ticho House, 7 Harav Kook Street *Tel:* 02 624-5068, is just south of Mea She'arim, between Ha'Nevim and the Jaffa Road. There are three disabled persons parking spaces near the Jaffa Road end. It was one of the first houses to be built in the second half of the 19thC outside the Old City walls, by an Arab dignitary. The Tichos bought the house in 1924, and it became an eye clinic for both rich and poor. It is accessed via a little pedestrian passageway on the left if you are coming from the Jaffa Road, and over a kerb 10m away, which is ramped. There is then a ramp bypassing +4 steps, and a further ramp bypassing another +4. At the end of the passageway, a cobbled path leads to the left, and around to the garden terrace. The museum has +1 [9cm] to the GF and the café, which has movable seating both inside and out. The museum is quite small, with +5 to a gallery with a display of watercolours by the architect. The upper gallery has +22 up a spiral staircase.

[P] [△] [A] [◢] E1N27 [&] 50% [&X]

Ethiopian Church, Ethiopia (Etyopya) Street which is a turning off Ha-Nevi'im. Flat access is via the car entrance, which is on the side nearest Ha-Nevi'im. If this is locked, you may have to ask at the main gate where the Lion of Judah is a feature. The main gate has a door in it with a ±1 [25cm] threshold, and a narrow door D57. The area around the church is an oasis of calm and tranquillity. To get into the church there are +6 steps and a ±1 [20cm] threshold at the top. Shoes must be left outside, and a strict warning on the door reads "No nude". A circular gallery goes round a central hall, and you can see the beautiful domed roof. Half of the area is for men and the other half for women, and we sensed that our visit was something of an intrusion. The tracks of dust on the carpet which were left by the wheelchair seemed to cause slight offence, and there was obviously a need to be sensitive to those who use the building for prayer and worship.

Time Elevator, Beit Agron, 37 Hillel Street (at the junction with Ben Shatakh) *Tel:* 02 625-2227 *Fax:* 02 625-2228. This is a new tourist attraction where there is a film/video about the history of Jerusalem from the time of David until the Six Day War. The seats move around, synchronised to the 'movement' in the video. Entrance +23 steps, although there is a step-free alternative from the top of the CP ramp to the right. This brings you to the main foyer with the ticket office and café. There are at least −5 to the seats. We were told that a chair user had to be accompanied "by a nurse!!"; that they were not allowed in at busy periods, and that they must be able to transfer into a seat. There is some fixed seating which does not move around for pregnant women, anyone with a heart problem or who suffers from dizziness. *Attitudes towards chair users and other disabled people clearly need to be brought up-to-date, and it was disappointing to find a new facility was not required to provide good access.*

Western suburbs, including Givat Ram

Israel Museum and Shrine of the Book, POB 71117, Givat Ram, 91710 *website:* www.imj.org.il *Tel:* 02 670-8811 *Fax:* 02 563-1833 are both on the same site, and signposted off Ruppin Road. CP with disabled persons spaces. Flat entrance to the large site. It is then some 200m to the Israel Museum up a gentle slope. A minibus with a tail lift (named Doris after its donor) runs a shuttle service to and from the museum. En route you pass a sculpture garden which has a mainly gravelled path and some split levels and slopes.

The **Israel Museum** houses the country's foremost collection of art and antiquities. Entrance +6 steps bypassed by a ramp. The museum is arranged over three floors, and is approximately 200m long. Its layout and arrangement seem quite complicated, but a plan is available at the ticket office. This plan shows some areas as being inaccessible when in fact they can be reached step-free (particularly the areas numbered 25-28). The two lifts (D140 W200+ L200+) are shown on the plan. There are many split levels, particularly on the main lower GF, level two, but virtually all are bypassed either with small open lifts or with platform stairlifts. This means that nearly everything can be reached and seen without steps. Distance, and the hassle of getting the lifts operated are the main problems. There is always a difficulty with the maintenance of lifts that are only used occasionally, and one of the platform stairlifts was not operational when we visited. There are benches scattered around. Two wheelchairs are available on loan if needed. The men's and women's toilets marked on the plan all have **wheelchair cubicles (D70+ ST70+)**.

The **Shrine of the Book**, with some of the Dead Sea Scrolls on display, is some 100m from the Israel Museum ticket office, and then via +8–26+1 steps. There is a clearly signed alternative way in for disabled visitors, without steps, using the main exit doors. The museum is quite small, and divided into three areas. One small exhibition is –21, and there are some further exhibits in a tunnel shaped area leading from the main entrance to the central exhibition hall. There are six separate steps and then +9 to the hall. The shop and **wheelchair cubicles (D75 ST80)** in both men's and women's toilets are step-free. They are near the disabled persons entrance, which is also the main exit.

Bible Lands Museum, 25 Granot Street, Givat Ram *see* www.bestj.co.il/bible *e-mail:* biblelnd@netmedia.net.il *Tel:* 02 561-1066 *Fax:* 02 563-8228 located opposite the Israel Museum. CP with disabled persons spaces outside. Step-free entrance, with lift (D80 W125 L130) which bypasses –18 and –37 steps to the lower floors. The exhibits trace the background to various Bible stories, and there is flat access throughout. The lower floor measures about 70 by 60m, and there are benches scattered around if you want to sit down. Restaurant and **wheelchair toilet (D75 ST75)** on the second of the lower floors.

Supreme Court, Shaarey Mishpat Street, Kiryat David Ben Gurion, Jerusalem 91909 *Tel:* 02 675-9666 *Fax:* 02 675-9648. It is probably worth ringing first to find out when tours, in English or Hebrew, start. The street map we were using didn't mark the new roads and we eventually found the main entrance to the building at the end of Kaplan. It is about 200m up a slope from the nearest parking. **The building itself is step-free almost everywhere, and the tour would take you a maximum of about 300m.** Our guide was most informative, and the visit was interesting. The architecture is stunning, and the significance of various features is fascinating. Lifts (D100 W150 L150) bypass the +30 steps just after the entrance. There are **unisex wheelchair toilets (D70+ ST70+)** just off the entrance foyer to the left of the stairs, and at the end of the huge hallway on the next floor up, past the courts. We did not have time to find the route down to the coffee shop to bypass the –27 from the hallway described.

The **Knesset** *Tel:* 02 675-3333 is Israel's parliament building, and can only be visited when parliament is not sitting (apart from attending in the public gallery). It is probably worth ringing first to find out when there are tours in English or Hebrew. If you are a foreigner, you need to bring your

MAP OF GIVAT RAM 139

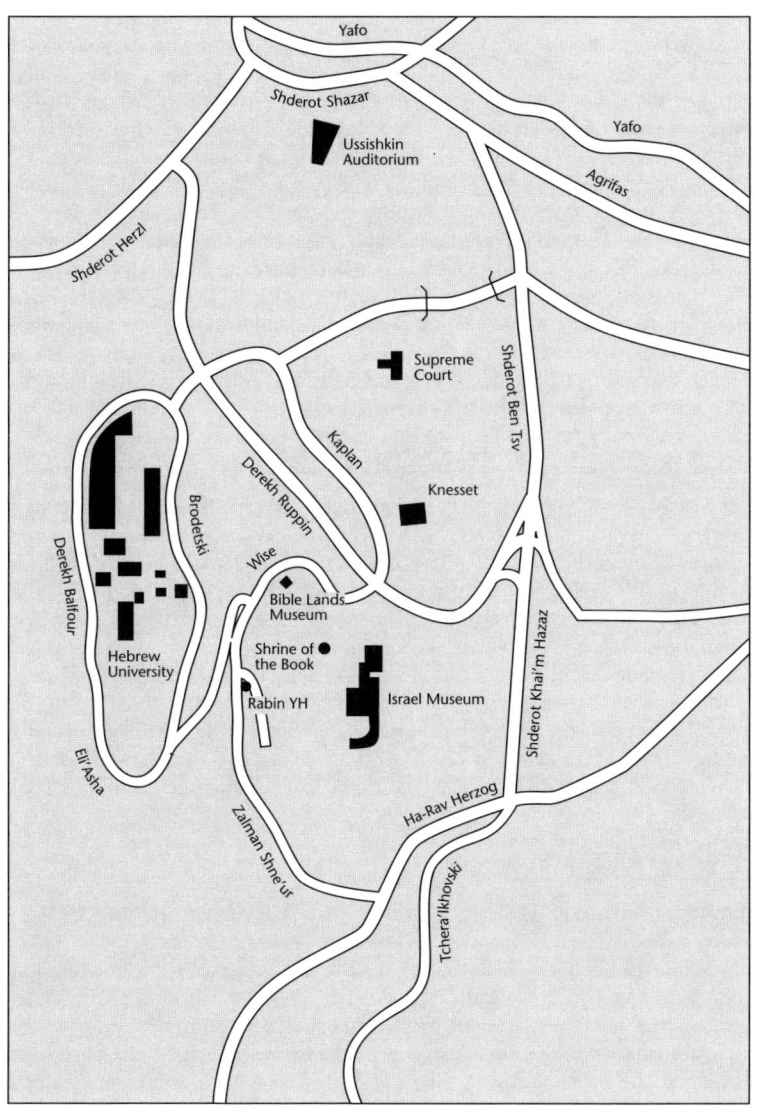

Givat Ram

passport. The entrance is off Kaplan, and at least 200m up a slope from the nearest parking. Going through 'security' involves +1–1 steps, but there's a bypass for chair users. It's nearly 150m across the wide and gently stepped plaza in front of the building. There are +9 shallow steps, which can be bypassed away on the left. Once through the doors, you go to the back of a gallery overlooking the main Knesset chamber for a presentation which explains the basic working of the chamber. Step-free at this stage. Inside there are –23, bypassed by lifts (D80 W120 L120), and –7 bypassed by a platform stairlift (W75 L80). Through the cafeteria area there's another +7 with no stairlift. This implies that a chair user would have to double back and retrace their steps before rejoining the tour. The next part is a visit to Independence Hall which contains some magnificent tapestries and a huge mosaic, all by Chagall. Perversely, the **wheelchair cubicles (D80 ST80)** in both men's and women's toilets are at the top of the +7 which does not have the stairlift. It was a fascinating tour giving an insight into the Israeli constitution (which has never been formalised) and the practicalities of decision making. **Chair users can get around OK though they have to take a few bypasses while making the tour**.

Ussishkin Auditorium and Jerusalem International Conference Centre, Givat Ram, POB 6001 *website:* www.iccjer.co.il *e-mail:* infoicc@iccjer.co.il *Tel:* 02 655-8558 *Fax:* 02 537-6448. The Ussishkin Auditorium is the largest in Israel, seating over 3000 people, and puts on a wide range of events. It is located at the north end of Givat Ram in the block bounded by Ha-Aliya, Weizman and Shazar. CP with disabled persons spaces some 60m from the auditorium. There is a ramped bypass to the steps at the entrance some 20m further on. This gives access to the third floor and to the wheelchair spaces which are at the back of the stalls on this level. Lift (D80 W115 L160) gives access to all other floors. **Wheelchair toilet (D70 ST75)** near the main entrance to the left of reception.

Botanical Gardens, Hebrew University, Givat Ram, Jerusalem 91904 *e-mail:* jubgdn@netvision.net.il *Tel:* 02 679-4012 *Fax:* 02 679-3941. Entrance from Yehuda Burla Street, next to the Supersol supermarket, and quite near the Israel Museum. On-site CP. The trail through the gardens goes up the hillside, and then back to the CP. The path is tarmaced, but there are some steepish slopes, and a chair user would need help. Our team described the slopes as *very* steep. The whole loop around the gardens might take you as far as 1km. There is a motorised buggy available for disabled walkers, and if you want to use this it might be worth ringing first to check availability. The Visitors Centre is approximately 100m on the left from the entrance. The +3 can be bypassed a ramp. Inside the door on the left is a **unisex wheelchair toilet (D80 ST80)**. The Florence Dworsky Conservatory is at the top of the hill, and has +1, bypassed by a steepish ramp. Inside, the path has a light sand covering over compacted earth. There is a small lip [5cm] at the exit. **Unisex wheelchair toilet (D85 ST80)** near the entrance to the conservatory. There are a good number of seats around the gardens. There are, in addition, some wood-chip paths which allow closer views of certain plants/shrubs etc.

South-western suburbs, around George V, David Street and Keren Ha-Yesod

The **Heichal Shlomo Complex**, 58 King George V Street is the headquarters of the Supreme Rabbinical Institutions and the seat of the two chief Rabbis, Sephardi and Ashkenazi. Small CP behind.

The **Great Synagogue**, POB 7440, 58 King George Street, Jerusalem 91073, is next door. It is reached via the flat entrance from George V. After the Western Wall, this is probably the most interesting and important Jewish site to visit, and allows some insight into the basics of Jewish custom and worship. Kippas (for men) are available at the door. There is a large foyer area, with some Jewish artefacts around. The synagogue is on an upper level, accessed by going right from the reception area, and there's a lift (D80 W125 L160) on your right. Men go to Level 1 which brings you into the washing room, then you go through the door on your left which leads to the synagogue with spectacular stained-glass windows. There are chair spaces at the end of each aisle, and the interior plan is a combination of Sephardi and Ashkenazi forms. Women's seats are in a large upstairs gallery.

The **Wolfson Museum** *Tel:* 02 624-7112 is to the left of the synagogue. Entrance +6+3 steps, leading to two lifts (D80 W145 L100) which give access to the museum on the third floor. There are four rooms, the best of which depicts scenes from the Old Testament.

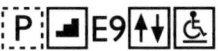

Montefiore's Windmill is in the Yemin Moshe Quarter, originally established outside the Old City in 1860. The windmill enabled the community to produce its own flour. It has recently lost its sails, and as a result is a less prominent landmark, but there's a good view over the city. It is located near the junction between David Street, Keren Ha-Yesod and Jabotinsky. Small CP outside with one disabled persons space. Entrance via −2+2+3 steps and over some bumpy surfaces. There are some pictures inside describing the life and work of Sir Hugh Montefiore.

 E7

Western outskirts, including Mount Herzl

Mount Herzl is to the west of Jerusalem. Herzl was the visionary journalist who founded the Zionist movement in Europe around the turn of the century. The sites include Herzl's tomb, a museum associated with him, and a military cemetery. The Military Cemetery is the resting place for many of the Israelis who have been killed in the wars since Independence in 1948. It is the centre of remembrance of recent Jewish/Israeli history. Many national leaders, including Yitzhak Rabin, are buried in the cemetery. On a neighbouring hill is the Yad Vashem memorial which is an important place to visit if you are to gain any understanding of the issues lying behind the rebirth of the Jewish state. To get to Mount Herzl from the Old City, travel west along Sderot Herzl (Herzl Boulevard) which becomes Kiriat Ha Yovel just before the CP for the cemetery. It is about a 15 minute taxi ride from the Jaffa Gate. The CPs for the military cemetery and for Yad Vashem are some 800m apart.

Mount Herzl Park, *Tel:* 02 651-1108. CP outside. Entrance +6–1 steps to the office and main courtyard, with rough flagstones. There is ramped access via a gate 30m to the right which, unfortunately, is normally kept locked. **If you ask permission at the office, disabled visitors can take their car in through this entrance, and can park/stop inside**. You have to ask for the gate to be opened, and this provides step-free access to the park using, initially, different paths from those leading from the courtyard. **Access around the park and cemetery areas is largely step-free, but quite long distances are involved, on sloping ground**.

Herzl's tomb is approximately 200m from the entrance, up a steady slope. The paths tend to be a bit rough and stony in places. The tombs of other national leaders are further on, with Rabin's grave reached via –14 small steps. Note that the graves are marked only in Hebrew, which makes it difficult to know which is which. Jewish practice is to put stones on the top of a grave, and this tradition is based on the idea that a stone is a permanent remembrance, whereas flowers (used within many cultures) last only a short time, and wither away. **To get out of the park without steps, you need to use the same route back that you used to get in**, and basically to retrace your steps. If you don't, you are likely to finish up in the courtyard area with steps, either up or down, for getting out (or by taking a huge 400m detour back around the park). The **Museum** was closed for major refurbishment when we visited.

 90%

Yad Vashem Holocaust Memorial *website:* www.yad-vashem.org.il *e-mail:* info@yad-vashem.org.il *Tel:* 02 675-1611 *Fax:* 02 643-3511 is a centre dedicated to the victims, survivors and heroes of the Holocaust. It contains a record of what happened to Jewish people in countries which came under Nazi control in the 1930s, and then during WW2. See IH p203 and LP p181 for a layout plan, and a discussion of the purpose of the memorial. Although it is, necessarily, a disturbing and harrowing place, **we strongly recommend that you make time for a visit**.

The memorial is spread out on part of Mount Herzl. The entire site is over 500m in length, but several of the main buildings are within a 100m by 80m area about 100/150m from the CP. There is a café by the CP with step-free access, and two **wheelchair toilets (D70 ST70)**. Kerb ramps tend to be steep, at a 45° angle. Great efforts have been made to accommodate chair users, but there are some slopes, some slightly difficult surfaces and quite a number of flights of stairs bypassed by platform stairlifts. Following a step-free route involves longer distances, as there are several places where you have to 'double back' to avoid the steps. There is a wheelchair available for use. *The use of stairlifts is associated with the usual disadvantages. When one of our surveyors went, the main one was not working, so we had to bump up +23 steps. The next lifts, each took the staff nearly a quarter of an hour to get going (first to find the key and then to fiddle endlessly with the controls to make it work).*

A site plan is available at the information kiosk and there is good signposting but not of the step-free route/s. The marked wheelchair toilets in the Historical Museum are outside just past the entrance, with +5 and no disabled persons toilets. The marking is thus completely inaccurate.

In the write-up we follow first the yellow route on the site plan, starting at the main CP. This takes you up the **Avenue of the Righteous Gentiles** commemorating those who helped the Jews during the persecution (including a plaque to Oskar Schindler). It leads to the main group of buildings. It is step-free into the **Historical Museum** where the Holocaust in Europe is documented. Two platform stairlifts (W75 L95) in the building bypass the +23+9 steps to the mid-level, and a further +12 to get into the **Art Museum**, an auditorium with chair spaces at the back, and the **Hall of Names**. From the mid-level, there is a third platform stairlift bypassing –20, and just behind these stairs, in the basement, are some toilets, including **adapted cubicles (D75 ST56)**. To avoid steps, you have to come back to the mid-level and leave on the far side of the buildings towards the Memorial to the Jewish Soldiers. There's some rough paving outside. A ramp bypasses +5 en route to the memorial. To get to the **Hall of Remembrance**, go round the perimeter road, and find the step-free route which involves following a path to the right which goes directly towards the building (some 30m before the yellow route turns right where there are +4). There is no sign.

To get to the **Children's Memorial**, follow the yellow route. The entrance has D72, slightly blocked by the door handles at H90 W55, which might be a hassle for a chair user. From the Memorial exit, there's a steepish slope for some 30m to get up and over the hill. It is just over 100m back to the CP.

The yellow route described will take you anything from 500-800m, depending on how much you include. Note that there are very few seats in the area, and most of those are benches with no back.

To follow the green route, there is an alternative CP some 500m from the main CP. It is about 300m uphill to the **Boxcar Memorial**, and coming down directly to the CP through the **Garden of the Righteous** would involve a total of −38. The **Valley of the Destroyed Communities** is bumpy and gravelly, but step-free. The **adapted toilet** there (**D70 ST50**) is hewn into slabs of rock.

Biblical Zoo (Tisch Zoological Gardens), Derekh Gan HaKhayot. POB 898, 91008 *Tel:* 02 675-0111/1025 *Fax:* 02 643-0122 The zoo is at the south end of Gan HaKhayot, in the southwest of the city, some 2.5km from the Old City. It features many animals mentioned in the Bible and runs a conservation program to protect endangered species. There is a large CP with disabled persons spaces, which, on public holidays, gets filled up early.

You get a map at the ticket office with a recommended route indicated by the exhibit numbers on the map. It covers 250 dunams (which is an interesting measure, and means that **it is quite big – about 65 acres) and is built on two levels**. The lower level is built around a series of lakes while most of the large animal pens are on the upper level. Between them is a significant hill.

The paths are mainly tarmac, smooth but there are slopes, and **the entire complex is step-free**. There are plenty of benches around. A recent innovation is the provision of a small train, which can accommodate wheelchair users as well as families with push chairs. This starts from outside exhibit (8), and you can either go for the entire trip, or get off either by the bears or by the elephants – and one way to use it is to go to the upper level in the zoo and then walk or wheel gently downwards back towards the entrance. Note that if the zoo is crowded, for example on major Jewish holidays, the train may not run 'for safety reasons'. Without the train, parts of the zoo are a real challenge to reach.

The Small Animals building (2) has large windows (70cm from the floor) looking into the enclosures. To view the Squirrel Monkey Island (7) a chair user can go on to the grass (which is flat) and get a clear view, alternatively, to get a little closer, there are –8+10 steps. The Marsh Aviary (11) has a set of two double gates with a path that is compacted earth for the first 3m then changes to a wooden path before returning back to compacted earth again at the exit and another set of double doors. The double doors all open outward and are to prevent the birds escaping.

To get into the Predatory Birds enclosure (19) there is a single metal gate and plastic strips curtain. The Tropical Avery (20) has two large doors that open outward (same on exit). Zoo announcements are only in Hebrew, and the café, by the entrance, which serves snacks and drinks only has a Hebrew menu. About 80% of the signs around the place have an English translation. For disabled walkers there are wheelchairs for loan, just go towards the toilets at the entrance and they are on your right in an alcove.

There are **three unisex disabled persons toilets** on the site (all marked on the map). One **(D85 ST85)** is just to your right from the main entrance, the second is by the Mandrill enclosure (16) and is **adapted (D85 ST60)**, but BE WARNED the headrest doubles as the flush! The third is by the South American Yard (28) and the Children's Zoo (33) **(D100 ST85)**.

The **Chagall Windows** are in the **Hadassah Medical Centre,** Ein Kerem. This is the largest hospital in the Middle East, and not to be confused with the Hadassah Hospital on Mount Scopus. The Medical Centre is well to the west near Ein Kerem, and reached by following the Hadassah signs from Arthur Handke Street into Henrietta Szold. From there it is impossible to miss, and the huge complex is just 500m further on. There's a security gate at the hospital entrance, followed by a strictly one way system, round to the right. The hospital buildings look pretty anonymous. At the bottom of the hill, you will pass the signed Sharett Institute. Carry on up the hill, and near the top there is a CP barrier on the right and a bus lane marking on the left. Turn left (90°) at that point, and the road goes up towards Ben Gurion Square in the centre of the complex. This is the main hospital outpatients and accident and emergency entrance, and so it's nearly always quite busy. There is, however, some supervised parking and drop-off space, although this is a site where you might sensibly consider coming by taxi.

The **Chagall Windows** are in the hospital synagogue, and you can see them directly in front of you as you come up to Ben Gurion Square. The synagogue is on a lower floor, underneath the square, and the windows (which let the light in) protrude above ground level in a rectangular structure. Flat access to the synagogue is possible by going through the main hospital entrance, beside the taxi drop-off point. Turn left, and go about 40m towards the hospital information desk. Just to the right is a set of eleven lifts (D120 W160 L260), serving the whole hospital. Take one of these to the next level down, and then proceed to go back in the direction you came in the GF corridor (ie back under the main entrance). About 40m along the corridor on the left is the Tourist Reception Centre (*Tel:* 02 677-6271), where you can buy a ticket. The synagogue is then at the end of the corridor. Ramped bypass of –3 steps, to where men can pick up a skull cap. There is a gallery all the way round from which you can see the windows which represent the twelve tribes of Israel. A single bullet-hole has been left in one of the windows to symbolise damage caused during the 1967 war.

The **Malkha Shopping Mall** is Jerusalem's largest shopping centre and is in Manakhat, off Golomb. It is right down in the valley with various other buildings, all of which are totally out of character with the rest of Jerusalem. Large CP. The mall measures about 150 by 100m and is on three floors linked by large lifts. Not all the toilets have **wheelchair cubicles (D70 ST70)**, but we found some **in the toilets on the lowest level**, right by the bottom of the escalators.

Model of Ancient Jerusalem, Holyland Hotel grounds, Mikha'el Avi-Yonah Street, Ramat Sharett, and well signposted off Eliahu Golomb. *Tel:* 02 643-7777. It is a 1:50 scale model of Jerusalem as it was at the time of the Second Temple. It enables the visitor to place the current Old City in its context, two thousand years ago, and in particular to see what the Temple probably looked like. CP some 50m to the right of the Holyland Hotel. From there it is about 150m of smooth path, 40m of which is up a steepish slope, to the entrance. The turnstile can be bypassed through an adjacent gate. **The path around the model is some 100m long, and a chair user can see most things**. There are two observation points for getting a better view from an elevated position. The first is to the left of the entrance with +4+6 steps, and a 100cm high wall around it. The second has +28, and a wall 80cm high. The cafeteria with movable furniture is to the right of the entrance, and is step-free. Nearby is the **unisex wheelchair toilet (D75 ST90)**, and, inevitably, you have to get the key from the ticket office. Our surveyors reported that the only major barrier were two Israeli actors pretending to be Herod and his wife – barking mad and very scary was their comment.

The Dead Sea

The chapter covers:
- sights alongside the routes 1 and 90 from Jerusalem to the Dead Sea.
- It includes, in order, **Qumran, Ein Gedi, Masada** and discusses the possibility of "swimming".

The Dead Sea is some 400m below sea level, and is the lowest place on earth. The Jordan river flows into the lake, and in the intense desert heat, the water evaporates, leaving a lake with a salt content of some 25%. *We reckoned that it is a place you must go, even if you only drive around the shore. A "swim" is an experience not to be missed if you can possibly manage it.* There are several organised bathing places, and swimming (or more accurately, floating) is possible at any time of the year. Getting into the water can be a problem, as it is shallow, and often with sharp salt encrusted rocks a little below the surface. **The height of the water has gone down significantly during the past few years, resulting in steeper rocky beaches leading to shallow water**. A few places provide some kind of floating jetty out over the water, but these were not particularly well designed or maintained. The partially completed developments at Ein Gedi could provide a good place for people with disabilities to go for a "swim", but it was not clear whether they will provide a paved route right into the sea when completed. Regrettably the probability is that they will not, but see the write-ups, and at Ein Gedi it is possible to get a car right down to the water's edge, while at the Ein Gedi Health Spa there is a ramp going down into the sea.

If you can, avoid going to the Dead Sea at weekends or over major Jewish holidays, as it tends to get very crowded. If you do manage to get in the sea, **it's important to wash with clean water as soon as possible after getting out**, otherwise you get encrusted with salt. If you swim/float, don't get salt in your eyes, don't swallow anything, and be careful if you have any open cuts, as they may sting. During the summer it is extremely hot (at 40°C+), and it's particularly important to drink lots of water at most times of the year.

There are various specialist spas and places where you can get mud treatments and sit in hot sulphurous water, all of which is said to be beneficial for certain conditions. The scenery is stunning, and there are some places where you can drive up into the hills alongside the sea. There is some accessible accommodation, particularly in the hotels at the southern end. In addition, Qumran now has good facilities for visitors; Ein Gedi beach is being developed, and the new cable car for Masada has been

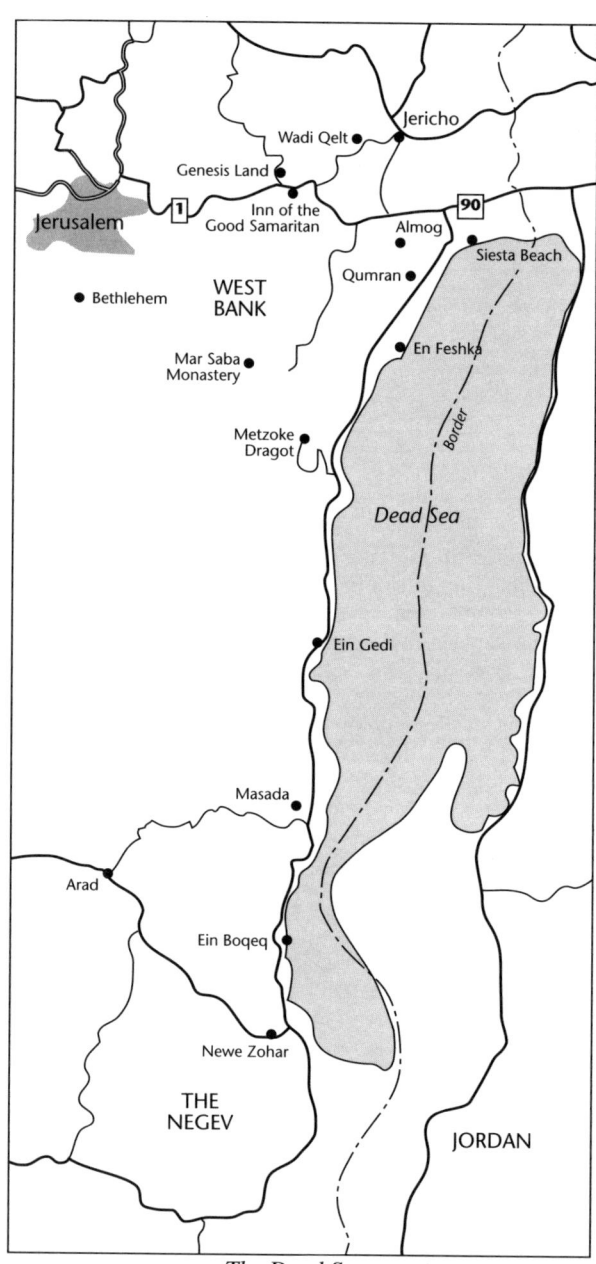

The Dead Sea

completed. These all represent significant improvements in the provisions for disabled visitors.

En route from Jerusalem to the Dead Sea

Genesis Land *Tel:* 02 997-4477 *Fax:* 02 997-4482. Situated off the road between Jerusalem and Jericho (route 1). It is signed on the 458 to Alon, just before you get to the Inn of the Good Samaritan, and is some 3km from the 1. It is signed again just before you reach the settlement. CP area, and a rough slope about 10m up to reception. They provide desert hospitality for pre-arranged travellers in 'Abraham's' tent. You start with a five minute camel ride, and they have a special saddle/seat for chair users to provide extra support.

The camels take you to the tents, from which there is a stunning view out over the desert wilderness. You are greeted by Eliazar, Abraham's slave, and there are various different programmes offered, with stories and readings, and with activities for children. Families are particularly welcome during Succot and Pesach, and the experience is the Jewish equivalent of hospitality in a Bedouin tent. For eating, people recline on cushions, but for elderly or disabled people, chairs could be provided. There are **wheelchair cubicles (D70 ST70)** in both men's and women's toilets near the tents. Access to the toilets is ramped. Elsewhere the site is slightly rough, as is the path leading down from reception to the tents (if you don't want to try the camel). It's an interesting option for a visit, but ring first to find out what is going on. They also offer jeep tours and longer camel rides through the desert.

Inn of the Good Samaritan. This is the traditional site of the inn, where the injured traveller was taken in Jesus' story about the man attacked by thieves. On the Jerusalem-Jericho road it is about half-way between them, just after the junction with the 458, and on the right side at the top of a slope. CP area outside with rather rough surfaces. A small business with a café seems to come and go on this site. It's quite a small building, and not particularly well maintained. When we visited, there would have been +1 [20cm] +1 [25cm] steps into the GF café area.

A little further down the road by Mitzpe Yerikho is the turning to the left towards St George's Monastery and Wadi Qelt. This takes the old Jerusalem-Jericho road, along which you can get a much better idea of what travelling was like two thousand years ago (when the narrow road certainly would not have been properly surfaced). It is described further on p170.

Siesta Beach, Kalia Beach, Northern Dead Sea *see:* www.siesta-deadsea.co.il *Tel:* 02 994-4111 *Fax:* 02 994-4040, some 7km north of Qumran, just off route 90. Follow the signs for the Water Park. **Siesta Beach has an entry in the *Guinness Book of Records* as having the lowest pub on earth at 410m below sea level, and it has step-free access!** The site also offers mud baths, a sea water jacuzzi and traditional Thai massage.

Large CP. Paths are generally well paved, and those running parallel to the sea are fairly level. Getting down to the sea shore is another matter. First there are –4 steps, followed by steep, loose gravel slopes which can be really slippery. Although the route is mainly step-free it really would be difficult for a chair user, and our team recommended that there should be as many as four helpers to enable someone to get down safely. The Thai massage area is only –1. **Adapted cubicle (D85 ST85 with an inward opening door)** in the men's toilets.

[P][A][!]

Qumran, Dead Sea *Tel:* 02 994-2235. Situated at the northern end of the Dead Sea, and clearly signed off route 90. It is the site where the Dead Sea Scrolls were found accidentally in 1947, by a Bedouin shepherd. He was looking for a goat who'd strayed into some caves, near the ruins of an Essene monastery. The scrolls are now kept in the Shrine of the Book in Jerusalem. Their interpretation is the subject of considerable controversy.

The facilities have been considerably improved and enlarged since our last visit, and are generally well designed.

Large CP. Ramps bypass the +3+4+5 steps up to the ticket barrier. Staff will open a metal barrier to bypass the turnstiles. In front of you there are +7 steps, bypassed only by going through the cinema on your right (through two unmarked wooden doors). It is rather an odd arrangement. The cinema shows videos in various languages about the history of the Scrolls. Our surveyor had a problem, as he didn't know about the film, the cinema was in darkness as he tried to wheel his way across to find the exit, and he didn't know quite what he was looking for! When you leave the cinema, the route is ramped gently upwards, and goes past some exhibits relating to the Scrolls. You emerge at the top of the 7 steps referred to.

To see the ruins of the monastery, the ground is rougher, and through the ruins themselves, there are (as one might expect) significant barriers, in the form of awkward steps. You can, however, see quite a lot, and can get a good view of the caves where the scrolls were found. **To avoid the barriers, what you need to do is to go off to the left, and go over some hard, slightly stony, level ground, keeping the ruins on your right**. You go past a low wall, and right past the monastery. There's a gap in the wall, with a loose wire barrier. Go through (under) this, and if you go on to the edge of the cliff, you can get a really good look at the caves. The whole route is about 150m. If you come back towards the ruins, you can see quite a lot – but to get back to the exit, you will need to retrace your steps.

If you took the standard route through the ruins, which our survey team did, you will encounter rough loose stone-chippings and occasional large rocks. To get to the observation point there are +22. Near the cistern, there's a wooden platform via +2–3, but chair users should watch out, as there are gaps in the slats which could easily trap a wheel.

The exit from the site is through the facilities by the CP. En route you will find a souvenir shop, which has quite narrow aisles. From there you can reach the restaurant/café. Near the shop are the clearly marked toilets with **wheelchair cubicles (D80 ST80)** in both the men's and women's. They were not locked when we visited (an unusual bonus), but they were not lockable from the inside either! You obviously can't have everything. To leave the site and bypass –15, you have to retrace your steps and go back through the ticket barrier, using the ramp you came in on.

Ein Zukim, En Feshka, Dead Sea *Tel:* 02 994-2355. Just a few km south of Qumran off the route 90. It is both a bathing place and a nature reserve. There are fresh-water pools as well as the sea. **Cars can drive right up to the picnic area near the sea shore**. The site has plenty of fixed tables and benches in shaded areas. The fresh-water pool nearest the picnic area has 5 rough steps going into it, and you will need to make up your own mind about the practicalities. To get down to the sea, there is a further 100m past the CP over a rough gravelled path. From this there is a steep, slippery and muddy ramp leading down to a floating jetty. Down the ramp, there's a handrail on both sides, but on the jetty, there is only a single central handrail. An alternative ramp, also steep and muddy, lands you in an area of oozy mud where you sink in about 0.5m. It is difficult to keep your footing.

There's a refreshment counter near the pools, with shaded (but fixed) seating and tables. The toilets are a little way up the path towards the exit. There is a **wheelchair toilet (D90 ST70)** behind, but our survey team reported that it had no seat, that the floor was slightly flooded, and that it gave off a 'pungent odour'. Be warned.

Metzoke Dragot, Kibbutz Mizpe Shalem, 86983 Dead Sea *e-mail:* metzoke@netvision.net.il *Tel:* 02 994-4222 *Fax:* 02 994-4333. This is the

International Centre for Desert Tourism, with a guest house, and desert tours by jeep or safari truck, rugged outdoor activities and the opportunity of listening to lectures and talks about desert life and survival. It is not, you might think, an obvious place to include in a guide for disabled people. The centre takes a different view, and offers activities suited to everyone, irrespective of age, level of fitness, or disability. If you want to do something or try something, talk to them about it, and they will see if it is practicable. It is well signed from route 90 as Metsuqe Deragot. The road is quite rough, and climbs steeply for some 5km, affording excellent views. Take the right fork at the entrance to the complex, which consists of several buildings, including a bar. The paths are quite rough, but there are plans to tarmac them. The auditorium is about 50m from reception, up a slope.

Ahava Visitors Centre, Mitzpe Shalem, MP 86983, Dead Sea *Tel:* 02 994-5117 *Fax:* 02 994-5122. Clearly signed from the route 90 and between Ein Feshka and Ein Gedi. Take the next right (about 300m along) into the Ahava factory gates, and the visitors CP is on your left. The centre includes displays and explanations of various Dead Sea mineral products, and a shop selling them. It is about 10m from the CP to the entrance, but there are +1−1 steps en route, and a narrow pavement. These can be bypassed by going under a metal chain to the right. Flat main entrance, with a factory shop on the right and a café and souvenir stall to the left. At the end of the shop there's a small video viewing area with movable seats. The video is about the making of cosmetics, and is in Hebrew. At the far end of the café, up a steep ramp, there are **wheelchair cubicles (D80 ST110)** in both men's and women's toilets.

The **Nahal David Nature Reserve** at Ein Gedi is some 500m off the route 90. CP with a disabled persons space by the entrance. Toilets by the CP have **wheelchair cubicles (D80 ST80 in the men's)**, but are kept locked, and used as store-cupboards. Key obtainable at the ticket office. The café nearby is in the open and has +4 steps and fixed seating. +1 to the small shop and ticket office from the CP. As there is a narrow gap W50 at the entrance, a chair user would have to go into the reserve through the exit, up a short ramp. **The first part of the reserve can be reached step-free over somewhat rough paths, and these take you to the first waterfall**. It's about 400m uphill. After this, the trail becomes very inaccessible with multiple rocky steps and rough paths up the side of the river, however the first stretch can be quite interesting. It provides a real contrast to other sights in the area.

Ein Gedi Beach is about half-way along the Dead Sea, with some substantial development work going on when we visited. There is a petrol station, CP, information kiosk and café alongside the road. There is a shaded picnic area near the CP. It is some 150-180m to the sea. At the back of the beach is a changing room/shower/toilet block with **wheelchair cubicles (D80 ST75)** in both men's and women's toilets. The one in the women's was hidden behind a sliding partition, so you may have to ask for access.

There is a paved path leading down towards the sea and a lifeguard's lookout. Unfortunately the development to the right, with more paved paths, has been abandoned as access to the sea has become more difficult/dangerous as the sea has receded. On the left side, there is still some 100m of rather rough stony ground to cover from the end of the paths in order to get to the sea.

It is possible to drive down to the edge of the sea if you get a gate opened on the left of the site. There are small boulders at the edge, and some of the stones are pretty rough. Walkers are advised to wear shoes. The beach shelves steeply once you've got in, so you don't have far to go before you're floating.

Ein Gedi Health Spa, Dead Sea *Tel:* 07 659-4760 has a wide range of facilities. There are disabled persons spaces outside, although no ramped kerb. Main CP 50m away down the slope. A ramp at the entrance bypasses +8 steps. Flat through to the changing and locker areas, and to two small sulphur pools. One of these has stepped access. There are no larger changing cubicles for changing. The standard ones have D50 and are quite small. There is a **wheelchair cubicle (D70 ST100+)** in the toilets attached to both the men's and women's changing areas, and you might have to use this as a changing place. In this main building there is a lift (D80 W100 L120) to get down to the restaurant.

From this part of the complex there is a ramped route down to the fresh-water outdoor pool, and a further 100m to the mud baths. The pool's water is level with the edge, and it has stepped access. The mud baths further on are like small metal skips which you either get into, or just gather handfuls of mud and cover your body (which was what most people were doing). The area around the baths/skips is –1, and inevitably gets incredibly messy and slippery. A chair user might want to get someone to fill a jug with the mud and use that, but note that after a quarter of an hour the mud must be washed off, so you need to have either a very old chair or to transfer to a plastic chair under the shower (–1).

The sea is some 400m away from the pool, and a small 'train' takes people there. Access to this is via +3, transferring to bench seats. If you can't manage the transfer, you may be able to negotiate taking your car down to near the sea. The arrangements for getting into the sea were the best we'd seen as there is a gentle inclined ramp with handrails on both sides going right out to where it is possible to 'float'. The only problem is that the ramp will often be quite crowded.

Masada/Mezada *Tel:* 07 658-4207 *Fax:* 07 658-4464 is about 20km south of Ein Gedi and just off route 90. Masada is a name that evokes great emotion for Jews. It is where Herod built an impregnable fortress and palace where he could get away from his rebellious subjects. More importantly, it is the place where Jewish rebels held out for years against the Romans, finally committing mass suicide in 70 CE when their position became hopeless. **A new cable car giving step-free access right to the top was opened in 1999, and a massive new complex is being built around it at the bottom**. There is lift access (D75 W110 L130) to the cable car, step-free transfer into the car itself, and a ramp at the top leading up to the rock itself.

Work is going on to provide some wheelchair accessible routes at the top, to some of the main areas of the fortress, but be prepared for roughish surfaces, some steep slopes, a long way to go and the blinding white light. You won't be able to get everywhere, as Herod was not designing his fortress for easy access, but you can certainly get a feel for the sheer size and complexity of the rock fortress. There are plans to provide a disabled persons toilet on the top of the rock, as well as several accessible models of what it was like some 2000 years ago. A key thing to remember about visiting Masada is that it is likely to be VERY hot, about 40°C hot, and you need to take a supply of water.

The new complex at the base will include a large UGCP with disabled persons spaces near the large lifts. It will also include restaurants and shops. Access has been thoroughly considered. **The plans show step-free routes everywhere and the provision of several disabled persons toilets in different locations. It looks as though it will become one of the best equipped sites for disabled people in Israel soon after this guide is published**.

Right at the southern end of the Dead Sea are two large hotel complexes at **En Boqeq** and **Newe Zohar**. The Newe Zohar ones are spread out along the shoreline, while several of those at En Boqeq are grouped around a small shopping centre. These hotels offer extensive spa facilities, and are generally quite expensive. There is nothing else immediately around to see or to do, but you can always use them as a base for further exploration, and, for example, Jerusalem is about a 1.5 hour drive away.

The hotels are written-up in the *Accommodation* chapter, and the only other site surveyed was the **Ahava/Petra Shopping Centre** at En Boqeq. A small circular market with shops, kiosks, bar and café, it has different signs/names on either side of the building It is just off the main road, and surrounded by some of the big hotels. CP outside. Ignore the entrance sign which leads you to +7 steps, and go round the other way (to the right) which is step-free. The centre is largely step-free. There's a lift (D90 W120 L200) up to the first-floor restaurant. **Adapted cubicles (D80 ST60)** in the men's and women's toilets on the GF, directly opposite the entrance.

The background to the changes in the Dead Sea

The Dead Sea is a lake, which is some 70km long and up to 18km wide. It is nearly 400m below sea level. It is primarily fed from the River Jordan, but upstream exploitation of the waters has led to a reduction in the amount coming into the Dead Sea. Consequently there has been a significant fall in the water levels, and a century ago it was some 12m higher than it is now. Much of this fall in level has taken place since 1960. With no outlet, and high ambient temperatures, water is lost steadily by evaporation.

Most tourist activity is focused on the northern section of the lake, particularly on the Israeli side. There are specially designated beaches, health spas and beauty treatment centres. The Dead Sea has special characteristics, because of the build-up of salts and chemicals in the water and surrounding mud as evaporation takes place. The chemicals include iodine, bromine and magnesium, all said to be associated with promoting the treatment of various conditions.

In the southern part of the lake, there are large evaporation pans on both sides for the extraction of potash and of other chemicals. It is difficult to know what will happen to the Dead Sea over the coming years, but there are imaginative plans. One is to bring water by an underground pipeline from the Mediterranean, using it to generate power en route. However, any such plan would have to be agreed by both Israel and Jordan.

It is to be hoped that the unique character of the area with its salt-rich waters can be maintained, as it is an extraordinarily beautiful and interesting environment for local residents, visitors and for local wildlife.

PNA areas

> This chapter covers:
> - the places south of Jerusalem, principally **Bethlehem**, Beit Sahur and **Hebron**
> - **Jericho**, to the west, and places to the north, including **Ramallah** and **Nablus**.
> - **Gaza**.

During our survey for the guide, we visited all the main areas under both Israeli and Palestinian control, including some which are regarded as particularly sensitive. We took local advice about the security situation and not only did we have no problems but we were welcomed almost wherever we went. For visiting some of the places you might like to consider using the services of **Alternative Tours** or of **The Alternative Tourism Group**, details below.

Alternative Tours, c/o Jerusalem Hotel, Nablus Road, East Jerusalem *website:* www.jrshotel.com *e-mail:* raed@jrshotel.com *Tel/fax:* 02 628-3282. The hotel itself is within easy reach of the Old City, and a number of 'Experience Palestine Tours' are run from it. These can include Hebron, Ramallah and Nablus, Bethlehem, Gaza, Nazareth and visits to refugee camps. We used AT to organise a visit to Gaza, and our guide was both interesting and helpful.

The **Alternative Tourism Group** (ATG), POB 173, Beit Sahur, West Bank *website:* www.patg.com *e-mail:* atg@p-ol.com *Tel:* 02 277-2151 *Fax:* 02 277-2211. The ATG and the Alternative Information Centre are grassroots groups that are striving to create a platform for Palestinian-Israeli cooperation. There are both Israelis and Palestinians who are working to create a society of peace and justice for both peoples, and the Alternative Tours Programme offers visitors a unique insight into some of the realities of life in the area. Some of the tours have a religious focus, some highlight the history and culture of the peoples, while others look at the latest political and social developments. Two of these tours are called: 'People in Struggle; Palestinians under occupation' and 'Palestine and the Other Israel; Meeting Israeli-Palestinian NGOs'. They involve people-to-people interaction, and can be tailored to meet any visiting groups specific needs. We used ATG to organise visits to Hebron, Nablus and Gaza, and found our various guides to be interesting, flexible and wholly constructive.

At the time of writing, the outcome of the Oslo Peace Process is still uncertain. It has sadly been delayed and bogged down time and time again, but there are some territories which can now display the Palestinian flag and are under the control of the PNA. Others, currently come under some kind of joint jurisdiction, while some of the occupied West Bank is under total Israeli control. The division of the land has brought all kinds of problems. Area A is controlled by the Palestinian Authority, but consists of a tiny part of what was (pre-1967) the West Bank of the Jordan. Area B is jointly controlled, and some of this territory may be handed over to the PNA as part of the negotiated settlement. Area C is the parts of the West Bank currently under Israeli control. Palestinians who live in these areas need permits to travel to other areas, and to Palestinian towns (in Israel) such as Nazareth. Local Palestinians cannot travel from Bethlehem to Ramallah via Jerusalem (the most direct route), and vehicles with Palestinian registration plates cannot travel outside their particular area without a pass or permit. It is not the function of a guide like this to comment on the politics, except insofar as they affect access, and the current borders between the areas under different jurisdictions do certainly make travelling around more difficult. During our surveying we visited the Princess Basma Centre for the Rehabilitation of Disabled Children which serves the Palestinian community, and is situated on the Mount of Olives in East Jerusalem. Its work was being severely hampered by the current travel restrictions. **We hope and pray that these and other problems will be resolved, so that the different communities in the Land can live and work together after a just settlement.**

During the writing of the guide, further agreement was reported on the implementation of the so-called Wye agreement. The map on p24 shows the outline of the territories to be transferred either wholly or partly to the control of the PNA, and some of the by-pass roads linking Jewish settlements in the disputed territory. The boundaries shown are not necessarily precise, and the details of the arrangements are complex. They lie outside the scope of this guide. In many areas there are levels of joint Israeli/Palestinian control. Talks aimed at settling all the outstanding disputes are taking place as we write, between Israelis and Palestinians – but there are many very difficult issues to resolve with any semblance of justice.

Driving up from Jerusalem through Ramallah and Nablus takes you through some magnificent rock-strewn and hilly Biblical scenery. **Signposting is relatively poor or non-existent, and can be confusing, as new Israeli settlements are better signed than some of the main towns. There is also an extensive network of bypass roads, not yet shown on most maps.** We managed to get off the main route from Ramallah to Nablus, thus seeing some wonderful scenery, but at one point the signs were so poor that we did a neat loop around the same roads, saying after a while "We've been here before!"

> One of the really nice souvenirs to take home (in our view) is some of the stamps issued by the PNA. Not only are they well designed and colourful, but they are a way of buying something that directly supports the local economy, even if only in a small way.

Bethlehem

Bethlehem is the most visited place within the PNA areas. It is the traditional site of the birthplace of Jesus, and this fact has distorted the economic base of the town, as it is heavily dependent on the tourist and pilgrimage business, see the write-ups in the IH p240-248, and LP p403-409. Note that because of the different calendars, there are three Christmas celebrations – the Roman Catholic/Protestant one, the Orthodox one and the Armenian one.

It's a relatively short taxi ride from Jerusalem, provided you can get one that is cleared to travel across the Israeli/PNA boundary (and agree the price before setting out). If you're driving yourself, even though it is only some 8km south of Jerusalem, it isn't that easy to find. You go south on the Hebron Road, and past the Mar Elias Monastery on the left. A little further on, you come to a major junction and traffic lights, with one of the new bypass roads going off to the right to Hebron. Extraordinarily, Bethlehem is not signed here, though in fact what you do is simply to go straight on. About 0.5km further on you meet the PNA/Israeli checkpoint, where there may be a queue. On either side of the border you will find service taxis, since many of those operating within the PNA area are not allowed to take their vehicle across the border. At a busy time, such as when Palestinian workers are either coming from or going to Jerusalem, the whole road can be bedlam, with many cars doing U-turns in the confined space and cutting across the traffic passing through.

Once inside the PNA area, navigating and finding your way is not easy, as there are very few signs and **because of the hills, two-dimensional maps are not always clear**. Manger Street is very long, and is not remotely straight. Two-thirds of the way along there's a huge U-shaped bend. The route we followed in order to find Manger Square was as follows. Follow Manger Street from the checkpoint, past Rachel's Tomb where there is a strong Israeli military presence with heavily armed soldiers. Carry on until you come to a four-storey brick building on the right by some traffic lights, above which you can see a three-tier bell tower. Turn up the hill towards a mosque minaret straight ahead, and you will reach the top of the hill level with Manger Square. There is a map of central Bethlehem on p162, showing the step-free routes around Manger Square and the Souq.

Because of the Millennium, there is a huge amount of building going on and hopefully, part of the plan will be to provide adequate signposting.

When we visited it was quite difficult, because the town is very hilly, and it is difficult to pick out any landmarks. Even if you see something that you recognise, it is difficult to know how to get there!

Rachel's Tomb, Manger Street is about 500m past the main checkpoint if you come in from Jerusalem. She was Jacob's second wife, and died in giving birth to Benjamin. In Jewish tradition she is regarded as the 'mother of the nation', and many Jewish women come here to pray for fertility or for a safe delivery. Parking is usually possible on the street outside. The shrine is a small synagogue with both a men's section (considerably larger) and a women's section, both of which are at ground level and separated by a curtain. Access is via a kerb +1 [15cm], and then +1 [6cm] step. Inside, a ramp bypasses the –4. Beyond the ramp, men need to put on a kippa (skull cap). The men's section is to the right and down a corridor where three sides of the black-shrouded tomb are exposed. The route is step-free. Women go a little further on, and access to their section is via –1–2.

A little further on up the road from the tomb is the new Intercontinental Hotel development, and on the other side of the road the new Modern Art Museum is being built. Hopefully, both will be 'accessible'.

The map on p162 shows the centre of Bethlehem with the step-free routes around Manger Square. Because the area is so hilly, the standard maps are difficult to interpret. Manger Street is very long. As it nears the town centre, after passing the Paradise and Bethlehem Hotels, it is well down the hill below the level of Manger Square. The diagram we show covers effectively only the top of the hill, although it does show most of the interesting part of the town. **Undoubtedly the best way to visit, is to stay for a night of two at the Casa Nova Guest House (if you can cope with the bathrooms) or to use the Bethlehem Hotel** which has well adapted rooms *see Accommodation chapter*.

From Manger Square, if you go up Paul VI Street which is across the square from the church, after about 100m you will meet a large flight of about 40 steps. If, on the other hand, you go up the next street and turn left around the back of the Municipality Offices, then turning right, there is a step-free route through much of the rest of central Bethlehem. This leads up Fawaghra to the **new Market/Souq**, which was still being developed when we visited. As shown on the map there are ramps to both parts of the Souq, although slopes are inevitably involved, because the town is built on a number of hills. There are relatively few sights of note, although the mixed Muslim/Christian culture is fascinating, and the attraction is the busyness and activity around Manger Square, and the shops and eating places along the main streets, mainly serving the local Palestinian community.

MAP OF BETHLEHEM

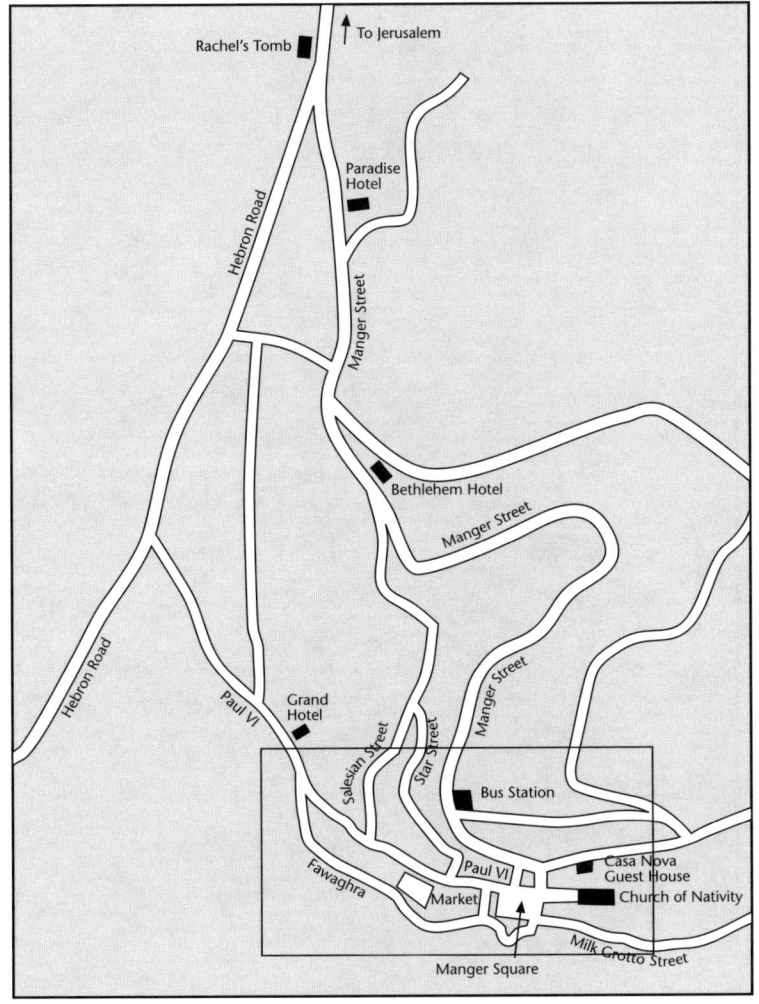

Bethlehem

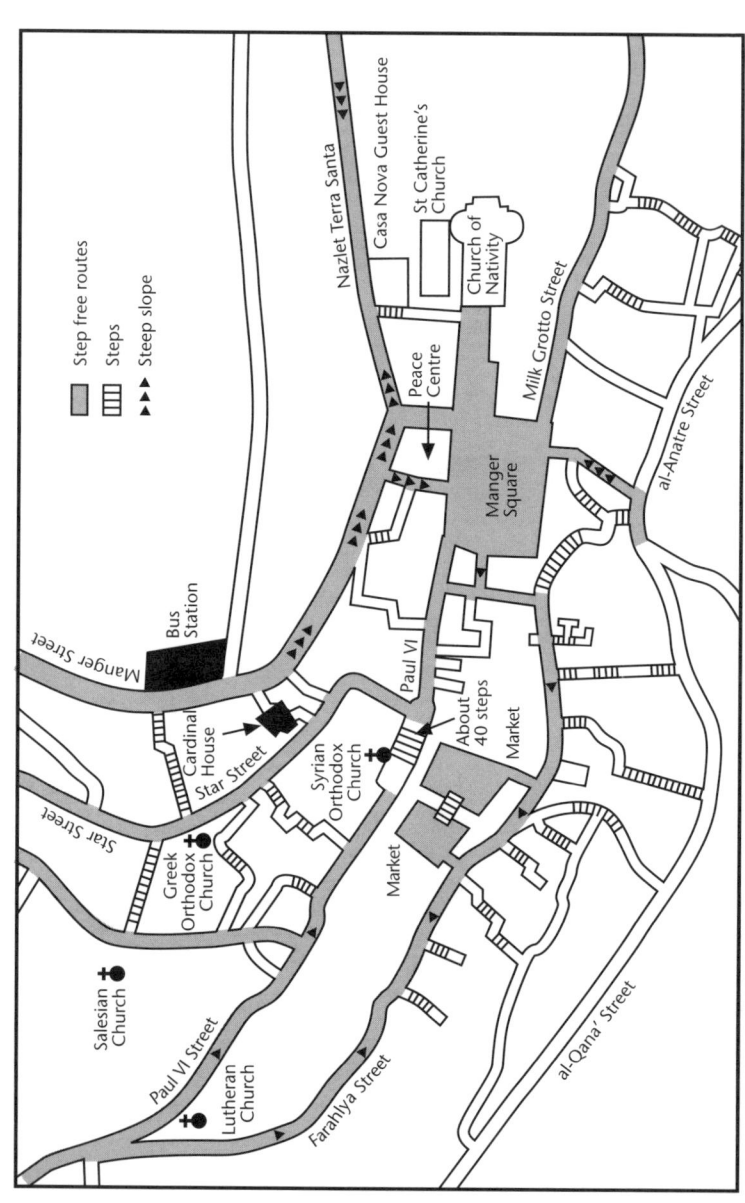

Central Bethlehem step map

There is a huge new building going up near the Church of the Nativity, and it was not quite clear what services will be transferred into it when it is completed. We believe that it will be called the Peace Centre, and may well contain an Information Office, and a Museum and Cultural Centre. If you want to visit the church when the tour groups are not all pervasive, go early in the morning – and you might consider staying in Bethlehem overnight, thus getting a much better feel for the place.

Manger Square is the central focus for Bethlehem. It was looking rather like a building site when we visited, as there were extensive preparations being made for the Millennium celebrations. It was being paved and pedestrianised. This is a potential problem for disabled visitors, as the square is at the top of a hill, and you used to be able to come up and park in the square itself. Accessibility is now affected by how close you can get with a car or taxi, and where you can stop, as to how easy it is to get up to the square. This will depend on how crowded it is at the time. Parking is difficult, less so if you come off peak. Down the road from the drop-off point by Manger Square, numerous small boys will offer to find you a space (possibly some way away), for a suitable fee – and they will 'watch your car'. The problem is that the roads around Manger Square are narrow and busy, and one way to tackle the problem is to park a little way away, and get a taxi in both directions, perhaps even from just inside the Israel/PNA border. You might find that reduces the hassle. Around the square are some shops which have ramped access from the end of the walkway in front of them nearest to the post office.

The **Post Office** is currently reached via +1–21 steps, and is in the corner of the square.

The **Church of the Nativity** is the oldest complete and working church in Christendom, and is built over the traditional place of Jesus' birth. It was restored by the Crusaders, and later again in the 17thC. There are plans on IH p244 and LP p406/7. The easiest way into the church for many people is via St Catherine's which is joined to the older church down one side. This route is not always available, particularly during a two-hour lunch time. However, there is a bell outside St Catherine's and usually someone is on duty to open up for easier access. The problem with the main entrance to the old church is over an awkward tall threshold, and through a low door H175. Apparently the low door was to stop people riding into church! It's really difficult for a chair user, even with two strong friends, and the St Catherine's route is certainly better. Once in the cloister, there are two ways into the Nativity Church, either over a rough threshold, or via a step. Neither is a major problem.

Inside the Church of the Nativity, the main nave is flat, with various old mosaics under the floor, and with fold-back panels in the floor. There is a raised area (+4) where the Armenian altar and worship area are. To get down to the grotto, there are some –15 large steps and a door 60cm wide. It is actually slightly easier for a chair user, and for some other people with disabilities to use the exit, as it is normally less crowded, and the door is slightly wider (at 65cm). An important difference.

P /H/ A ■N15 &:50%

St Catherine's, the Franciscan Church next door, is flat, with access via the courtyard (a medieval cloister) which was described above as part of the route for getting into the Church of the Nativity. It is where the service which is broadcast around the world takes place on Christmas Eve, December 24th. It is quite a modern building, decorated, not unnaturally, with Catherine Wheels in remembrance of the Saint who was martyred on such a wheel centuries ago. There is a separate access to a grotto area underneath via –28 to the main section, and then a few more steps to other parts.

P /H/ A ■N28 &:60%

Milk Grotto Church, Milk Grotto Road about 300m from Manger Square (with –1 [15cm] step en route). It is the traditional site of the Holy Family's hiding place before the flight to Egypt, and has a serenity lacking in the Nativity church. Entrance +1–18 to 90% of the church, and a further –2 to the rest.

P /H/ ■E19

Beit Sahur

Beit Sahur is a village some 2km from Bethlehem, and is the place where, traditionally, the angel appeared to the shepherds. Hence there are a number of **Shepherds' Fields**, though none have any historical basis. It is also the home of the Alternative Tourism Group, see p157. The road to Beit Sahur is very badly signed, like that to Bethlehem. We found it by taking the left fork just past Rachel's Tomb, and then taking a right turn down a steepish hill at a junction. The approach road to one of the churches was being rebuilt, and we didn't manage to get to that one.

At the **Franciscan Shepherds' Fields Church** there has been considerable development. Tourist buses drop you off some 200m away, but it is possible to drive a car into the CP. The easiest access to the main church is up a 100m long slope, then there's a really steep ramp to bypass +3 steps, then +1 [12cm]. It is flat inside. There are a number of excavations taking place around the site, and two small chapels have been opened up below the main church. The smallest is −8, although you can see in from the top, while the other is a little larger and has −5 shallow steps. The Byzantine excavations can be seen from the CP.

The **Greek Orthodox Shepherds' Fields Church** nearby has flat access to the courtyard, although you may have to ring the bell to get the gate opened. It is a modern church with some beautiful icons. Entrance +4 steps, then level inside. The ancient Byzantine crypt chapel is about 80m away with a mosaic dating back to the 4thC reached via +1–25. You can see much of the church ruins above the chapel without any steps.

Beit Jala

Beit Jala is another village on the opposite side of Bethlehem from Beit Sahur. **It is built on the side of a really steep hill**. This makes getting around quite hard work. As elsewhere there was extensive rebuilding and landscaping going on for 2000. We saw the **Latin Catholic Church of the Annunciation**. Small ±1 [4cm] to reception. Into the church there was +1 [8cm] from outside. At **St Mary's Church**, some way up the hill, there was +1±1 [10cm] into the church.

En route to Hebron

Solomon's Pools are just off the Bethlehem–Hebron road some 5km south west of Bethlehem. Associated with both Solomon and Herod, these pools and the aqueducts attached, supplied Jerusalem with water until the early 1950s. They are currently being renovated, and were empty when we visited. The three pools stretch for over 500m, with a road running alongside, gently downwards. **A new tourist centre is being built near the main road, which will have a CP, café and shops**, and, hopefully, toilets. It is possible to park beside the road, and surfaces are currently a bit rough if you want to get near the pools. Most of it can be seen from the road.

Hebron

Hebron is one of the oldest inhabited places in the world, and is sacred to Jews, Christians and Moslems alike as the burial place of Abraham. For all its troubles during the past century, and even though it is where the Israeli military presence is most acutely obvious, it is a fascinating place to visit. The background is well explained in the IH p256-262, LP p411-415 and RG p407-413. Life has been disrupted by the security precautions taken and the closure of roads and routes. The main street is no longer a through route.

The main shrine, the **Cave of Machpelah/Haram al-Khalil/Tomb of the Patriarchs**, dominates the town centre. It includes the tombs of Abraham, Isaac and Jacob and their wives. The walls are those of Herod, but there are Crusader and Mamluk structures as well. It is one of the world's most disturbing religious sites where prayer and piety go hand in hand with violence and sectarian hatred. **Access to the Moslem side and the Jewish side is controlled separately, with very tight security**. We were not even allowed to take our tape measures in, because they had sharp edges! Unfortunately **there are between 35 and 70 steps at each entrance, and no way of bypassing them**.
> CP outside, if you can get past the security at the entrance. To get to the mosque, there is a steepish slope, and +2–1 steps and then +3 through two stages of security checks. The steps can be bypassed. There are then +31 to the mosque, with –1–1 to the tombs. To reach the synagogue there is a separate entrance, +24, then +1–1–1 (which can be bypassed), +21 +40 and +1–2. Inside there are ±1 thresholds between different areas.

The **Souq** area, some 300m away from the shrine **has flat access throughout**. Surfaces are slightly bumpy, and it's quite busy, but unspoiled by tourism. The area nearest the shrine has been closed, because of pressure from Israeli settlers. The souq continues for more than 500m, and is a compendium of Mamluk and Crusader facades, with vaulted ceilings, tiny shops and narrow alleyways. We had a fascinating visit, and one of the more remarkable sights was the butcher's shop selling camel meat. The camel's head was still attached, with a remarkably bored expression, in spite of the fact that its carcass was being sold off in pieces. We were so taken aback that we didn't have the presence of mind even to get a picture!

The Hebron area is famous for its glass and pottery production, and the various factories make an interesting visit, and provide good value souvenirs. We went to the **Al Salam Glass & Pottery Factory**, some 2km north of Hebron, on the road to Bethlehem. It is a sizeable building, with blue doors. The factory entrance had a ridge [5cm], and the shop has +1 [10cm] step.

Other sights south of Jerusalem

Herodion

Herod moved the top of one mountain and put it on the top of its neighbour and then built a palace on top (hence, perhaps, one of Jesus' stories about moving mountains). There are interesting ruins in the lower area by the main road which are currently undergoing further excavation. These can be seen easily. The ruins of the palace itself are inside the hilltop. CP part way up the hill, with fine views, and a café with +4 steps. There is a steep slope about 200m long up to the top with +3+6+5+41+9 and roughish surfaces en route.

Mar Saba Monastery

Situated some 15km east of Bethlehem in the middle of the desert, it is set right above the Kidron valley as the river makes its way towards the Dead Sea. St Sabas' monastery was founded in the 5thC, and is a spectacular sight, even from outside. The road leading to it offers some spectacular views.

It is possible to park nearby, and get to a viewing point about 200m further on. The route is quite steep, and potentially slippery for the first 2-3m from the road. Then there's some 50m of very uneven path, and 150m with a smoother surface. Finally a rough steepish ramp leads to a really good viewpoint. It's worth a little effort.

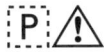

West of Jerusalem

Jericho

Jericho is a sleepy town some 10km north of the Dead Sea, and is an archetypal desert oasis. It is a thriving agricultural settlement based on local springs. At 250m below sea level, it is the lowest town on earth, and is also one of the oldest settlements in the world. **It is flat**, and therefore poses none of the access difficulties encountered in other places. See IH p272-277, with a map on p272 and LP p398-402. Some new hotels are being built in the surrounding area, and there's an ambitious cable car project described below, which is up and running.

As you drive into town, there are large street plans showing the location of all the major places of interest. These are excellent, and hopefully the idea will be copied by other places in the PNA areas. The central point is Palestine Square.

Post Office, Al-Karamah, *Tel:* 02 232-3574 just off Palestine Square. Street parking, then +2 steps at the entrance.

The **Sycamore Tree,** which is supposedly or traditionally the one climbed by Zacchaeus the tax collector in order to see Jesus, is at the junction of Ein Al Sultan Street and Al Jumaizah Square. There is a plaque there just off the pavement, with the story quoted on it. It is a place to remember the acceptance of the outcasts by Jesus.

About 2km along Ein Al Sultan Street, is Tel Jericho. Opposite is Elisha's Spring (Ein Al-Sultan) with the new tourist complex and cable car station alongside it.

Tel Jericho is some 2km north from Palestine Square, up Ein as-Sultan Street which bends to the right, becoming Jiftlik Road. The Tel is the supposed site of the ruins of the ancient walls of Jericho that fell down under Joshua's attack. CP outside. Being a gravelly hill causes obvious access difficulties. There are +15 steps leading to a steepish gravelly path leading to the top which bypasses a further +49. From here, uneven sloping paths lead step-free to some 90% of the site, including most of the more important excavations. A chair user with two strong friends could probably make it.

The **Sultan Cable Car and Tourist Center**, POB 12, Elisha's Spring, Jericho *e-mail:* sultan@sinokrot.com *Tel:* 02 232-1590 *Fax:* 02 232-1598 goes from the terminal opposite Tel Jericho up to the mountainside near the Monastery of the Temptation. It must be by far the most significant investment in a tourist facility in Palestinian territory. When we visited the cable car was operating, but the rest of the complex was under construction, and very well advanced. It includes the cable car station; a large restaurant and shop; and a hotel. It is planned to include some adapted rooms in the hotel.

To get to the cable cars, there were +4 steps at the entrance, bypassed by a ramp. **Adapted cubicles (D65 ST50)** in the mens and womens toilets at ground level, but when we surveyed, the door opened inwards. The management said that they would change this. There is lift access to the upper station level, but we only saw the lift shaft, as the cabin had not been installed. At the upper level, for boarding the cable cars, the small gondola cars come to a complete halt, thus facilitating transfer. The door into the cars had D70, with 63cm between bench seats on either side of the gondola. One car, No 2, has a slightly larger gap to facilitate a chair user, but you may have to transfer to the seat.

At the upper station there is a platform around the cable car unloading point. Everywhere else, there are steps. There are −15 to the caves and −25 to the main seating area. In total there are about −100+100 steps to get to the monastery, which is just around the corner of the cliff. The views back over Jericho during the trip are magnificent, especially with the evening sun behind the car.

At the bottom, the link from the upper level to the restaurant involves +1–7, which are bypassed by a steepish ramp. Off the restaurant, there were some toilets, with a potential unisex wheelchair toilet (D85). They were about to install the toilet in the centre of the cubicle, thus preventing ST from either side, but if they have taken our advice, and installed it at the side, there should be ST70. The cubicle was big enough to accommodate this.

Khirbet al-Mafjar (Hisham's Palace) *Tel:* 02 232-2522, see IH p277 LP p400. Some unusual and interesting remains which are thought to be those of Caliph Hisham's hedonistic palace completed around 744 CE and destroyed in the 749 CE earthquake. It is about 2km north of the town. If you are heading south on the 90, turn left at the Jericho Resort Village where it is clearly signed, then take the next left. It is about 1km from the resort. The site is only partly developed, and measures about 100 by 150m with stony paths. CP outside. From the entrance, it is about 50m to the arched entrance on the left with +3–2+1 into the main courtyard and surrounding rooms, some with ±1. From the courtyard, it is +9 to the next collonaded area, and +1 to the impressive bath house.

It is, however, possible to see most of the ruins by going straight from the site entrance, keeping the main buildings on your left and the ornate swimming pool on your right. There is then only +1 to the bath house.

On the old Jericho-Jerusalem road

If you possibly can, take the old road, which branches off the route 90 near Mitzpe Yerikho. It is just wider than a single track, and takes you through the wilderness and desert, giving a much better feel for the 'road from Jerusalem to Jericho' than the new dual carriageway does. In terms of the story in the New Testament, you can see how easy it would be for a small band of thieves to hide only a few metres off the road, and to ambush travellers making the long trek.

Monastery of St George of Koziba, Wadi Qelt, near Jericho. A very scenic route between Jericho and the main Jerusalem road uses a narrow (but surfaced) road through the wilderness. **The monastery is set in a spectacular gorge, but without a direct view from the road**. An archway has been built where the road turns off to go down to the monastery, but this is only for those with strong nerves, as it is steep and without any guards at the edge of the road. The view of the gorge is dramatic, but you still have some way to go at the bottom before you can see the monastery. It's about 100 m further on from a small parking spot, and involves about 40 steps. An alternative way of getting a view is to park by the archway, and take the rough path upwards for about 200m. It's quite rough and quite steep at the start, but it leads to a viewpoint over the gorge from which you can look down on the monastery. There's a slightly easier spot further along the road towards Jerusalem. It's where there is a cross on top of a square brick base, painted white. This is quite a steep and gravelled slope up about 75m from the road, and there's an alternative some 100m back down the road. A chair user with a couple of determined friends could probably make it, and the view is spectacular.

Ramallah

Ramallah is a large town, almost due north of Jerusalem. Nearby is the Birzeit University, which is the leading Palestinian academic institution. An interesting place to visit if you have the time. It is possibly the most affluent Palestinian town, and there are plenty of eating places and shops. The centre of Ramallah and the main shopping streets such as Shari Rokab, Shari Nadha and Shari Al-Quids are fairly flat, or at most gently sloping. There's a major meeting point of roads at the Midan Manara. There aren't really any standard tourist sites, but it is an interesting town in terms of its economy and Arab lifestyle.

The **Post Office** in Park Street, is about 80m down quite a steep hill, with +3 steps at the entrance.

Nablus

Nablus (Shekem) is the largest city in the West Bank area, and is a bustling Arab town. It was in Shekem that Abraham received the possession of the land of Israel. It is now one of the centres of Palestinian industry and

NABLUS 171

commerce. It is in the northern part of the PNA area and is quite hilly. It contains only a few sites of tourist interest.

The principal commercial area with some of the larger slopes is along King Faisal Street which is the main street going East/West through the city. It slopes gently southwards towards the West. There is also the old city and souq area to the South, which is far more atmospheric. The souq is largely flat and well paved and is unspoilt by tourism. For a street plan see LP p417.

We found a good CP just along Ghazzali Street which is one way going East. It was on the right when you could see the blue-domed mosque straight in front, and well signposted.

From the CP, we came back to the municipality office on foot/wheel and turned left down Hitten Street towards the souq. One of Nablus' specialities is its sweets and we stopped at Alaker Sweets (+3 steps at entrance) where we tried some Knafah, which is toasted sugar around a local cheese! Going on to Jamaa al-Kebir, to the right, you reach Martyrs Square with a tall white clock-tower labelled number 20 in the LP map. We crossed it and went along An-Nasir Street along to the right. This route through the souq is flat and paved and you can buy almost anything you might want.

The **Post Office**, Faisal Street, is +7 steps at the entrance and is located under the sign for Palestinian Telecoms, opposite the Municipality office and some attractive fountains in the middle of the road.

The **Municipality Office** has ramped access and a lift inside. Both are situated where King Faisal Street splits into almost parallel one way streets.

On the left, about 300m along An-Nasir is a sign pointing to **Turkish Baths**. These are the oldest working **Turkish Baths (Al-Shifa)** *Tel:* 09 838-1176, originally built in 1480 and well restored. Entrance is +16 steps, but it is well worth the effort to get up these if you possibly can. You enter a large room with cushion-strewn platforms to sit or recline on where you can take tea or puff a nargila. Both the steam baths and sauna are accessible without steps, and even the full treatment with a massage is very cheap. The baths are used by men only for most of the time. Women can use them on Wednesdays during the daytime.

Jacob's Well *Tel:* 09 237-5123. Coming into Nablus from the south, follow the road towards the town centre, until you come to a very sharp turn to the right. You almost go back in the direction you have just come from. About halfway to the mosque which is part way down the hill is a small sign indicating Jacob's Well on the left. The site was being extensively rebuilt, with a new church on top of the crypt containing the well. Through the main entrance there are –20 steps to the level of the church which can be bypassed by using another way in which is for vehicles. The church will be flat throughout, but the Byzantine crypt chapel with the well is down –18. When we visited, building work was going on, and all the surfaces were really rough. **We were told that it will all be paved on completion of the work, and that a disabled persons toilet will be provided**.

Samaria/Sebaste

Some 15km north-west of Nablus, off the Route 60 is Sebaste. Incredibly, the access road is not signed off the 60, and the turning is opposite a Hebrew advertising board with a red stripe, on which three radio frequencies are listed. If you are coming from Nablus, it is just before a Z-bends sign, and you can just see some remains on the top of the hill. As with other places, there are various names for the place. Samaria was built by King Ahab, of the northern Kingdom of Israel as a capital to rival Jerusalem. After its destruction by Nebuchadnezzar in 722 BCE it was rebuilt by Alexander the Great, and then enhanced by Herod the Great as Sebastia. It remained occupied well into the Byzantine period. Only about 20% of the site has been excavated, but **the visible remains are impressive and substantial**, and there are spectacular views from the top, illustrating the strategic importance of the site. The Roman and Herodian city walls, city gate and cardo remains are all seen easily from the car, before the entrance to the site.

Sebaste excavations CP just past the entrance. Adjacent to the CP are the remains of the basilica, and then it is some 100m up a slope to the right over slightly rough ground to a well-preserved Roman theatre and a Greek tower. Thereafter, the path becomes increasingly steep and rutted. To get to the top, an easier route is to backtrack to the CP, go to the right, and then go right again from the other corner of the CP. By this route it is about 300m to the top, and it is only the first 20m that is really tricky (for someone pushing a chair). Even this route is quite rough, and it's steep in parts, but it is slightly less difficult than the alternative path leading from the Roman theatre. At the top is the ruined Byzantine church of St John which contains John the Baptist's traditional burial cave. Access is over rough paving stones. A recommended shortened tour is simply to take in the basilica and the theatre, together with what you can see from the road.

The **Holyland Sun Restaurant/Souvenir Shop** to the right of the CP is down a short ramp, over a bit of rough ground with a sharply ramped step, a ±2cm threshold and –1 [12cm] step to the restaurant. We had a superb lunch there, eating local food.

Mount Gerizim is just to the south of Nablus, to the right off route 60. There are excellent views out over the valley from the road leading up the mountain-side. The road leads to a village called Brakha. It is **the sacred mountain of the Samaritans**, who are one of the smallest religious communities in the world. They number about 450, and differ from the Jews in that they recognise as sacred texts only the Torah (the law in the first five books of the Bible) and they venerate this mountain as being the place where Abraham offered Isaac as a sacrifice. They follow a strict policy of not marrying outside the group. The community is outwardly prosperous, and the men wear distinctive grey robes.

After going up the hill, turn right and then right again, and the **Gerizim Centre and Museum** is on your right. Entrance +9 steps. Alongside the Centre is the Sacrificial Area with a ±2cm threshold and then –8. It is where a lamb is ritually sacrificed at Passover in accordance with the traditions of the Torah.

Gaza

While there are not many obvious tourist sites in Gaza, it can nonetheless be a fascinating place to visit. It boasts the third oldest church in Christendom and some interesting mosques. Beyond that, it can be enjoyed for its markets and atmosphere and its genuine hospitality.

It is one of the most densely populated places on earth, with some one million people boxed into a narrow strip of land. More than half the population are refugees. Various groups will provide a guide, and/or organise visits, including **Alternative Tours** and the **Alternative Tourism Group**, see p157. We used both, and found the local guides to be very interesting and informative, and they added an enormous amount to what we learned from the visit.

Some of the refugees have been in camps in Gaza for just over fifty years, and there are many second and even third generation refugees. Gaza must be one of the most sedentary and fixed populations anywhere in the world, because most of the population cannot travel anywhere, and the territory itself is tiny. While we were writing the guide, the 'safe route' from Gaza to other parts of the PNA areas was opened. While it is only a partial and temporary solution to the question of freedom of travel, it does at least

174 PNA AREAS

enable some Gazans to visit other parts of the Palestinian Territories, and possibly to see friends and relatives for the first time.

The crossing point from Israel is at Erez at the north end. As a visitor, you have to leave your transport in the CP and walk/wheel for up to 1km, passing through the Israeli and Palestinian security procedures. With a foreign passport, you bypass most of the queues, and pass en route through a so-called VIP lounge in a Portacabin, which is simply an office (with +1 step) with a couple of desks in it. It is pretty simple for non-Israeli and non-Arab passport holders and is step-free from one side to the other. There is little or no signposting, so you may need to ask an official for directions. When the border is open to Palestinian workers, there are taxis to Erez from Ashquelon and Jaffa, but you have to get another taxi in Gaza. Visits to the refugee camps can be organised through UNRWA, the United Nations Refugee agency, who run a large clinic and several schools. There are separate crossing points and separate roads if you are wanting to visit one of the Israeli settlements in Gaza.

UNRWA (United Nations Relief and Works Agency for Palestinian Refugees), *Information Department Tel:* 07 286-7044 is in Gaza City, opposite the Islamic University on Al-Azhar Street, just off Talatin Street. You can identify it by the large blue UN flag. Depending on their work load, they may be able to organise a visit to one of the refugee camps, and if you want AT or ATG to organise such a visit for you, make it clear that it is a high priority on your visit. **Remember that 'taking tourists around' is not, and should not be, a major priority for a hard working and very effective relief agency**. Modest dress is essential, and UNRWA advises against wearing any olive green or military style clothing. Generally, the Palestinians are delighted to welcome visitors, and appreciate outside interest in their living conditions. If you cannot go on an organised visit, LP advises that Beach Camp on the fringes of Gaza City is a place where you can probably visit on your own.

There is step-free access to the public information office through the large blue gates. There are +15+3+2–2+1 steps inside, which can be bypassed by a walk of about 200m. To do this, ring 07 677-7260 on the telephone to the right of the gates to get someone to come down.

British War Cemetery, 3km before you get to Gaza City on the road from Erez (Sharia Salah al-Din). It is opposite the 7up factory which precedes the Pepsi factory. There is general parking outside and step-free to the beautifully maintained graveyard 200m by 200m, flat with neatly trimmed grass. Cemetery Register Enquiries: Ramleh War Cemetery, Ramleh *Tel:* 08 922-1220.

Gaza City is some 7km south of Erez, and the main sights are around Palestine Square in the Old City. The area is flat, although surfaces can sometimes be a little rough. There's a huge amount of building work going on, with associated disruption. Finding your way around can be quite difficult, as we found that hardly anyone knew what the street names were, apart from the major ones. This may be due to the fact that the population is almost entirely static, and everyone there knows their local area without the use of names. The people are really friendly, providing that you are not Jewish, and the place is completely unspoiled by tourism.

Just to the south of the square is a delightful market area, and although there are 1 or 2 steps into most of the small shops, the displays of goods spill down on to the roadside.

Main Post Office, Ministry of Post and Telecommunications, Ministries Complex, al-Mokhtar *Tel:* 07 282-9202 *Fax:* 07 282-9231. An imposing building opposite the Municipal Park. Entrance +9+4 steps to the counter. Souvenir stamps are sold in the office to the left.

[◢|E13]

Ministry of Tourism, off Al-Yarmouk (see maps IH p428 and RG p452) *Tel:* 07 282-9461/2 *Fax:* 07 282-4856. On the third floor, reached by +4 steps and a lift (D80 W140 L140).

[P|◢|E4|↑↓]

The **Sayid Hashemi Mosque** on Sharia Yafa is the burial place of Mohammed's grandfather. Entrance –1–1–1 steps to an area where you can see the whole courtyard. There's a stone barrier ±1 [27cm] to surmount to get into the courtyard, then +1+1–2 into the mosque.

[P|◢|E3N]

The **Great Mosque (Jamaa al-Akbar)**, Omar al-Makhtai, is 400m south of Palestine Square. It was originally built by the Crusaders as a cathedral dedicated to St John the Baptist. All visitors need a permit from the Ministry of Awqaf. The easiest entrance for chair users is from Desariah Market, with –4–4 steps. After removing your shoes, there is a further +1[21cm] –4 into the body of the Mosque.

[P]

One of the most interesting sites in Gaza is **St Berferjos/Porphyrios Church**, which claims to be the third oldest church in Christendom, dating back to 425AD. It is located less than 500m south-west of Palestine Square and is approached from Rass'a Al-Tale'a Street in the Zeitoun area. It is a Greek Orthodox Church with parking outside. The principal entrance is from the courtyard via +7 steps, which leads to the gallery from which you can get a pretty good view of the church. To get to the lower level there are −19 awkward curved steps from the gallery, or you can enter from outside by going to the left of the church and via −5−11+1 wider and easier steps. You can see everything from this level. The priest commented with some affection that the only thing disturbing the peace was the call to prayer from the mosque next door.

The **Welayat Mosque** has been built alongside Berferjos/Porphyrios Church, and dates back to 1432. The church and mosque typify the good relations between Moslem and Christian. As we passed, a local Muslim in an electric wheelchair was waiting to go in, and a portable ramp was immediately available inside to get over the −3 steps at the entrance. He rolled in and went straight on to the carpet inside.

Napoleons Fort is now part of a girls' school and much of it can be seen from outside.

The **Shujayya Market** is nearly 1km south of Palestine Square and is a large straggling local market particularly for vegetables, fruit and meat. Surfaces are somewhat uneven in places, and many of the shops have 1 or 2 steps up to them. You can do most of your shopping or window shopping from the road.

PLO Flag Shop, Al-Wihda Street *Tel:* 07 286-0401. Located 100m south of the junction with An-Nasser St. +1 step leads to some glorious tack and assorted Palestinian odds and ends.

We found a very good place to eat in the **Garden of Akadraa Restaurant**, near the junction between Jala Street and Omaral Maker Street. It had a 20m slope up into the garden +1 [10cm] step. The toilets were accessed via +1 (4cm), but the door was W59.

South of Gaza City

Heading south-west from Gaza City leads you past more refugee camps and more Israeli settlements to Khan Yunis and Rafah, which are the next two main towns after Gaza City.

The **Haifa Restaurant** *Tel:* 050-399624 is a pleasant restaurant, inexpensive by Western standards, on the seafront road just past the Netsarim Jewish settlement. From the sandy CP there is a steep 20m ramp HR on both sides to the restaurant with moveable tables and chairs. Unadapted toilets, step-free, with D70+.

Khan Yunis has most to offer around Khan Yunis Centre Place where most of the shops, cafés and market stalls are step-free or have a small lip from the pavement. You can see a seven-hundred-year-old wall and arch that is the remains of a castle built by Sultan Barkook. There is a colourful Bedouin market on Wednesdays and Thursdays.

Rafah also has a Bedouin market which happens on Saturdays and Sundays. Rafah, unfortunately was split in two in 1979 meaning that a portion of the town, including some 5000 people, became part of the Sinai. As it is nearly impossible to visit the other part of the town, the only form of contact for separated families and friends is, sadly, to shout to each other over a high wall across 20 metres of no mans land.

Gaza International Airport *Tel:* 07 213-5696 just outside Rafah is now open for international flights, most of which are to and from the Arab nations, with some flights from Europe. We could not survey the airport at the time of our visit, but we heard that the building is all at ground floor level so access should not be too difficult after leaving the plane.

Around 10 km north of Khan Yunis, there is a **British War Cemetery** in El Zweida Village near the Abu Zayed Horticultural Nursery. It is beautifully kept by a Palestinian gardener. It is flat with neatly trimmed grass and covers an area of 150m by 150m.

178

Tel Aviv and the surrounding area

This chapter covers:
- Tel Aviv; Jaffa;
- nearby inland sights such as **St George's, Lod**; the **Weizmann Institute** and **Neot Kedumim**;
- the coastal sites of **Netanya** and **Caesarea** to the north.

Tel Aviv is by far the largest city in Israel, and has grown steadily since 1909 when it was founded by Jewish immigrant families building their houses on the shores of the Mediterranean. It has become Israel's most important commercial and cultural centre. It is a bustling and modern city, with little of historical importance, and for the tourist the main interests would be the shops, the nightlife, the beach, and some of the major museums. It has relatively little to offer the pilgrim to the 'Holy Land', apart from sites in the adjacent town of **Jaffa**. See LP pp206-251, IH pp435-478 RG pp71-100. However, it does have Independence Hall from whose steps Ben Gurion proclaimed the establishment of the Jewish state on May 14th 1948 when the British Mandate ended.

The city is basically flat, apart from the hill on which Old Jaffa is built. Driving can be difficult, because of the city rush, the number of one-way streets, and the lack of signs and good maps. If you're hassled by traffic, this may be a place to rely on the use of taxis. If you want to stay, then your hotel location could be particularly important, relative to either the beach or to the shopping and entertainment centre around Dizengoff Square.

One of the attractions of the city is the array of distinctive neighbourhoods, which reflect the diverse backgrounds of its inhabitants who have arrived from many different countries. It is also a major seaside resort, with sandy beaches, cafés and bars in abundance along several kilometres of sea front. There are numerous hotels along the seafront (in Hayarkon Street) but these inevitably tend to be quite expensive. Some have well adapted rooms. Hotels set back a short distance from the sea front are considerably cheaper. Its layout is fairly straightforward, with a grid of streets bounded on the west by Hayarkon, and on the east by a motorway called Ayalon. At the north side there is a large park and the river Nakhal Yarkon and Tel Aviv University campus lies to the north of the river. Old Jaffa is to the south. The streets don't always go straight, and there is a story that Allenby was originally meant to be a main north-south link but that it was diverted, to reach a coffee house on the beach. Around Tel Aviv there are extensive suburbs, for example on the east side of Ayalon, and the ribbon development along the coast southwards to Ashkelon and northwards through Herzlia and Netanya.

Tourist Information Office, City Hall, 69 Ibn Gvirol Street, 64162 *Tel:* 03 521-8500 *Fax:* 03 521-6423. City Hall is in Rabin Square. From the square, there are more than 20 steps up to the first floor level where the office is. To reach it from the pedestrian level in the square, go round the building to the right towards the Rabin Memorial, and near the bottom of some other steps there is a door marked with a 'wheelchair' sign. Alongside the door is an intercom, and this should enable you to get the door opened and get access to a lift. The building was closed when we visited, so we didn't use this route.

Tourist Information Office, New Central Bus Station, 6th floor, next to platform 630 *Tel:* 03 639-5660 *Fax:* 03 639-5659. The new bus station is a huge and confusing building just south of Lewinski. It is well south of the city centre. The building resembles a large shopping centre, and it is crossed by a motorway-type flyover linking it to Ayalon. It has many bus platforms and a considerable number of shops, spread out over six floors. If you are coming by car, parking is on level three, and is approached from Wolfson Street. Three pairs of lifts (D100 W145 L135) give access to all floors and any split levels are bypassed by ramps. As the system of corridors is quite confusing, we describe one route for finding the Tourist Office. From the main taxi drop-off point, at the east end of the station, by David Tsemakh, there is a kerb [12cm]. Then access to the lifts is step-free, and is well signed. This level is the fourth floor. Take the lift to the sixth floor, and follow the signs to bus platform 630/631. It is nearly 100m, and is step-free into the office. The staff on duty did not speak much English, and the amount of information for a disabled visitor would be very limited.

Post Office, 132 Allenby Street *Tel:* 03 564-3760 at the junction with Yehuda Ha-Levi Street and Mikve Yisrael Street. Step-free throughout.

American Embassy, 71 Hayarkon Street *Tel:* 03 519-7575. Security in and around the embassy is extremely tight. Parking immediately outside may be possible if you make an appointment and highlight any disability. If not, there are some nearby public CPs. Entrance is through a very heavy door to a security point, where you can outline your business. We were told that the building complied with US regulations regarding access, and that there were some disabled employees, one of whom used an electric chair.

British Embassy, 192 Hayarkon Street *Tel:* 03 524-9171, located on the corner of Arlozorov. Entrance +1 step, bypassed by a ramp. Note that the consular section is on the sixth floor, Migdalor Building, 1 Ben Yehuda Street *Tel:* 03 510-0166. We did not visit this.

The seafront **Promenade** stretches for more than 2km. Just north of Ben Gurion there are a number of expensive hotels, with their own swimming pools and facilities. Several have been surveyed, and these are described in the *Accommodation* section. From where Ben Gurion finishes, by the Gordon Swimming Pool, there are stretches of public beach, with numerous bars and cafés behind. There are a number of small CPs just off Hayarkon and/or Herbert Samuel. The Shlomo (Cheech) Lahat Promenade covers the Gordon and Bugrashov beaches. It is paved with small stones set in concrete, and consequently is quite smooth. There is access to the sand via a number of ramps. The sand is of quite high quality, and kept reasonably clean. It is retained by series of artificial sand bars jutting out into the sea, and the area had improved enormously since our last visit/s some ten years earlier. The whole system seems to work very well. There are shaded bench seats on the promenade.

In the write-up we have used the two Orange Route walking tours set up by the Tourist Office, and described in the IH. A simplified version of the maps is on p182/185.

Orange Route I

Bialik House (2), 22 Bialik Street *Tel:* 03 525-4530 is at the far end of Bialik off Allenby. It was the home of Chaim Bialik who was a prominent Hebrew poet and Zionist. There are +7 steps to the small garden, then +6 to the front door. Inside, the first floor is +25. Unadapted toilets off the garden.

Rubin Museum (3), 14 Bialik Street *Tel:* 03 525-5961 in the house of the painter Ruben Rubin. Entrance +2 steps bypassed by a ramp. The GF, with a permanent exhibition, is step-free. Temporary exhibitions are held on the first floor +24, and second floor +21. It is well worth a visit if only for a fascinating introduction to the history of Tel Aviv and of Bialik Street from the friendly and informative staff. Past reception are **unisex adapted toilets (D85 ST28)** which would be usable by many chair users, even though ST is only 28cm.

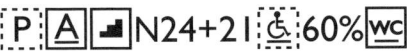

182 TEL AVIV AND THE SURROUNDING AREA

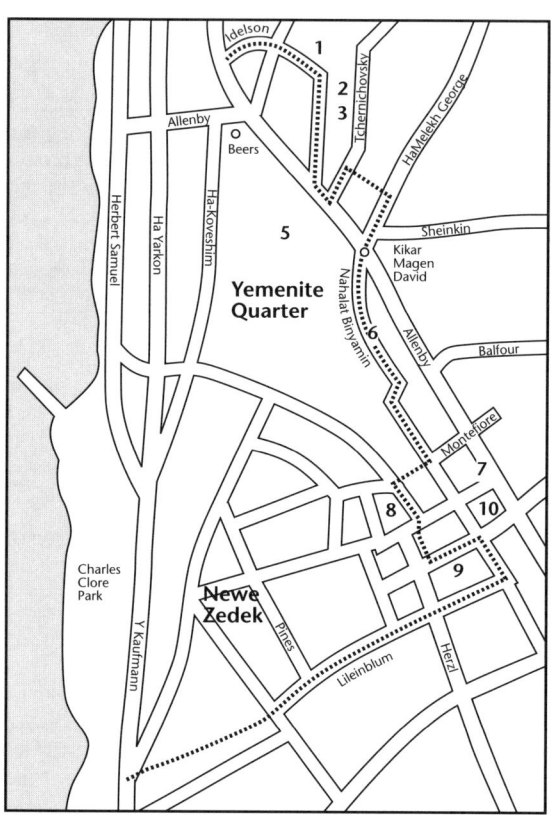

Key

First Town Hall (1)
Bialik House (2)
Rubin Museum (3)
Carmel Market (5)
Nahalat Binyamin (6)
Great Synagogue (7)
Shalom Tower (8)
Independence Hall (9)
Haganah Museum (10)

Orange route 1

Carmel Market (5) is a lively open air market consisting of a network of streets selling almost anything and everything. The main street runs about 400m from Allenby to Daniel, and the whole area can be quite crowded. Slightly hilly in parts.

Nahalat Binyamin Street (6) is lively and part of it is pedestrianised with lots of street cafés and craft shops. There are sometimes street entertainments. It is over 250m long, and slopes down gently from the southern end, and then goes slightly more steeply up towards Allenby.

Great Synagogue (7), Rehov Har-Sinai with +14 steps at the entrance. There is flat access to the men's section but the women's balcony is +22, and the balcony itself it tiered. The building was closed when we visited in 1999, so we have used our ten year-old information.

[P]E14N22

The **Shalom Tower** (8) is an imposing 1960s tower, mainly consisting of offices. It straddles Herzl in between Montefiore and Ahad Ha'an Streets. The main attraction is the observation platform on the 34th floor from which there's an impressive view over the city. Step-free entrance to the lift (D90 W150 L170) in the east wing which provides access from street level to the top. There is a **unisex wheelchair toilet (D75 ST120)** in the west wing on the GF. It is not marked, and you need to go through the doors in the mosaic wall, and then turn right. To get to the shops on the first floor you have to use a lift in the west wing.

[P][M][↑↓][&]90%[&wc]

Independence Hall/Eretz Israel Museum (9), 16 Rothschild is some 50m down the road from the junction with Nahalat Benjamin, just past the memorial and fountain in the middle of the street. Entrance +9 steps then –6 to the main auditorium and to some other exhibits. We didn't see it all as it was supposed to be closed.

[P][◼]E9N

Haganah Museum (10), Beit Eliyahu, 23 Rothschild *Tel:* 03 560-8642. Located some 30m from the junction with Nahalat Benjamin. Parking difficult. It is an exhibition of the history of the pre-independence clandestine Jewish defence force, the Haganah, and is in the house of one of its former leaders. Entrance +4 steps, with a ramped bypass. Step-free to the living quarters on the GF. Lift (D80 W105 L140) to the historical exhibitions on the other three floors. All step-free apart from two small areas on the first floor which have +1. Unadapted toilets –15 from the GF.

90%

Orange route 2

Dizengoff Square (Kikar Dizengoff) (15) is the central hub of Tel Aviv. It is a pedestrianised area built over the intersection of three roads, Dizengoff, Pinsker and Zamenhof. The wide tree-lined roadways leading to the square, with its shady benches, shops, cafés and its spectacular glass-fountain, make it well worth a visit. Ramps bypass the +13 steps up to the fountain.

The **Dizengoff Centre** (16) is about 100m away, up Dizengoff Street. It has CPs both above and below ground. The best one for a disabled person is on level –2 where the bays are large enough to allow a chair user to get in and out of the car easily. The centre is on eight levels, and lifts (D90 W135 L210) and glass fronted elevators (D85 W110 L180) go to all of them, including the CPs. It is full of shops and eating places. There are **wheelchair cubicles (D70+ ST70+)** in the mens and womens toilets on each level, clearly indicated on the information boards.

The **Habima Square Complex** includes Israel's National Theatre, the Habima (18); the Helena Rubenstein Pavilion (19) and the Frederic Mann Auditorium (20), principal home of the Israel Philarmonic Orchestra. It is located near the eastern end of Dizengoff, and the various venues are grouped around the Ya'akov Gardens between Tarsat and Huber Mann. There is a large CP in the centre, accessed from Hubermann. Just to the side of the Habima Theatre entrance is a **café**, which has ramped access from the CP or from Tarsat. This has a **unisex wheelchair toilet (D75 ST100)** by the top of the ramp from Tarsat.

Habima Theatre (18), Kikar Habima *Tel:* 03 526-6666. Check *What's on in Tel Aviv* for listings, but note that most performances are in Hebrew, although sometimes an English translation is provided through headsets. Ramped kerb from the CP outside. Flat entrance to box office over a small threshold [±3cm]. **The theatre has four auditoria**, only one of which has some seats and wheelchair spaces which can be reached without steps.

The accessible one is the **Robina**, which is also the largest. The main entrance is up a long curved ramp which bypasses +19 steps. The back

Map of Orange Route 2

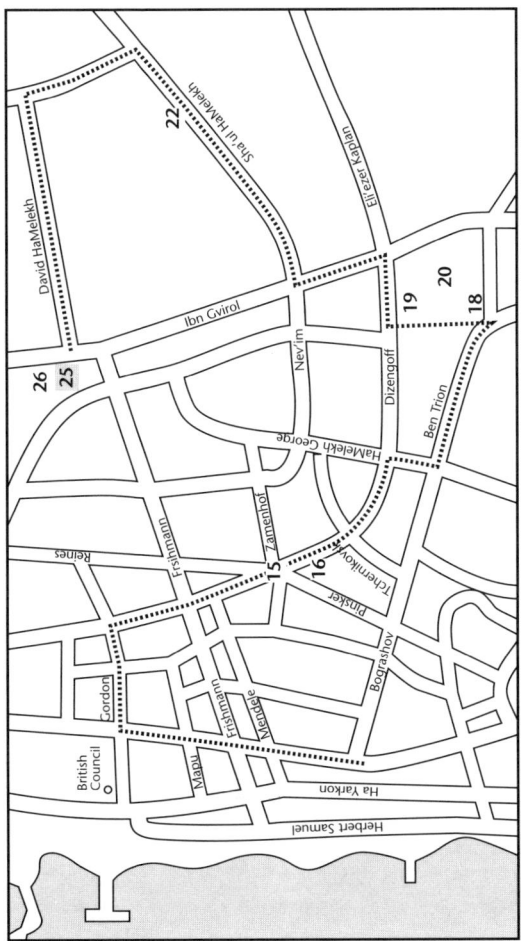

Key
Kikar Dizengoff (15)
Dizengoff Centre (16)
Habima Theatre (18)
Helena Rubenstein Pavillion (19)
Frederic Mann Auditorium (20)
Tel Aviv Museum of Art (22)
Rabin Square (25)
City Hall (26)

Orange route 2

of the stalls can be reached without steps by using the ramp. The stalls slope gently towards the stage. As there are fold-up seats at the end of each row, a considerable number of chair users can be accommodated. The bar is +16.

P A A &

The **Maskin** is entered at street level, to the right of the box office. It has a lift (D120 W170 L120) to an upper level, but a minimum of +9 to reach any seats.

P A ◢ N9+

The **Heineken** is more of a cabaret venue and the seating is bar-style, around tables. From street level there are −23 to the entrance.

P E23

The **Bertonov** is entered from Tarsat, and there are at least −7 to reach the theatre area, but we were unable to see this one.

P ◢ E7+

Helena Rubenstein Pavilion (19), Kikar Habima *Tel:* 03 528-7196. A venue for temporary modern art exhibitions. Flat entrance from Tarsat. The GF is step-free, but there are +12+12 to the upper floors and −12 to a basement area. They say that they are planning to provide a platform stairlift, but they've been saying much the same for the past twenty years, so don't hold your breath. Unadapted toilets −12−7 from the GF.

P A ◢ N24 & 40%

Mann Auditorium (20), Kikar Habima *Tel:* 03 525-1502 *Fax:* 03 525-3695. Home of the Israel Philharmonic Orchestra. The front entrance is flat into the lobby and ticket office. Chair users (and others) can use the artists entrance about 50-60m down Hubermann to bypass the steps after the lobby. Inside there is a lift (D100 W100+ L100+), allowing step-free access to the front of the hall where there are chair spaces and/or people can use the front row seats. We were told that there is an adapted toilet, but we did not see it. We were also told that disabled people came regularly to concerts.

P A ↑↓ &

Tel Aviv Museum of Art (22), 27 Shaul HaMelekh Street *Tel:* 03 696-1297, is near the junction with Weizman. It houses an extensive collection of interesting impressionist and post-impressionist art. It's quite big, measuring something like 100 by 100m. Parking in the street, up to 100m away, with some disabled persons spaces. If you ring you may be able to park in the staff CP off Berkovitz Street.

There's a big plaza in front, with about 75m from the road to the entrance. **Flat/ramped access almost everywhere in the museum.** The lift (D90 W150 L100) to the right of the entrance links all three floors. The ramp from the entrance hall gives step-free access to two mezzanine floors. Wherever you encounter some steps, they can be avoided by either coming back to the ramp or the lift and going up or down a level as appropriate. The auditorium is reached via −13 steps from the entrance, with a platform stairlift to bypass them. There are chair spaces at the back and it is step-free to row 15. In the basement there is a café, and a children's 'creative' area. **Adapted toilet (outerD68, D70+ ST60)** near the café, with the key kept behind the counter.

The museum is due to be enlarged by about 20% with a new wing.

Rabin Square (25), formerly the Kings of Israel square. It was renamed following the assassination of Israel's Prime Minister Yitzakh Rabin during a peace rally in 1995. It is a rather featureless concrete plaza, overlooked by the City Hall. The square houses a memorial to the holocaust and to the rebirth of the Jewish nation. Four steps in the middle of the square can be bypassed by going along the pavement on the side. The **Rabin Memorial** is at the site where he was shot, at the bottom of a flight of steps behind City Hall on Ibn Gvirol and near the corner of Ben Gurion. The memorial is set in the pavement, and the stones seem to rise up in revolt against the crime committed on them. On the wall across the road there is a large picture of Rabin and quite a lot of graffiti and popular remembrance.

City Hall (26) with the Tourist Information Office, see p180.

Other Tel Aviv sites

Gan Ha'ir Shopping Centre on Ibn Gvirol is just 30m north of the Rabin Memorial. UGCP on level −2, and flat entrances from Ibn Gvirol and Hadasa. It is about 100m square, and on four floors, including two levels of shops and a UGCP. Glass sided lift (D100 W160 L160) in the central atrium goes to all floors. There are two other lifts 20m away. Toilets with **wheelchair cubicles (D75 ST80 in the mens)** on level −1. Turn left out of the glass-sided lift, go through the glass doors in the corner of the central area and as the corridor bends right, the toilets are in the far left corner. The Enav Cultural Centre is on the roof and has step-free access.

Ben Gurion Exhibition Centre, 17 Ben Gurion Boulevard *Tel:* 03 522-1010. It is located off HaYarkon and was the home of Israel's first Prime Minister from the early 1930s until his death in 1973. It contains his extensive library with over twenty thousand books. Four parking places for visitors immediately outside. Entrance +3 steps. First floor +19. Outside the house, around the back and down a steep slope, there is a unisex toilet (D75 opens in) which may be usable if a chair user had a companion to take the chair out after transferring. There is no ST space.

[P] [◢] E3N19

The **Azrieli Centre** is by Hashalom station and also the Ayalon junction with Kaplan which runs into Ha'Tachmoshet on the bridge over the motorway. It is a huge shopping complex with a number of cafés, over a massive UGCP. This can be approached from several different sides, including one off Ayalon south. There are many disabled persons parking spaces on level –2 *with* a good space alongside the car for getting out! There are several blocks of **lifts (all D100+ W130+ L200+)**. On the two shopping floors there are three main legs stretching out from a central plaza. These legs vary in length from 50m to 120m, which gives an idea of the sheer size of the place. In the toilet blocks on each floor there are **two unisex wheelchair toilets (D70+ ST70+)** built to a good specification. We found more wheelchair-accessible toilets in this one building than we did in the whole of the rest of Tel Aviv! It is certainly a good place for shopping, and might even be a place to spend time on a rainy day if you've nowhere else to go.

Northern Tel Aviv

Diaspora Museum, Tel Aviv University campus, Klausner Street *e-mail:* bhwebmaster@bh.org.il *Tel:* 03 646-2020 *Fax:* 03 646-2134. The museum is in the centre of the university campus in the north of Tel Aviv. It records the life, culture and faith of the Jewish diaspora throughout the ages. CP about 100m from the entrance, or near the Matatia Gate (No 2) about 150m. The site is flat. It is step-free to reception, and all the floors can be accessed by a lift (D80 W150 L130). This is staff controlled, and you will have to ask to use it each time you change floors. It bypasses the +19; +23; +27 and +27 steps which separate the various floors. Flat access almost everywhere from the lift. It would take nearly 100m on each floor to go around and see all the sections. Signposting to the lift is good, and there are plenty of benches. Cafeteria on the GF. Adapted cubicles in the toilets on the lower GF were locked when we tried to survey as the museum was about to close, but the 1988 guide describes them as 'large'.

Eretz Israel Museum, 2 Haim Levanon Street *Tel:* 03 641-5244 *Fax:* 03 641-2408. The museum is located just to the south of the university campus in north Tel Aviv. It is a large multidisciplinary museum including the ethnography, history and culture of the land of Israel, together with a state-of-the-art planetarium, and philatelic and numismatic displays. There is also an archaeological site. CP near the entrance with five disabled persons spaces. **The museum is housed in a series of pavilions with the site measuring some 500 by 900m**, although several of the pavilions are within 250m of the entrance. An excellent scaled map is available, showing where most of the steps are, and, generally, the routes to bypass them. The site has been well adapted to provide step-free access almost everywhere.

In the Postal Museum a lift (D85 W100 L160) bypasses the –22 steps. The Migdal Gallery has an observation tower, with a lift (D120 W140 L145). The Man and his Work centre has +3 which can be bypassed by taking the path to the right and going in through the second door you come to. Access to the Planeterium is up quite a steep ramp. The Tell Qasile excavations inevitably involve rough paths and slopes. The Flour Mill has a flat entrance nearest to the tennis courts, if you want to avoid the hump back bridges. The site has several seats around the place. There are **wheelchair cubicles (D80 ST70)** in the toilets near the entrance.

South of Tel Aviv

Etzel (Irgun) Museum *Tel:* 03 577-2044 at the south end of the Charles Clore Park. This is dedicated to the history of the Irgun, specialising in the years 1947–48. It is a modern construction within the shell of one of the old buildings of Jaffa's former Manshieh Quarter. CP about 100m away, but some carelessly strewn boulders partially block access from near the CP entrance. There are other ways around, taking you a little further. Entrance +5+3 steps bypassed by a ramp, but using the ramped entrance involves getting a door unlocked and a desk moved. 90% accessible without steps, but +17 to a small section. Film/video room with movable chairs. **Wheelchair cubicle (D80 ST70)** in the men's toilets and reached via two slightly narrow turns (W70). It is not signed, and was locked (!).

Just north of the Etzel Museum is **Alma Beach** with the possibility of swimming, and with a café behind. It is step-free to the beach, and about 50m across the soft sand to the sea. They have tried to block off step-free access to the café, but you can get in from the north side without steps. Just across from the café is a toilet block with a **wheelchair cubicle (D85**

ST80) in both mens and womens toilets, but with the annoying bar which will not stay retracted – common in Israel.

Jaffa

Old Jaffa is just south of Tel Aviv, built around the original port of Joppa. It is a harbour-side town situated on a hill and extensively redeveloped as a tourist attraction. There are maps in RG p87 and LP p235. The development has been done in 'ye olde worlde' style and, as in other places in Israel, rough paving slabs have been used throughout the pedestrianised areas. Combined with occasional steep slopes and many more gentle slopes, this leads to the area being something of a challenge access-wise. In our view, Jaffa is a little over-rated in the guidebooks, but if you have a free half-day in Tel Aviv, it's probably worth a visit.

If you come from Tel Aviv, one of the first sights is the Ottoman Clock-tower just before Yefet Street. On the hilltop is Kedumin Square, which is pedestrianised, and from this focal point most of the places of interest are scattered around within about 350m distance. Down the side of the hill towards the harbour and going down to the port, there is a maze of narrow alleys, some with slippery steps. On the other side of the square there are the Rameses Gardens, with both steps and steep slopes, and a little to the south is the artists area. New Jaffa is the rather more run-down area around the bottom of the hill. Jaffa is supposed to be the nightclub capital of Israel. Unfortunately we were too busy writing-up our survey forms to be able to find out!

Kedumin Square. There is on-street parking nearby, and two small CPs, one at each end of the square off Mifratz Schlomo. It is surrounded by restaurants, snack bars, jewellery and souvenir shops.

The **Visitors Centre** *Tel:* 03 518-2680 is under the square. The −22 steps at the entrance are bypassed by a well-signed ramp from the opposite corner of the square. This is quite steep, and leads to a door into the centre. Inside there is an exhibition about Jaffa's history and some excavations with a 60m long walkway running around them.

 90%

The **Jaffa Museum of Antiquities**, 10 Mifratz Schlomo Street, Old Jaffa *Tel:* 03 682-5375 is about 300m north of Kedumin Square, down the hill. Street parking outside. Entrance +3 steps bypassed by a ramp to the front courtyard. +29 to the small museum.

P ⬛ E29

St Peter's Church, 1 Mifratz Schlomo is located on the north side of Kedumin Square some 50m from the Visitors Centre. Small CP outside. Main entrance +1 [6cm] and then a ±1 [13cm] threshold into a small anteroom. The door only opens to 45° and is D60. Our chair using surveyor just scraped in. The 17thC church has beautiful marble walls, but the lighting is poor, and the paintings and side altars are not well lit.

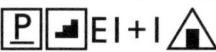

The **Artists Colony** around Mazal Arie is on the hillside, and consists of cobbled pedestrianised arcades containing somewhat touristy (and rather expensive) shops. Access is generally difficult. There is ramped access into some of the arcades, but all are sloped, with 2/3 steps every 20m or so. Most of the shops have a step at the entrance and a narrow door.

Ilana Goor Museum, 4 Mazal Dagim Street, Old Jaffa 68036 *Tel:* 03 683-7676 *Fax:* 03 683-6699. In a hilly area with rough paving. Street parking possible. Built in 1740 for Jewish pilgrims, it now houses a large collection of modern sculpture on three floors. Entrance is possible either through the shop in Mazal Arie Street at GF level or from Mazal Dagim leading into the first floor. There is a small lift (D75 W100 L75) in which a chair user would probably need to remove their footplates. This links the floors and gives step-free access to all the GF, and about 60% on the first and second floors. The remainder is +4 in each case.

 60%

The **Flea Market** off Hagareh Square lies between Rehov Bet Eshel and Rehov Olei Tziyon. Very limited parking. The walkways are flat but uneven, and can get very crowded. Most of the shops have a step at the entrance. The Market has a good atmosphere, and is worth a visit so long as you can cope with the (minor?) access hassles. It covers about 100m square.

 80%

The Great Mosque, Mifratz Schlomo, Jaffa is about 20m from the junction with Mifratz Yefet. The sign just inside says 'No Entry for Strangers' and, in general, non-Muslims are not welcome. Entrance +1, and then a rounded ±1 [20cm] threshold, followed by –4.

◢ EI ± I

There are two accessible toilets, both on Mifratz Schlomo. One is opposite St Peter's Church, where there is a **wheelchair cubicle (D115 ST80)** in the men's. We were unable to check the women's as the attendant spoke no

English. South of the Square, and just over the hill, there is a **unisex wheelchair toilet (D90 ST70)** next to the Muscat Restaurant and just before Mazal Dagim.

We also found the **Abouelafia Restaurant**, 4 Mifratz Schlomo *Tel:* 03 681-4335, situated 150m north of Kedumim Square down the hill. Entrance +3 steps with a ramped bypass. Wide entrance door and movable furniture in the restaurant. **Adapted unisex toilet (D58 ST63)**; the door would be too small for some, but as it opens outwards, it is better than many.

Around Tel Aviv

Carmel Winery, Ha Carmel Street, **Rishon Le Zion (Tsiyon)** *Tel:* 03 964-2021 *Fax:* 03 967-5974. Located just south of route 1 on the 412. The winery is just off Herzl Street and 30m down Ha Carmel, on the right. The cellars were completed in 1897, and it is a kosher winery, founded by Baron de Rothschild. Book in advance for a guided tour, and they may be able to organise on-site parking if you ask. The tour takes you about 300m around the slightly rough tarmaced perimeter road, visiting various rooms en route. The first room has –3 steps. The wine vats are reached via –15–15, and the steps are somewhat slippery. There is a ramp and then +1 [5cm] to the ageing room. You can reach the factory floor in the bottling and packaging room. There are +22 to a viewing gallery but you can see a fair amount of the action from the ground. To get to the tasting room there are +9, but you can also taste/drink at ground level if you want to!

Weizmann Institute of Science, Rehov Herzl, **Rehovot** *Tel:* 08 934-4500. Named after Israel's first President, the Institute is well signed off the route 412, coming from Tel Aviv. There are some sixty buildings spread over a large site. The central road is about 1km long. CP, café and **unisex wheelchair toilet (D70 ST70)** by the Levinson Visitors Centre. This was unfortunately closed when we visited, but you can get a good site plan there. Visitors tours start from here, and cover about 1.5km. Our survey team went for a walk through the grounds, and described it as 'lovely'. The only barrier was the occasional kerb. Four other disabled persons toilets are marked on the plan, and the one by the main entrance to the Garden of Science was a **unisex wheelchair toilet (D85 ST80)**. The others were locked, but on the basis that the two we saw were good, it is likely that the others are as well.

At the end of the road is the Memorial Plaza, reached via +15 steps. There are a further +37, spread over some 500m, to the Weizmann House. These can be bypassed by taking the road from the roundabout by the memorial. The house was being completely refurbished when we visited.

St George's Church, Lod (Lydda). This houses the tomb of St George, who was a Roman conscript, martyred for tearing up a copy of Emperor Diocletian's decree forbidding the practice of Christianity. Richard the Lionheart was so taken with his story that he adopted St George as the patron saint of England. St George is also revered by Muslims as a human manifestation of a spirit known as Al-Khader, originating from Elijah who ascended to heaven in a fiery chariot. St George's rescue of the damsel from the dragon is very much in the style of Al-Khader. The church is just south of the bus station, and you can find it because it has a tall white spire visible above the buildings around. Parking within 50m. If the church is locked, use the bell on the door just across the pathway, and someone will come to open the church. Entrance –3 steps, and then most of the church is flat. There are –17 to the small crypt with the grave. The church has a fine collection of icons, Byzantine apses, Crusader arches and Islamic columns.

Almost next door to St George's is a **mosque**, which can be visited, with permission, but not at the hour of prayer. Entrance to courtyard via –4, then +1 into the mosque.

P ◢ E4

Neot Kedumim, The Biblical Landscape Reserve, POB 1007, Lod 71100 *web-site:* www.neot-kedumim.org.il *Tel:* 08 977-0777 *Fax:* 08 977-0766. It is located and clearly signed just off the 443 about half-way between Jerusalem and Tel Aviv and near the extensive Modi'in developments. CP outside, and a welcoming sign for disabled visitors (!) saying that information is available at the desk in reception. A 20m ramp bypasses +10 steps up to the reception area. There is another CP for disabled persons, further on inside the reserve. There are three step-free trails through the reserve described as fully accessible. They are well marked, and there is a clear map to go with them. This, however, doesn't currently show where the hill is towards the centre of the site, probably towards the far end of Trail B. Descriptive booklets highlighting things of interest en route, and/or an audio guide in Hebrew or English are available when you have chosen a particular trail.

We looked at Trail A which is 2.4km long. Trail B is somewhat shorter, but more hilly. The routes are paved, but you will have to get used to slopes, as the whole site is quite hilly. You can, however, see quite a lot without going along a full trail, although you will definitely miss out on part of the experience.

By the disabled persons CP inside there is a second reception area where **you can pick up a two seat electric buggy** to go around one of the trails. The seat is a bench seat, and if has a rectangular sunshade to stop you from getting burned (or wet!). These are ideal for many disabled walkers, and for some chair users. They have six such buggies, and if you ring first you can be sure of getting one reasonably quickly.

The snack bar is up a modest slope. There are **three unisex wheelchair toilets, all (D70+ ST70+)** on the site. They are fairly close together. One is some 50m down the slope from reception. The second is near the building opposite the disabled persons parking spaces and the third is just down the hill from the snack bar.

Emmaus Monastery, Latrun *Tel:* 08 925-6940. An imposing monastery building up a hill overlooking the flat plain and just by the Latrun junction on route 1. Entrance via a rough steep path about 150m long, but if you ask at the gate, you can get permission to drive up. Note that it's quite a steep path to get the 20m or so up to the kiosk by the gate. You might have to attract attention by gently hooting! Near the bottom, and the site entrance, there are the ruins of a Byzantine church. From the CP at the top there are +8 steps to the chapel, followed by +11 tight spiralled steps to a viewing platform. We were told that the +8 could be bypassed by going through a back entrance to the monastery, and that it is possible just to stay at the chapel level. The chapel is beautifully decorated with icons and with a modern altar backdrop, but it is primarily a place for prayer, and it is important to respect the purpose and sanctity of the place.

Netanya

Netanya is a seaside resort some 32km north of Tel Aviv. It has a number of good features, as **the town centre is flat**, it is relatively quiet and uncongested compared with Tel Aviv, and there is some accessible accommodation. See LP pp248-251 or RG pp156-159. The beach, however, is at the bottom of a cliff which has about 100 steps down and up. The town would provide a relaxed centre for making exploratory day trips either to Jerusalem or Galilee, and it would be about a 1.5 hour drive to either. As with a number of other places, many people there do not speak English.

There is a pedestrianised area with shops and cafés on Herzl once you get past Dizengoff, and this leads on to Kikar Ha'atzma'ut (Independence Square) which is a large open square. The rest of Herzl has more shops and cafés, and near the post office is the Hasha'on Shopping Mall. It is all fairly spacious and relaxed.

Beyond Ha'atzma'ut there is a long **cliff-top promenade** going in both directions in front of the line of hotels and appartment blocks. As there are roughly a hundred steps down to the beach, you may prefer to use the road down which is accessed from the end of Matityahu Dankner near the junction with Baruch Ram. The road with a barrier across it leads back down the cliffside and then turns along the back of the **beach**. There is parking and step-free access from near the tunnel. There are then –1, –2 or –3 steps down on to the sand, and it is 30-40m to the sea. Around the paved area there is a restaurant and bar, and there are numerous shaded open tent-like structures to provide some shade. If you go through the tunnel there is a further beach area, and it is possible to drive right out to near the water's edge if getting over the hot soft sand is a problem.

Tourist Information Office, corner of Ha'atzma'ut and Gad Machnes *Tel:* 09 882-7286 *Fax:* 09 884-1348. Parking nearby is possible, and the office is in one of the sea-side corners of Independence Square (Kikar Ha'atzma'ut). The office is step-free, and has a striking design. They have a really good street plan and an accompanying leaflet, but little or no information specifically for disabled visitors. The main administrative office is at 15 Herzl Street *Tel:* 09 860-3324.

The main **Post Office** is at the junction between Herzl and Raziel just across the road from the Hasha'on Shopping Mall. As the office is up a steep hill from the road, the best approach is from the Mall, using its lift to the second floor. There is then a bridge over Herzl and a ramped route to the post office. The route involves just over 100m from the lifts. The post office is step-free. Just across the area in front of the post office is the **courthouse**. This is also ramped, so if you commit a serious enough offence to appear in court, you will not be able to complain about the poor access!

Hasha'on Shopping Mall on the corner of Herzl and Petah Tikva. UGCP entrance off Haportzim which is itself a turning off Petah Tikva. Lifts (D110 W120 L200) to the shopping centre, but these do not serve levels 4 and 5 of the CP. Step-free pedestrian entrances both from the corner of Petah Tikva and Herzl, and the corner with Haportzim. There is also an upper level footbridge over Herzl, leading to the post office and courthouse, from which there is a long steep ramp back down to Herzl. The centre is about 100m from end to end. **Wheelchair cubicles (D80 ST80)** in the men's and women's toilets on level two, and in the CP level 3 (or more correctly –3).

Built into the cliffside, just past Ha'atzma'ut Square is an **amphitheatre** where there are various music performances and cinema shows throughout the summer months. There is step-free access to the back, and also a ramp leading to a tier about half-way down. The seats are in the form of stone steps with no backs. Two or three chair users could be accommodated at the lower level, and/or there is plenty of room around the back. It's a dramatic setting, with the sea at the bottom of the cliffs behind the stage.

[P] [&]

Just by the amphitheatre there is a block of toilets, but in spite of there being a substantial number of local disabled people there was no provision of a disabled person's toilet or cubicle, and the only ones we found were in the shopping mall.

Netanya Diamond Centre, 90 Herzl Street, Netanya *Tel:* 09 862-4770 *Fax:* 09 861-5106. Located about 200m from the route 2 freeway, Netanya interchange. **It is Israel's largest diamond processing centre, and you can see the craftsmen at work**. CP in front, but it can only be approached if you are heading out of town as Herzl is a dual carriageway. Ramped entrance, with ramps leading to the exhibition, film, workshop and shop. Outside there's a café with movable furniture. The complete tour is less than 100m in length and while some of the ramps were an afterthought, and a little rough, the staff are helpful. No adapted toilets.

There is a **unisex adapted toilet (D74 ST64)** off the lobby in La Promenade Hotel, 6 Gad Machnes. The +7 steps at the hotel entrance are bypassed by a ramp, then there are +3 to the left of the lobby bypassed by a ramp.

Caesarea

There is a large and developing residential area in Caesarea, together with two important and impressive historical sites in the Caesarea National Park. There are also extensive remains of a Roman aqueduct just to the north of the Park. Caesarea is situated off route 2 between Tel Aviv and Haifa, just north of the Hadera power station. You leave at the junction called Qesariyya, and the National Park is clearly signed.

Caesarea National Park, *Tel:* 06 636-1358 *Fax:* 06 626-2056, is a large area lying for some 2km alongside the Mediterranean. There are two distinct sites with three entrances two of which provide easy access, see the map opposite. You are given a detailed site plan at the ticket office, and the numbers referred to here are those on that plan. There is parking by the southernmost entrance, and in the large rectangular CP between this and the middle entrance. There is a further CP opposite the northerly entrance.

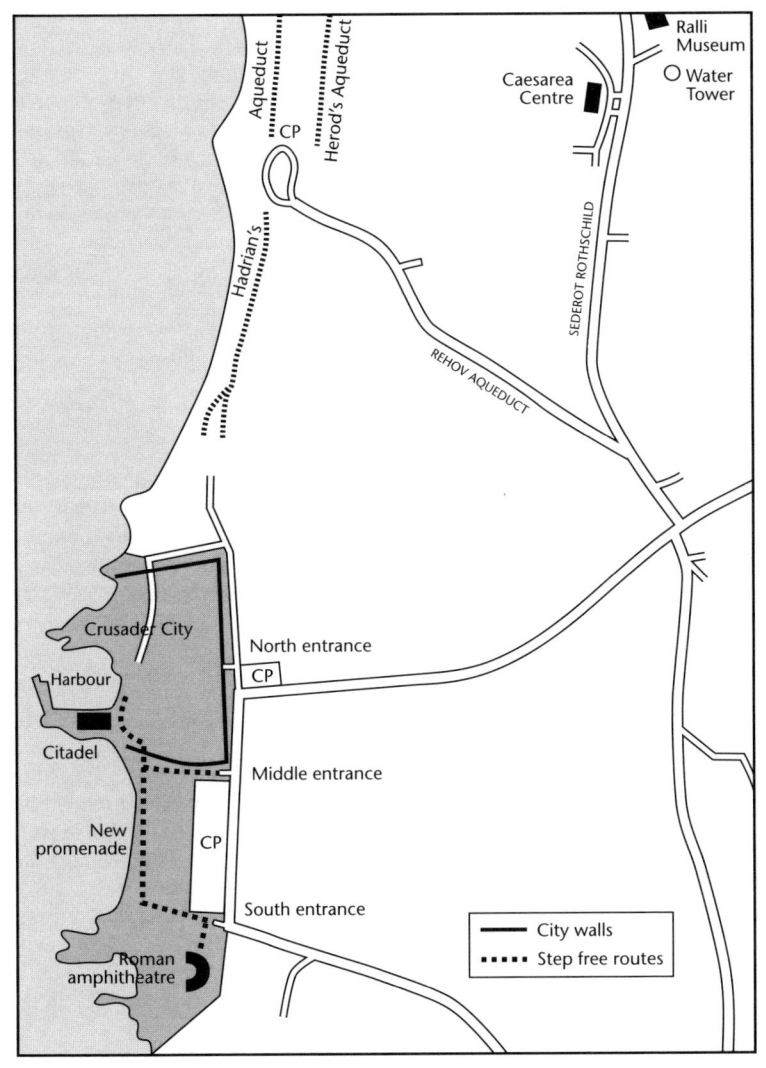

Caesarea

The larger site currently, is the **Crusader City**, whose walls can be seen from the road outside. **The easiest way into the City is from just outside the walls, using the middle entrance**. From this, a paved and ramped route, slightly steep in places, leads down outside the walls towards the harbour. You reach the harbour and the City by going through an archway in the walls on your right. Inside the City the area by the harbour is flat, and many of the paths are paved. Development and building was still going on when we visited. Around the harbour there is a mosque minaret, restaurants, shops and a good view of some of the excavations. To visit most of the site using this route would involve a distance of about 800m.

To reach the City from the northern entrance involves using a really rough and bumpy path, with some quite large awkward steps en route. It is an original path from Crusader times, and access was not a particularly important consideration. There is, however, an even easier way of getting there, useful for anyone for whom distance is particularly important. This involves using the road which runs alongside the walls going north from the northern entrance. There is a bar across it, and you will have to ask for it to be opened at the ticket office. However, by this route, you can drive right round to a CP which is less than 50m from the flat harbour area.

Around the harbour, the Crusaders Restaurant has flat access, while there is −1 [5cm] step to get into Charley's Café/Restaurant. The shops are quite small, and several have +1 at the entrance. There are +3 to the glassblowers. Although the toilets nearby do not currently have a disabled persons cubicle, we were told by the developers that it was planned to provide one by the end of 1999.

A large area where there was a Herodian Amphitheatre (3) between the two sites is being extensively developed, and you will be able to reach it from the middle entrance, but when you get near the sea, you turn left, instead of going right through the arch into the Crusader City. The plans here include a seafront promenade which will lead all the way past the Roman amphitheatre (13) nearly 1km to the south. Currently the southern site is more compact. If you ask, you may even be able to park inside the gates, but there is also parking outside. The main sight is the well restored **Roman amphitheatre**, which is impressive in itself, and where there are performances from time to time. With the backdrop of the sea, these could be impressive. Someone in the ticket office will open the gate to bypass the turnstile. **From the entrance, it is about 100m to the theatre**. The best place to get a view is to go to the left, up the slope (slightly gravelly) and go through entrance number two into the theatre. This takes you through an archway over some bumps to the top of the first circle in the amphitheatre. Note that there are no barriers on or around the tiers of steps/seats, but you get a wonderful view, and at least an idea of what it was like to come to a performance.

To get down to the stage area, go back towards the site entrance, and then round the outside of the theatre. There is a route which involves –2–1 steps and a somewhat uneven passage with some slopes and rocky bits.

Wheelchair toilet (D80 ST80) about 100m from the site entrance, towards the sea, and +1 [5cm] en route. Café by the entrance, +1 [5cm].

With the redevelopment of the whole site, it is planned that there will be step-free access from the Roman amphitheatre site alongside the Herodian amphitheatre to the Crusader City. However, bear in mind that it's a long way, and you may feel that the best way to visit is to see the southern site (the Roman bit) and then park near the middle entrance or even drive along the road at the north end right round to the harbour area, as described above, and this would certainly involve much less walking or wheeling.

To see the **Roman Aqueduct**, go into the residential area, turn first left, and then fork left again by the sculpture (which is an inverted U) soon afterwards. It's about 2km altogether. If you get to the Caesarea Centre, you've gone too far. There's a CP near the sea, where the remains of a massive aqueduct can be seen.

Haifa and the north coast

This chapter covers:
- **Haifa city**; the Carmel Centre; and western Haifa.
- Sites to the south including Atlit and Bet She'arim are described.
- **Sites** to the north include **Acre**, **Nahariya**, **Rosh Hanikra** and the Yehi'am National Park.

Haifa is built on the side of a steep hill, and stratified on three main levels. The lower level is around the port, with the railway and bus stations. Above this is Hadar Carmel, which we refer to as central Haifa. At the top of the hill, is the Carmel Centre, home to the upmarket hotels, and the more trendy shops and restaurants. There is a further area away from the centre, referred to as Western Haifa which includes Elijah's Cave, the beach and the cable car up to the Carmelite Monastery.

Israel's third city and its most important port is the centre of considerable industrial activity, especially along the coast towards Acre. Haifa grew as a result of its fame for shipbuilding and its Talmudic College in the 10thC. It was captured by the Crusaders and then recaptured by Saladin, although the main Crusader centre was Acre, just up the coast. It was held by Mamluks and then the Ottomans. The port continued to develop and was enhanced by a jetty being constructed for the visit of German Emperor, William II, in 1898. In 1948 it was the main port of entry for Jewish immigrants from Europe.

There is some fine scenery in the Carmel Hills to the south (an area called Little Switzerland), along with a good beach and, of course, the area is very much associated with the Biblical prophet Elijah. There are also several Druze villages to the south.

We managed to visit most of the sites of interest, but as we were there during Pesach/Passover, some places were closed for several days.

Near the port the main shopping area is fairly flat but the rest of the town, including many of the sights, is on the steep slopes of Mount Carmel. There's little of special interest except, perhaps, the Bahai shrine with its distinctive dome, and some of the museums. A so-called underground railway links the lower part of town with the Carmel Centre at the top. In reality this is a mountain railway with steep stepped stations, and in no way can it be described as 'accessible'. The Tourist Information Office have put together a number of walks, rather like the Orange Route walks in Tel Aviv. However, **the principal walk is called the Thousand Steps Way as it uses the numerous flights of stairs that link Haifa's different levels, illustrating some of the difficulties facing the disabled visitor to Haifa**.

Large parts of lower Haifa were being rebuilt when we visited. This included a petrol station with a large UGCP in a new complex opposite Bank Hapoalim in HaPalyam Avenue, 50m from the junction with Khatib Street. Outside they advertised disabled persons facilities. Just by the pumps there was a **unisex adapted toilet (D80 ST0)** also used as a store cupboard. ST would be about 50 without the bar and toilet-roll holder that effectively reduce it to 0. The small snack bar attached to the petrol station has +4 steps and no bypass. Regrettably this illustrates that even brand new facilities are not designed to be 'disabled-friendly'.

Tourist Information Office, Central Bus Station (Lower Level) *Tel:* 04 851-2208. It is simply an information kiosk whose staff are mainly Hebrew speaking and which has no reliable access information. The main office is at 48 Ben Gurion Avenue *e-mail:* haifa5@netvision.net.il *Tel:* 04 853-5606 *Fax:* 04 853-5610.

We found two **Post Offices**. One is at 152 Yafo at the junction with Elomar Street. Entrance +1 step with a ramp bypass. The other was at 19 HaPalyam just 100m from the subway station (Paris Square). The +12 steps at the entrance are bypassed by a ramp.

The **Carmelit Subway** links lower Haifa with the top of Mount Carmel, but it is more like a mountain funicular than an underground railway. It is not by any stretch of the imagination 'accessible'! At the Paris station at the bottom there are –33 steps to the platform, although there's an escalator to come up to street level if you are getting off the train. On the platform there are eight pairs of steps matching the train which is on a permanent incline. For the minimum number of steps, if you're going to the top, go to the front of the train (ie +16). At Gan-ha'em station at the top, the incline is much steeper and there are eight sets of six steps between the front and back of the train. After that there are +36 to the street level bypassed by an escalator. The stations en route also involve steps, but a detailed survey didn't seem worth the effort.

Lower Haifa

Railway Station, situated behind the **Bus Station** on the main coastal road, Route 2 (or Sederot Hahaganah). There is a junction with Hel Hayam where you can turn in, heading for signs to Bat Galim. Straight-ahead is a roundabout, which you should use to turn around completely, allowing you to turn onto a slip road on the right leading to both Bus and Railway Stations. Our surveying teams felt that the trains were not accessible as there were steps to nearly all the platforms.

There's a fabulous view of the Bahai Shrine from Ben Gurion, as the street goes directly upwards towards the gardens, and the domed building stands out on the hillside above.

We didn't manage to survey the Railway Museum, Dagon Grain Silo and the Israel Edible Oil Museum, as we were there during Passover, and they were shut.

Central Haifa

Bahai Shrine and Persian Gardens, Sederot Hatzionut. Located some way up the steep side of Mount Carmel and it is well worth taking a trip up there. **The golden dome of the shrine is one of the city's most notable landmarks**. The Bahai Faith originated in Persia in the mid-19thC. It's founder was a Moslem, Mizra Ali Mohammad, who declared himself El Bab, the Gateway to God, in 1844. He was declared a heretic and killed in 1850. In 1909 his remains were brought secretly to Palestine where a suitably splendid place of burial could be built. The religion has no ministers, no ritual, and prayers are largely silent. It is based on universality and brotherhood of man and doesn't seem to imply rejection of the beliefs of others. The Shrine is only open from 9 am to 12 noon.

At the time of the survey there was a small on-site CP off Shiphrah Street (turn right going up Hatzionut, before the tunnel) that a disabled visitor can use with permission. It's then +12 steps to the start of the Gardens. From June 1999 there should be parking on Hatzionut in front of the Main Gate with a smooth ramped concrete path (50m) down to the start of the Gardens. There are then two routes to the Shrine; one is over 125m of large gravel stones, which are very rough requiring at least one, maybe two, able-bodied helpers for a chair user. The other is over 90m of smooth pebbles with +5 followed by 35m of the rough stuff again. **The public only has access to one small room in the shrine which is +1 [15cm], and is very peaceful**. Visitors must remove their shoes and a chair user must at least dust down their wheels.

The view from the Shrine over the Gardens is stunning. They are still building the gardens, but when they are finished, in two years time, there will be nineteen levels stretching over 1km down the hillside with 1,700 steps and no ramps! There is an unadapted toilet (D64), −7 from the small CP outside. The Archives are not open to non-Bahais.

Ursula Malbin Sculpture Gardens, Beth Benovember. A small public garden with twenty- two bronze statues of naked women, and some men, by a former refugee from the German Nazis, located just past the Bahai Shrine and Gardens off Sederot Hatzionut (indicated by an orange sign).

CP immediately outside. Entrance +2 steps. There is access to the first third of the garden along a rough uphill path (40m long) and the rest is up a large number of steps. There is lots of grass and plenty of benches but because the gardens are on the hillside, access is tricky. There are fine views of Haifa and the Mediterranean Sea.

[P] [/H] [■]E2 [&] 30%

Beit Chagall, 24 Hatzionut Street *Tel:* 04 852-2355, was the house of the artist Chagall and contains some of his works along with those of other artists. It is just by the junction with Hagafen (and diagonally opposite the Haifa Museum); there is street parking 20m away in Abbas Street. Entrance +2 steps bypassed by a ramp on the immediate left. The displays are on two floors each consisting of one 10x10m room. There are +9+8+5 with one handrail between floors and an unadapted toilet D58 on the left through the entrance.

[P] [/H] [■]E2N22

The Israel National Museum of Science, The Historic Technion Building, Shmaryahu Levin Street, Hader Hacarmel *Tel:* 04 862-8111 *e-mail:* sci–muse@netvision.net.il. Despite the stuffy title this is a fascinating "hands on" science museum with over two hundred interactive exhibits where the surveyors could have spent many hours.

Entrance to the site, by foot, is off Balfour Street. By car, follow the signs from Herzliya Street. There is an on-site CP in front of the building. The entrance is up a lot of steps but these can be bypassed by parking around the back, near the Jet Fighter and Tank. When we visited, one of the staff noticed that there was a wheelchair in the back of the car and directed us round the side and opened the gate. However, you may need a friend to run up the entrance steps and ask at reception to open the side gate so that you can get round to the back. Access from the rear CP is over some gravel and a +1 [15cm] kerb. Both can be bypassed by parking right next to the kerb. There is step-free access through a sliding door to reception on the right. Here you will need to exchange some ID (like your passport) for a key to the lift. The stairs between floors are for the general public; the lift which goes to all floors, is only for disabled people.

The Museum is on three floors, each of which are based around a wide corridor 100m long off which there are large rooms containing the exhibits. Smooth surfaces everywhere. **Unisex wheelchair toilet (D70, sliding, ST100)** in the basement. It is near the main central stairs, and signed.

[P] [/H] [A] [↑↓] [&] 90% [&wc]

We didn't survey Wadi Salib, the old city district, the Wadi Nisnas neighbourhood, nor the Hadar district and its pedestrianised Nordau Mall. We also didn't survey the New Haifa Museum, as it was closed during both our visits. When we visited in 1988, there was +1 step at the entrance, and most of the exhibits were on upper floors. There was no lift and no adapted toilets. The mezzanine was +15, the first floor +32, and the second floor a further +25.

The Carmel Centre, on top of Mount Carmel

Panorama Shopping Centre, Hanassi. A large shopping complex next to the Dan Panorama Hotel near the summit of Mount Carmel. There are two floors of shops and restaurants (with flat access and movable tables and chairs). There is an octagonal lift (D105, W110, L165) between floors, which also gives access to a large UGCP and a viewing point on top of the building. The viewing point outside is obstructed by a 105cm high barrier, but there are some perspex (see through) sections, and it's worth some effort as the view is spectacular. There is an unadapted toilet (D59) on the upper level, but a much better option is the **unisex wheelchair toilet (D90 ST80)** in the adjacent Dan Panorama Hotel. The hotel has ramped access from the street or the Shopping Centre. Access to the UGCP is at the rear from Yefem Nof Street, parking fee levied.

Haifa Zoo, Gan ha'Em Park, Carmel Centre. The entrance is 30m off Hanassi Street opposite the Panorama Centre. There is on street parking outside the Centre with one disabled persons space. To get to the entrance there is a ramp bypassing −6−11 steps, with a good accurate map nearby showing the position of steps within the Zoo. It is built on a hillside, and most of the paths are sloped, some of them steeply. Some 80% of the animals can be seen in their cages without using steps. There are plenty of seats about and also a café with flat access and movable seats. Our visit was curtailed by a thunderstorm so we were unable to check out all the exhibits including the three museums, which are housed in the same building within the Zoo. The nearest accessible toilet is in the lobby of the Dan Panorama Hotel.

The Mané-Katz Museum, 89 Yafe Nof Street *Tel:* 04 838-3554. Mané-Katz was given the house by the Municipality of Haifa so that, in return, he would bequeath his works of art to them. The collection includes watercolours, oils and gouache paintings along with drawings, and sculptures in bronze and plaster. There are also collections including clay toys from Eastern Europe, antique furniture and oriental carpets. The house is built close to the crest of Mount Carmel and has a panoramic view of the bay and of the hills behind. There are −16−13 steps to the entrance. There are three small rooms with step-free access throughout. Unadapted toilet +2.

The **Tikotin Museum of Japanese Art**, 89 Hanassi, Carmel Centre *Tel:* 04 838-3554 is approximately 300 metres down the hill from the Panorama Hotel. It is housed in an imposing building with interesting permanent and temporary exhibits of Japanese Art. There is street parking, including one disabled persons space outside the building. Although there are +20 steps to the entrance there is an alternative gently sloping wooden ramp to the left of the stairs. Through the door, reception is immediately to your left. We suggest you go anticlockwise (i.e. turn right) for step-free access. There is a lift to the first floor where there are **wheelchair cubicles (D75 ST80)** in both the men's and women's toilets. The first floor also has an auditorium reached via +4. A chair user can sit at the back to avoid the steps down to the front.

We didn't survey the Observatory on the top of the Eshkol Tower, nor the Ruben & Edith Hecht Museum at the bottom

Western Haifa

Cable Car 1km west along Route 2 to Tel Aviv from Haifa Central Bus Station, the Cable Car crosses the road. You can't miss the three ball-shaped compartments that run across at regular intervals. To reach the bottom station, head towards Bat Galim at the junction of Derech Yofo and Hel Hayam. At the roundabout on Hel Hayam you will need to turn left onto Ha'aliya and continue straight on until you reach the Cable Car Station. There is a restaurant complex at the bottom, on the coast, and the cars go up to the Carmelite Monastery past Elijah's Cave.

The ticket office is on ground level, and then there are +19+13 steps to get to the cars (to the left of the restaurant entrance). **The ramp which bypasses these has been deliberately blocked off (we were told) to discourage and prevent disabled people from using the cable car!!!** The implication was that the management thought that disabled people caused 'too much hassle' – a view that left us speechless. The cars themselves are quite small (diameter 105cm) with +1 [25cm] to get in. In principle, transfer would be perfectly possible for a reasonably strong paraplegic. At the top a turnstile has blocked the exit, and it is deliberately immovable, so there is no way out for a chair user, other than lifting the chair across the barrier. In days gone by we have done just such things ourselves, as we do not accept the validity of such barriers, nor of such attitudes. If you do happen to make it over the assault course, there is, ironically, a zigzag ramp leading up to the roadside. The restaurant at the bottom has step-free access and there are **adapted cubicles (D70 ST60)** in the toilets to the left of the doors into the restaurant.

Clandestine Immigration and Naval Museum, 204 Allenby *Tel:* 04 853-6249 *Fax:* 04 853-7672. It is located just across the main road (route 4) from the cable car station. The museum covers the clandestine immigration from 1934-1948 and some of the naval encounters of the Israeli Defence Force (IDF) since that time. The roads around were being extensively rebuilt when we visited, and parking may be difficult when this is complete. You may have to park some 200m up the hill near the Maritime Museum. There is a lip [2cm] at the entrance. Most of the inside area is flat. There is –1 [9cm] step to the outside exhibits. The boat is reached via +21−1 and then +19, and there are more steps inside the boat itself. The museum is compact, and even the outside area does not involve going much more than 100m.

The National Maritime Museum 198 Allenby Road, *Tel:* 04 853-6622 is situated just up the hill from the cable car station. Coming from Haifa Bus Station along route 2, turn left at the junction beside the Cable Car Station, then right. There should be a parking space outside the museum. The road beside the Maritime Museum, linking it with Route 2, was still being built when we surveyed, so it was a temporary dead end. The exact road layout and parking arrangements may therefore change. Kerb [12cm], and then the entrance with +3 steps bypassed by a ramp. To the left of the entrance, lifts inside (D90 W120 L140) bypass ±22 to the two other floors, making the entire museum accessible. The lift goes down to a UGCP, which may be needed if street parking becomes impossible. Ordinary toilets only; on the ground floor.

Elijah's Cave is approached from the road going past the Maritime Museum. From the Museum, walk around the hill towards the dual carriageway and take the second of two sets of steps on the left (marked by handrail supports coming out from the side of the wall). It is the traditional place where the prophet Elijah hid from King Ahab, after killing all the prophets of Baal on Mount Carmel. It says in the IH, that it is one of the few places where you may see Jews, Muslims and Christians praying in the same place. There is a large hollow to the left where Jews pray for Elijah's return, which will precede the coming of the Messiah. For Muslims, a prayer niche is located just past the hollow, and Christians can just pray anywhere. We visited during Pesach when it was clearly being used mainly by Jews.

Unfortunately, **access is difficult. There are +51+22 steps to the first sign to Elijah's Cave. There are a further +22 to the entrance**. The cave itself is a little area up +3, to the left of the main chamber. This chamber has been made into a synagogue when we visited, and at the far end tapestries are draped against the wall, beside a covered lantern.

The Carmelite Monastery on the hillside is probably much better reached by car. It is situated by the Stella Maris Lighthouse, on Derech Stella Maris. There is flat access from the road and a small CP. The entrance is to your right as you approach the main building with a ±1 [7cm, 4cm] threshold. Beautiful murals around the chapel depict Elijah's ascent to heaven in his chariot, and many other Biblical scenes. There is a magnificent statue of Our Lady of Mount Carmel above the altar. Directly ahead of the entrance are –6 steps to a hollow in the rock, dedicated to Elijah. Most of the cave, and the statue of Elijah in it, can be seen from the top of the stairs by a chair user. Stepping back, you can see the altar, which is raised, above the cave. The **Carmelite Museum** was closed for refurbishment when we visited.

Gallery Shopping Centre. Located west and south of Haifa, off route 2 towards Tel Aviv and by the junction signposted Tirat Carmel. It is next to a futuristic-looking big green conference centre. There is both ground level and UG parking. The GF entrance has +3 steps, bypassed by ramps. There are lifts down to the UGCP (D110 W130 L200), clearly signed. There are two main floors of shops, many of them are discount and electrical stores, and a big lift solely moving between these two floors operates in the middle of the mall. The entire length of the shopping mall is about 150m. There is a **wheelchair cubicle (D80 ST75).** In the toilets on the second floor near the fast food area.

Haifa beaches

There are a number of sandy beaches just to the south and to the west of Haifa, away from the port area. As you leave the route 2 for Tel Aviv, you go past a number of them. We visited South Dado Beach where there was an extensive development with a paved strip stretching for over 1.5km with CPs and cafés along the path, and shaded areas on the sand.

South Dado can be reached by one of three routes:

- from the north, the turn is Ha Tzedef, by a petrol station about 2km south of the Cable Car, and takes you past the Carmel Beach Hotel;
- the next turn is 2km further on; go right at the Tirat Carmel junction, and a seafront sign reads South Dado Beach;
- the third turn is another kilometre beyond the second. Join Route 2 from Tirat Carmel. After the road crosses the railway you will see an undeveloped end of the beach on the right and an unsignposted turning will take you into the southern end of the beachfront road. There are also two CPs at this end, and a small road festooned with no-waiting signs will take you to within 10m of the sea. This could be useful for some.

Around 1km from the northern entry to the beach road, **a large 'wheelchair' sign indicates an extraordinary specially built area by the sea, with parking for around 30 cars**. There is flat access to a rather dilapidated shower and toilet block built especially for disabled users. This consists of a communal changing room with wooden benches. There is a small toilet cubicle with hand-rails. A larger cubicle has a roll-in, string operated shower with no transfer seat and a **toilet (D85 ST125)**. A corner of the communal area, set apart by a wall, has two similar showers (basically raised taps connected to strings again) with two fold-up wooden transfer seats, one of which is completely broken, and the other is not much better (ST115). It appears that the entire block has not been cleaned or serviced for several years, and only succeeds in demonstrating the folly of setting apart the areas for disabled people from other facilities.

Further on from this block the builders have had another wry chuckle, by constructing a wooden drinks bar right across the ramped access to a nice little restaurant (bypassing +3).

There is however, a good ramp from the special changing area to within 30-40m of the sea, but then there are ramps at several other intervals along the seafront which are 90% step-free.

South of Haifa

Atlit Immigration Camp, Atlit. About 100m from Atlit Junction (Route 2) on the right. Well signposted. There is parking in front. The largest detention centre for Jewish migrants and refugees during the last 10 years of the British Mandate, housing anything up to 3,000. In October 1945, over 200 were liberated in a Palmach raid led by Yitzakh Rabin. It is step-free at the entrance and throughout the site but over rough surfaces. A guided tour (about 100m) takes you past a model of the camp (H100), a reconstruction of a residential barracks, +1 [4cm] bypassed via a ramp at the far end, and a disinfecting centre +1 [10cm] bypassed via a ramp. At the far end a film is shown (ramped access). The whole site is about 200m square, but you see almost everything on the tour. **Adapted cubicles (D80 ST50)** in both the men's and women's toilets next to the picnic area; 10m over rough ground from the ticket office.

Bet She'arim National Park *Tel:* 04 983-1643, *Fax:* 04 953-1551, near Kiryat Tivon, is quite well signposted off route 75. The area includes the remains of an ancient Jewish city and the National Park is set amongst a large cemetery. The various tombs date from 2nd to 4th Century CE. There is a large CP with a café and toilet nearby, up a rough paved ramp. **Adapted unisex toilet (D80, ST30, restricted by a basin)** behind the café and at the entrance to the men's toilets; locked when we visited so we had to ask for the key. On the site, the lower route marked on the plan provided at the ticket office is about 150m with a level gravelled path. From the path it is possible to see several of the tombs and caves without going over steps. If you want a closer look then there are −24 rough steps to the coffin; +3+2±1 (bumpy) −2 to the catacomb of the sarcophagus; +1 and a ramped bypass to −6 to the grave of Rabbi Yehuda Hanassi. The upper route shown on the plan involves many steps and some rough ground as it takes you up the steep hillside. Some of the names used in the plan provided are confusing as they differ somewhat from the signs by the various tombs. The café has step-free access and a varied menu and there are pleasant picnic areas around. A major comment on the accessibility of the site relates to the use of gravel for the main path as this presents significant problems for chair users.

Acre/Akko

The main place of interest in Acre is the Old Walled City. This is an atmospheric, largely Arab town, which at one time was the Crusaders' principal foothold in the Holy Land. Many of the current buildings are the work of Bedouin Chieftain Ahmad Al-Jazzar in the late 18thC. A sprawling new town with associated industrial area has grown up in the 20thC. The major sites described here are within the City Walls. *See* LP p274 and RG p221.

There are two main parking areas, one in the north at the beginning of Al-Jazzar Street and the other in the south by the lighthouse. Most of the City is fairly flat and the slopes there are gentle, but the surfaces are somewhat variable. There is some tarmac, and a bit of quite rough, paving and unmade ground.

The Old City is relatively compact and is very roughly a 500m square. Distances are therefore fairly short and most steps on the various routes can be bypassed. There are numerous shops, cafés and alleyways which add character.

From the northern CP the main sights are:

The **Souq al-Abyed** runs east–west just by the CP. Ramped entrance at the western end near the City Walls. The eastern entrance has –3 steps. The surface throughout is of very rough flagstones.

The **Al-Jazzar Mosque** is off the pedestrianised Al-Jazzar Street that is lined with cafés and small shops. Admission charged. There are +13+1 steps into the Courtyard. To enter the Mosque there are +1+1+1. No adapted toilets in the area.

The **Tourist Information Office** was closed when we visited, possibly permanently, entrance +4 steps. It seems that the ticket office at the Crusader City doubles as the information office *Tel:* 04 991-1764.

The **Citadel and Subterranean Crusader City** is entered from Al Jazzar Street opposite the Mosque. There are extensive excavations but ensuring the stability of the various structures is extremely difficult, so the work is ongoing. **Efforts are being made to make a substantial part of the City wheelchair accessible, but this work was incomplete when we surveyed**. The Halls underground form a vast complex of buildings which Al-Jazzar later used as the foundation for his Citadel. Entrance +1 step to the ticket office, then –6 bypassed by a very steep ramp. There are toilets at this level including a ramped **adapted unisex toilet (D90, ST60)** which was locked but the staff opened it for us. After the first hall, there are –16 to the Knights Hall. These can be bypassed by taking the wood bridge to the left +2 –1 and then a further –4 +1 into the Hall. From the bridge you can also enter the Fortress Courtyard from which the Crypt is –3 (with a ramped bypass) –1. The route through the tunnels was surveyed for an earlier edition and involved –13 difficult steps with a 90° turn at the bottom. At one stage the tunnel narrows down to only W53. There were a further +15–6+20 to get out. Quite how our survey team made it we're not sure. The chair had to be partially folded to get through the narrow bits. If you opt to avoid the tunnel then you have to retrace your steps to the main entrance.

A related site is the **Municipal Museum** just south of the Citadel and about 50m from the Crusader City entrance. The museum entrance can be reached step-free by passing the steps to your left and going around the outside of the Museum building turning left three times. Shortly after passing the steps there is a door labelled Turkish Baths House. This is normally the exit but provides the easiest access to the bath area, which is the most interesting room in the Museum, via –3. If you go around to the Museum entrance, as described, there are +3 +6 to the reclining room used after taking a bath.

P △ ■ E9/3

The Museum of Heroism was closed when we made our visit.

To get onto the City Walls, go down Salah al-Din Street by the Souq to the Land Gate. There is a gravel path running north along the base of the wall. The first ramp (which goes north) you come to is very rough and steep. The second one about 100m further along (which goes south) is also steep but much smoother. It is possible for a chair user with one or two strong friends to get up and down safely. This provides a good view of the Old City.

From the southern CP

The main sights are reached via the street at the southern end by the City Walls. Follow this round past **the restaurants, which are highly recommended, with good views across the Bay**. After about 80m the Khan al-Umden is on the right with –3 steps. However, if you follow the walkway round the outside there is flat access to the right through the arch under the clock tower off Venezia Square. A Khan was a pillared courtyard which provided a shopping place for groups of travellers and traders with space for their pack animals. There are three other Khans in Acre, but this one is the showpiece, and you would be justified in giving the others a miss if pressed for time.

At the north end of the lighthouse CP is a Bahai Temple. Go down the street to the right and through Genoa Square to St George's Church. Entrance +1 [10cm], closed at the time of our visit.

To get on to the southern City walls there is a steep ramp with ridges behind the lighthouse. There is a good view over the Med'. A ramp to the left takes you to St John's Church with –3 to the entrance. It was closed at the time of our visit. A little further on is the **Fishing Port** from which there is a pleasant walk around and behind the sea wall past the lighthouse which is flat, and suitable for chair users.

From Acre to Rosh Hanikra

Lohamei Hageta'ot Holocaust Museum, Kibbutz Lohamei Hageta'ot, Western Galilee 25220. The Kibbutz is well signed from Route 4. Go through the main gate and turn right immediately, into the CP. The main entrance to the Museum is on the opposite side of the building via –6+7 steps, however there is a flat entrance marked "Seminar" about 50m to the left of the CP. This is normally manned by a security guard, although their English isn't great so you may have a problem getting understood. Inside the lobby there is a **unisex wheelchair toilet (D80, ST100)**.

To get to the Museum, turn right down the corridor. The lift (D80 W90 L220) in the corridor, goes to the 1st floor and the upper split level of 2nd floor. Another lift (D70 W110 L110) from the 1st floor serves the lower GF, GF, and 2nd floor lower split level (there are –5 between the 2nd floor levels). The only parts that are not accessible on the flat are the Saloniki and Jews of Holland exhibits on the lower GF which are +8 from the lift.

Yad Layeled is in a separate building. It is a memorial to the children who died in the Holocaust. It is mostly underground and best reached from the unsurfaced, gravelly CP down the road to the right just before the kibbutz gate, as there is no step-free route from the main museum. From here there is a step-free path to the entrance, well signed, the exhibition takes the form of a downward spiral path around a stone memorial inscribed with the names of children who died in the Holocaust. About 60% is step-free, thereafter there are –3 steps, a 64cm gap and railway tracks to negotiate. Before these obstacles, however, you can leave the spiral, going into the Temporary Exhibitions Hall adjacent (step-free) where there is a key-operated lift between the two levels. This can take you to the bottom where approximately the last 20% of the spiral can be seen step-free. Exit the way you came in. There is an **adapted cubicle (D70 ST60)** in the women's toilets on the upper level of the Temporary Exhibitions Hall.

Bahai Shrine and Garden. Off Route 8510 about 200m from Akko North Junction (Route 4), about 3km north of the centre of Acre. The home of the Baha'Ullah whilst under house arrest until his death in 1892. Parking outside on rough ground, then about 1km through the gardens through deep gravel which our team of one chair user and one able-bodied person found extremely difficult to negotiate. The house was closed when we visited but we were told it would involve lots of steps with no ways to bypass them.

Nahariya

A seaside resort on the north Mediterranean coast, founded by German Jews in 1934. Recently the promenade along the sea front has been spruced up and there are numerous cafés and restaurants along the beach. The town of Nahariya sprawls considerably but the only areas of interest to the visitor are the beach and the tree lined Haga'aton Street which runs 1km from the beach to Route 4, this is the main shopping street. The town is flat throughout and there is quite a lot of on-street parking.

Tourist Office, Municipal Building, Haga'aton Street *Tel:* 04 987-9800. Set back from the road in a pedestrianised square. Closed when we visited, but we think it is step-free.

Municipal Museum, Municipal Building, Haga'aton Street *Tel:* 04 987-9863 was closed when we visited, but in the 1988 guide is described as being on the 5th, 6th and 7th floors. The entrance is flat, and there is a lift (D75 W145 L90) to get up to the museum.

Post Office, Haga'aton Street *Tel:* 04 992-0180 50m from Weizman Street and step-free.

Nahariya Railway Station: by junction Haga'aton Street and Route 4. Ramped access from Haga'aton Street.

North of Nahariya

Akhziv National Park is a small seaside park, perfect for picnics. It is just north of Nahariya on Route 4, next to a Club Med resort, and well signposted. CP at the front, right by the main road. A ramp to the right of the entrance avoids the +8 steps (the ramp gate should be open). The park contains some archaeological remains and a sheltered bathing beach. The total area is about 200m sq. There are steep hills but the paths are mostly good, except by the sea. By the sea there is a restaurant (–6–2). The toilets near the restaurant include a **unisex toilet (D90, the key is at the Ticket Office but our team couldn't coax it from them)**. A 50m path which is very rutted, slopes down to the water's edge.

Next door is **Akhzivland**, declared an independent state by local eccentric Eli Avivi and his wife. He told us that he was 185 years old, and the Turkish coffee we were offered was supposed to help you live 184 years! His house contains a sizeable assortment of archaeological remains, wall paintings and other assorted items collected over the years. CP in front, up a rough road from the National Park CP, and past the 'Parliament'.

Entrance +6 steps. The narrowest ground floor gap is W60 with +1 [20cm]–1 [10cm]. About 40% can be seen without further steps. There are rooms upstairs for campers equipped with sleeping bags, +14 or +14+12 or even +14+12+12. However this is not advisable in stormy weather as the upper half of the building is made from rough timber and partly open to the elements. The whole construction resembles a haunted house out of an American Western, liberally draped with chains and anchors. Staying alone is not recommended in several guidebooks, especially not for female travellers, although Eli and his wife seemed to be a pleasant and intriguing couple. Even if you can't make it into the house, it is worth a visit just to see the place and get your passport stamped. One of our surveyors left his in the car and was threatened with three days in prison!

Yehi'am National Park and Judin Fortress are situated near Kibbutz Yehiam and can be reached from the Nahariya – Ma'alor Road from route 89 and route 8833. The main feature of the Park is the fortress which was constructed by the Crusaders as part of a defensive line to protect the area around Acre. It was also used in the Israeli War of Independence in 1948. *See* plan in IH p605.

CP at the entrance where there is a shop with +2 steps. Nearby are the toilets. These are unadapted, and have inward opening doors, but quite generously sized cubicles (D75 ST80) in both the men's and women's. As the fortress is built on a hilltop, there is a steepish tarmac path about 200m long leading up to it.

Through the hall, the Fortress Bar/Café has +3 with a ramp bypass. You can go through the café to get into the Mosque via the courtyard.

To see the fortress, there is an inside route via +40 steps, but there is an alternative way around the outside. This takes you over rough loose stone and gravel and there are still +3+1+1+7 en route. There are +33+55 to the top of the Keep!

From the Mosque a route involving −2−3+7−8 via a difficult rocky undulating path takes you around the back of the Fortress, the narrowest point is 59cm wide. It leads around the outside to the front of the Central Gate.

Rosh Hanikra *Tel:* 04 985-7109 *Fax:* 04 985-7107. A cliff-top site right on the Lebanese border. The main attraction is the cable car which goes 100m down the cliff face where you can see two tunnels built by the British as part of the short-lived Haifa-Beirut-Tripoli railway. There are also some caves. In the summer there is a short excursion on a little motorised 'train' along the coast at the bottom of the cliffs.

As you come up route 4, the first sign you come to points "To the grottos and little train station", with a 'wheelchair' sign attached. If you follow this sign, go right at the first junction and right again when you get to the fork with parking to the left. This leads to a small CP outside the end of one of the tunnels. By the metal gates there is an encouraging sign that says "disabled visitors ring the bell". Unfortunately the bell and attached intercom are well hidden behind the gate at H145! During the summer, when the train is running, this entrance is staffed. In the winter you are reliant on the intercom to contact a member of staff who may take a little while to come and open the gate.

From the gate you can enter the first (southern) tunnel which has a slightly gravelled surface, and is about 100m long. This brings you to the bottom of the cable car and the entrance to the grottos. Our survey team assessed the grottos as being scarcely practical for chair users, involving –4+8–7 steps, steep slopes and rough, slippery rocks. The narrowest gap is W56.

The specially constructed viewing points for looking up and down the coast are between the tunnels and near the cable car stop. They have either +4, +5 or –1, and why they are not ramped is a mystery, in view of the efforts made to make the site more accessible. In the new toilet block near the bottom of the cable car there is a **unisex wheelchair toilet (D80 ST70)** although ST is difficult because of a retracting bar which will not stay retracted – a relatively common feature in Israel.

Past the viewing points is the northern tunnel which houses an audiovisual display with movable chairs. The projector was playing up when we were there, so we didn't see the show. The distance at the bottom from the southern tunnel to the little auditorium is less than 100m.

If you go past the sign on route 4 and climb up to the main CP at the top, the area is often congested. There are **wheelchair cubicles (D75 ST75 with a movable handrial which won't stay upright)** in the toilets by CP at the top. At the top of the cliff, adjacent to the border crossing, is the On the Border restaurant, with step-free access, movable tables and chairs and a very good salad bar. **Unisex wheelchair toilet (D75 ST110)** by the other toilets, down a steep 20m ramp alongside the cliff face. It's one of the more imaginatively sited facilities that you'll find!

The Ticket Office near the top of the CP has +4 steps and an awkward turn to go past the window. From there it is a 70m uphill slope to the entrance for the cable car. To get into the car, there is a very steeply ramped –4 steps, then 40m downhill. The 60cm gap can be bypassed. Carriage door width 66cm. At the bottom (level with the tunnels) there is a shallow ramp. Coming back up in the cable car, there are +2 at the bottom and +4+9+9+14 at the top. These can be bypassed by using the way you came down. The whole visit is a slight challenge, but not impossible for some.

Feeding back information

A guidebook like this is based on information collected in person when we visited. Things change, our report may be incomplete, and you may have a different experience from the one that we had. The guide itself is inevitably incomplete, and if you can add to it, we would be most grateful.

Information from users can be of considerable value, as we intend to publish some of the information here on the web, which is a medium which can readily incorporate updated data.

Please bear in mind that most of our information is factual. It covers location, parking facilities, distances (accurately assessed by pacing or measuring them), details about the surfaces and slopes involved, steps are counted and lifts measured. We also give precise details about toilets for disabled people with measurements of the door width (for an outward opening door) and of the free side transfer space. We try to describe places, so that people who have not been there before will know whether it is a hilly park, a three storey building or a group of buildings scattered around a square. Basic descriptions like this are very important for someone who has not been there.

If you would like to add to (or correct) our write-ups, this is the data we need. It would be helpful if you would say a little about who you are and the nature of your ability/disability. Please say when you visited, and whether you were alone, or with friends, family or a tour group.

Information about any problems you have faced while flying or in finding and booking adapted transport would be of interest, but please give full contact details of any organisations or companies you refer to (with a contact name if possible, address, telephone, fax number, and e-mail). Details about accessible accommodation would also be welcome.

Please send your information, surveys and comments to:
Access Project, 39 Bradley Gardens, West Ealing, London W13 8HE, UK
e-mail: gordon.couch@virgin.net

Galilee, Upper Galilee and the Golan

> This chapter covers the Galilee region which we have divided into three areas:
> - **Nazareth** and the surrounding area west and south of the Sea of Galilee, including Cana, Mount Tabor, Zippori, Megiddo, and Bet She'an;
> - **Tiberias** and the sites immediately around the Sea of Galilee; and,
> - **Zefat, Upper Galilee and the Golan**.

Fertile, hilly **Galilee** is one of the most attractive areas of Israel and, particularly to Christian visitors, one of the most evocative. As the focal point of Jesus' ministry, there are numerous pilgrimage sites, particularly around the Sea of Galilee and in Nazareth, the site of his family home and a lively, largely Arab town. The area also has a number of important Jewish sites, particularly in Tiberias, with its rabbis' tombs, and Zefat, a centre of Jewish mysticism. If you have a car it is very easy to get away from the crowds and explore the countryside, with many remains dating back to Old Testament times.

To the east and north of the Sea of Galilee, the **Golan Heights** are of strategic importance to both Israel and Syria. Taken by Israel in 1967, they remain disputed territory with the many uncleared minefields the most obvious reminder. Discussions were restarted in 1999 with a view to a possible long-term agreement between Israel and Syria to exchange of land for peace. This may affect access into the area in the future.

Galilee is a mostly rural area, and unless you are with a tour group, a car is essential, particularly if you want to see some of the less obvious sites. The towns are generally quite hilly, and a car will probably be useful there as well. However, there is a much better range of accessible accommodation in Galilee than anywhere else in the country. Karei Deshe Youth Hostel and Nof Ginosar Inn both offer cheap, comparatively accessible accommodation, and there are a number of Kibbutz Inns and hotels with accessible rooms in different surroundings. These include the Nof Ginosar Hotel and the hotel at Kibbutz Lavi.

Nazareth

Although it is one of the most important sites in Israel for Christian visitors, Nazareth remains a difficult place to visit. The streets are narrow, giving rise to serious traffic problems, the town is hilly, and parking is difficult, but not impossible if you are both cheeky and lucky. The pavements (a kind description) are a nightmare, but with a little determination, you'll get around. The main shrine, the Basilica of the Annunciation, is well worth considerable effort to visit.

Nazareth is home to some 60,000 Christian and Muslim Palestinians, and is one of the larger Palestinian communities in Israel. The new development nearby at Nazareth Illit is a Jewish city built in the late 1950s. It houses some 45,000 people in a modern development. *See* IH p613-623, LP p286-291 and RG p175-184.

When we visited, a lot of building work was taking place in various parts of Nazareth in preparation for the Millennium. A number of new hotels were being built, and roads were being resurfaced. The rebuilding was most noticeable in the **Souq** (with its entrance at the top of Casa Nova Street near the Basilica), which had recently been repaved and is now a much more practicable proposition for chair users, at the expense perhaps of some of its atmosphere. It has quite a steep slope, but one route, going to the left, is step free for quite a long way up. Further improvements will continue during the lifetime of this book. Unfortunately, some of the building work close to the Basilica had caused inter-communal tension between Christians and Muslims, with some violent incidents in early 1999. It is not something that should deter anyone from a visit and the community seems intent on rebuilding relationships and trust.

Brown and green signs and signposts have appeared everywhere. They are potentially helpful, but (as elsewhere) the lettering is too small to read if you are driving past not knowing where to go. In addition, they are traffic signs and do not necessarily show the shortest pedestrian routes. It's a bizarre but well intended mix.

Nazareth was not designed for the tourist coach, nor for hoards of visitors. It would be ruined by the construction of a dual carriageway and the massive parking facilities that 'tourism' seems to demand these days. A new traffic and parking plan is being implemented to reduce the amount of through traffic on Paul VI Street and to improve parking. In due course Paul VI will become a one-way street with a parallel route going the other way.

One way to ensure a relaxed visit is to use the nearby Religieuse de Nazareth guest house which has a small CP or to stay at the Galilee Hotel (see *Accommodation* chapter), and then visit the Basilica early in the morning before it is full of tour groups. It is a much better way to experience the town than arriving on a coach for a standard thirty minute visit. Another possibility is to get a taxi from a more remote hotel, and get the driver to drop you off up the hill by the Basilica CP. As Casa Nova Street is one way, this means approaching it from behind and above, which should not be beyond the skill of a local driver. Even if you are not staying in the guest house, the idea of going really early is sound, as you will find parking is easier as well.

Tourist Office, Casa Nova Street *Tel:* 06 657-0555 *Fax:* 06 657-3078. Parking is difficult, and it is on the slope leading up to the basilica. Casa Nova Street is one way, downwards. Entrance +2 steps. They have no information about access, but can be helpful about opening times and other things like that.

Post Office. The main office is up the hill from Mary's Well. Follow the curved road around to the left past St Gabriel's. Go straight for about 50m and then turn right up street 6077. Entrance +2 steps, then flat.

The description here of the sights on or near Paul VI Street is based on starting at the Galilee Hotel at the south-west end, and leading up to Mary's Well at the north-east end. Paul VI Street is fairly flat from the Galilee Hotel to the bottom of Casa Nova Street (about 400m) and then it slopes gently up towards Mary's Well (about 600m). The Basilica is reached up quite a steep slope on Casa Nova Street with the Souq off to the left; *see* the detailed write-up. Similarly St Gabriel's Orthodox Church above Mary's Well is up quite a steep (but shorter) slope. Near the hotel is the **Church of the Nazarene** *Tel:* 06 655-4315 but this is not normally open. Similarly we did not manage to visit **Notre Dame de l'Effroi** this time, but according to our 1987 survey, there was a small CP outside. Entrance +5 shallow steps. Access inside was flat, with +3+1 to the altar. A display dedicated to Fr Charles de Foucard was −1 from the CP.

On the pavements, you come across the occasional split level, like the one opposite the end of Casa Nova Street where there are +5−3, so you may need to take your life in your hands and use the road! Many of the small shops and restaurants have +2 or +3 steps at the front, but there are enough with just one step or even no steps for you to be able to buy both food and souvenirs.

The **Basilica of the Annunciation**, Casa Nova Street, *Tel:* 06 657-2501/655-4170 is a dominating modern structure, part way up the hill. It is wonderfully decorated inside the upper church, and around the lower outside courtyard, with various mosaics and paintings donated by churches from all over the world. It is built over the place where, traditionally, the angel Gabriel appeared to Mary. Casa Nova Street slopes up to the main entrance, which is level with the grotto. Further up the street is the entrance to a CP, which disabled visitors may be able to use, with a little judicious negotiation. You reach it by a somewhat tortuous and narrow route from behind the Basilica. The CP area allows access to the Church of St Joseph (see below), and to the upper part of the basilica, which is where the normal services are held on a Sunday. Access from the CP is via –15+2 steps which are fairly gentle. Part of the rebuilding work for the Millennium involves a ramp to bypass all these steps, and construction was under way in 1999. It will make a visit much easier. There is plenty of space for the ramp. Inside the upper part of the church the mosaics dominate the walls, and there's a hole in the centre where you can look down into the grotto.

To get to the lower church and the outside courtyard, there are either –52, or you can go back up the ramp to the CP, and then about 100m down the slope outside to the main entrance, with +3–1+1. This enables you to see the courtyard with more donated art, and to get to the grotto chapel, with a further –12 if you want to go all the way down. We are not sure whether the steps at the main entrance are going to be ramped as well as those down from the CP.

St Joseph's Church is some 50m up the slope from the Basilica CP, and is built on the traditional site of Joseph's carpentry workshop. Steepish ramps bypass +15 en route, and then there are +1 [8cm]+1 [20cm] into the church. Inside you can see most of it, but there are +6 to the pews, and –14 to a crypt chapel.

The Synagogue Church is a Greek Catholic Church in the Souq, step-free from Casa Nova Street. Jesus is thought to have attended the synagogue here. Entrance ±1 [8cm,3cm], then –7 to the synagogue, which is plain stone underground room with an altar: however, pretty well everything can be seen from the entrance without going down the stairs.

Also in the Souq are the **Maronite Church of St Anthony** and the nearby **Mensa Christi Church,** where Christ is believed to have dined with his disciples after the resurrection. Both were closed when we visited, but each has +2 steps at the entrance, and there are +6 and +28 steps respectively from the rest of the souq.

At the top end of Paul VI Street the triangle around **Mary's Well** has been resurfaced and rebuilt. The 'Well' is a new structure with –1 step to the water outlet and trough. There are some remains visible from the back. Step-free access to the triangle is from the western corner.

St Gabriel's Orthodox Church is a little way up the hill from Mary's Well. To get there, avoiding the steps, take the new road which curves around to the left through 180°. At the top you can get on to the plaza step-free. Church entrance, –1 step at the gate, –4–1–1 at the door to the nave, and then –7+1 down to see the well/spring. It's well worth a little effort, as the icons and decoration are magnificent, and it's a rather more homely size than the Basilica.

Just to the left of St Gabriel's Church is a new development with ramped access to a new disabled persons toilet. In view of the lack of any toilets in Nazareth, we hate to think what may happen to this, and it's the only one we can think of that might justify being locked. There is a plan to provide step-free access to a museum associated with the church, and then a lift up to a cafeteria/restaurant above. The whole facility looked as though it will be very good from an access viewpoint.

We are told that the Holyland Restaurant near the Basilica and behind the Casa Nova Hospice has a disabled persons toilet, but we did not have time to visit.

Cana

Famous as the place where Jesus turned water into wine at a wedding feast, there are three shrine churches, and various souvenir shops. The semicircular path leading to the Franciscan church is really too narrow to drive up, and you are advised to park on the main road – or send a scout first to check on stopping possibilities nearer the church.

Franciscan Church of the Wedding Feast was closed when we visited this time, so the description here dates from the 1988 edition. It almost certainly hasn't changed. Entrance +2+2 steps, and you can see quite a lot from here. Inside there are –12 to the old shrine, or +7 to the 1890s church above. There are some fine paintings inside, especially around the dome.

There is a souvenir shop opposite with step-free access, selling, inevitably, Cana wine.

Greek Orthodox Wedding Feast Church is about 75m away, with +1 [10cm] step at the entrance gate, then a threshold ±1 [5cm] to get in. The interior is flat.

[P][■]E1±1[&]80%

Meiron

Meiron has the tombs of several prominent Hebrews dating from the first century BCE. Driving along route 89 from Nahariya, you come first to some signs pointing to old synagogues in a village just before Meiron. These, however, are not easy to find. Just after the village of Meiron, there is a viewpoint on the left over the area where an orthodox Jewish community has been established. Further down the road, a sign to old synagogues pointing to the left indicates a track leading into the hills. The first synagogue is right by the turning with +20 steps to the site, but you can see most of it from the area by the turn-off. The second synagogue is right alongside the track on the right and easily seen. To reach the third synagogue, go up the hill and take the right fork. The synagogue is up some +150 on the left further up the hill. The whole area has a number of remains of ancient place of worship, but since the descriptions are all in Hebrew it is difficult to tell which is which.

Megiddo

The site consists of the ruins of various forts and palaces built on a hilly outcrop overlooking a vast plain. The hilltop has been strategically important for thousands of years. The trade routes between many different civilisations in Africa, Asia and Europe came across this plain. Repeatedly fought over in ancient times, Megiddo (or Armageddon) is referred to in Revelation 16:16 as the site of the last great battle, in which the forces of good will triumph over evil. A lot of visitors are expected during the Millennium period.

Entrance just off route 66, about 2km north of the junction with route 65. Large CP. Entrance to the museum has +1 [12cm] step, where there is a video. The main museum is –2 which can be bypassed either by heading for the men's toilets, or by going to the far left of the room which takes you on a circuitous step-free tour around the building. **Unisex wheelchair toilet (D90 ST85)** just before the men's.

Access to the excavations is via a 150m-long steep rough path, including the occasional step. The excavations are impressive, with an amazing view over the plain, and are spread out over an area of approximately 100 square metres. The area is rough with steps throughout. To reach the underground tunnels used to supply water in sieges, there are –200 steps: however, if you drive to the exit of the tunnels (about 600m from the main reception), then there are "only" –70 steps.

Mount Tabor

The traditional site of the Transfiguration of Jesus. Following route 7266 up Mount Tabor, there is a fork at the top: the left fork is to the Church of St Elias (closed to visitors). Take the right turn towards the Church of the

Transfiguration and Terra Sancta Convent. When the Church is open, parking is available by the gates in the taxi rank.

Entrance to the Church +2 steps, bypassed by a ramp. Inside, there is a large mosaic of the Transfiguration. The crypt is –14, with seating and impressive stained glass: this is visible from the top of the steps, however. Viewpoints by the church are +2+4+10 or +15+2–1+1–1.

60%

Shibli

Off the route 65, there is a turning to Shibli on route 7266. This is a Bedouin village with a population of over 2000 all from one extended family, called Shibli. They are increasingly encouraged to marry outside the tribe to avoid the risks of inbreeding.

The **Bedouin Heritage Centre** on the right, coming from route 65 is typically poorly signed. It is in the middle of the village after you have passed the mosque, and almost opposite the Shibli Local Council Office. There's a red arrow on a sign with Hebrew and Arabic writing, followed immediately by a pedestrian crossing. Parking opposite the entrance. It is a small site measuring about 50m by 50m, with a slope down from the road and slightly rough gravelled surfaces. Museum +4 rough steps. Our surveyor was taken around by a young girl who made the family tents and Bedouin lifestyle most interesting. When she discovered the reason for the visit, she gave back the 12 NIS he had paid for entry. It was a magic moment.

There's an old oak tree by the entrance which it is said once had the power of healing. It became a place of pilgrimage where offerings were made and the local leaders would meet to make important decisions. It seems that as the Bedouin lifestyle has changed and become less nomadic, the tree has lost its powers.

80%

Further up the road from the Heritage Centre is a **Bedouin Restaurant**. CP outside with a gravelled surface just 20m from the entrance to the tent. Eating is either from/on cushions on the floor or on tables with movable chairs. Having a Bedouin-style meal and/or some Bedouin is 'something else'. It's all flat and compact, although the surfaces are slightly rough.

80%

Grave of Nabi Shu'eib

The holiest shrine to the Druze. Nabi Shu'eib is also known to the Jews as Jethro, Moses' father-in law. About 12km from Tiberias, on the edge of the

Horns of Hittim. As you approach on route 7717, there is an enormous CP in front. Ignore this and drive straight up to the three-storey building, where a steep ramp to the left leads up to a disabled persons parking space to the rear, avoiding +30+5+29 from the CP level. The shrine is reached by a flat route around to the front, followed by ±1 [20cm, 5cm]. Shoes must be removed, and chair users may need their wheels dusted. Outside is a cloister area (+1 or –1).

Sepphoris/Zippori National Park

Signposted off route 79 between Nazareth and the intersection with route 77. From here there is about 4km to the park itself. Sepphoris was an important Roman city and was subsequently occupied well into the Middle Ages. Excavations of the twenty-five or so layers of occupation are ongoing, so it is advisable to stick to the paths.

Zippori National Park *Tel:* 06 656-8272 is spread out over some 2km, including the ancient reservoir. The main site is about 500 metres square, and is no more than about 50% accessible. There are two parking areas, one nearer the entrance, and the other up by the reservoir. The IH has a map on pp630-1.

As it is so big and presents a few access problems, we recommend the following route:

From the CP near the entrance, there is a path labelled for chair users which is steep and gravelly and leads to a café with rough paving and movable tables and chairs. There is +1 [18cm] step to a small shop and a **unisex wheelchair toilet (D78 ST75)** that should be unlocked. To get to the Roman theatre (no 3 on the leaflet handed out at the gate), ignore the chair users' path and carry on round the hill to the right, where a gentler sloping path leads to it. The theatre has a large stage, recently restored, and much of the seating remains. A very steep path then leads past the "luxurious home"(no 7) to the citadel (no 6).

The citadel houses the **visitors centre** *Tel:* 06 656-8272. Entrance, inconveniently, involves a ±1 [25cm,7cm] threshold then –1 [12cm] to a visitors centre on the GF. Thereafter there are +29 to the information centre and a further +18 to the observation centre.

The mosaics which are the park's principal attraction are in several buildings, although some of the best are in the luxurious home (no 7), and in the Nile building (no 9). There are two entrances to the luxurious home. Both involve steps, but the easiest one is marked "no entrance" and is nearest the citadel. A gallery with a view of some of these mosaics can be reached by +2+5–1. The Nile building is more than 800m away, and the best way is to go back towards the CP and then go towards the colonnaded street (no 8) via –8. There is then a good smooth ramp, then a further –2–8+1 to the rest of the mosaics in the Nile building (no 9). This is a dead end, so you'll need to get back the way you came in.

To get to the **sunken aqueduct** or "tunnel of the shafts" (no 12) drive about 1.5km along a narrow road from the first the sunken aqueduct or "tunnel of the shafts" (no 12) to the second CP. There is +1 [5cm] to a flat, slightly gravelly path from where you can see more or less everything. If you want to get down to the caves and tunnels, there is –45, a 40m passage of W60 with height 105cm and +54 at the other end. This is for the intrepid only, as to get back to your car you will need to retrace your steps!

Bet She'an

Bet She'an National Park and Ampitheatre *Tel:* 06 658-7189 or Tel Bet She'an lies alongside the rather nondescript modern town about 16km south of the Sea of Galilee. It has a history spanning almost 6000 years, and includes the best preserved Roman-Byzantine town in Israel with a fine ampitheatre. There is a good site plan in the IH p650. Follow the signs, and turn off the Rehov Shaul Hamelech past the Bank Leumi. The CP is some 250m further on and directly outside the main entrance. Note that the signs in the town are quite small and difficult to read so, if you're driving, go slowly, to give yourself enough time to read them.

The site with the amphitheatre and the remains of the town is generally accessible, although sloping gently. It is quite large, spreading over an area of some 500 by 500m. There is step-free access to at least 80% of it. Some of the paths are somewhat bumpy, but you are going over flagstones laid over 1500 years ago! The Byzantine Baths have +10 steps, and the Tel itself has +150. Apart from that the only obstacle is a fallen pillar which restricts the width of one of the paths to 42cm, but this can be bypassed by coming from another direction.

A hop-on, hop-off open-sided buggy goes around, which is particularly useful for disabled walkers. There are few benches, and little shade on the site. **Wheelchair cubicles (D80 ST200)** in the toilets near the entrance.

Kochav Hayarden National Park (Belvoir Castle). A turning off Route 90 between Bet She'an and Tiberias leads some 5km up a winding road with spectacular views over the Jordan valley. At the site there are the remains of a major Crusader castle, and the Igael Tumarkin Sculpture Park. Large CP. The paths are generally rough, gently sloping and gravelled. One leads to the castle ruins just over 100m away, via a wooden bridge over the moat. It would be quite possible to drive a car up to near the bridge when it's quiet by simply rolling one of the stone barriers aside. There's a small step off the bridge. It's about 500m to go all around inside the castle. The site is basically flat, but the surfaces are gravelly and rocky. There are +3 steps into the inner keep and a ±1 inside, but it's worth a bit of effort, as this is the best preserved bit. Snack bar and (ordinary) toilets by the CP, +1 [10cm]. We are reliably told that there is an adapted toilet there and you have to ask at the snack bar for the key.

From the CP it's about 200m past the sculptures (which are in metal and stone) via a path to a fine viewpoint over the Jezreel valley.

Tiberias

Tiberias is now the only town on the Sea of Galilee. It was founded in honour of a Roman Emperor, and was famed at the time for its hot springs. As one of the four Jewish holy cities, it was the burial site for a number of influential rabbis. It is now a centre for tourism. The town is built on a hillside, but the main area of interest to visitors is the lakeside and the shopping centre behind it, and all this is fairly flat. There is a lakeside promenade, and two of the streets leading to it have been pedestrianised. These slope gently down towards the lake, and while the steps on the Midrahov have been ramped, this has been done in a zig zag fashion, with more thought to symmetry than to those who might use the ramps. The steps are grouped in threes down a wide street with many pavement cafés, and the ramps are placed alternatively on the left and then on the right – making it quite a tortuous route for a chair user. Also, some of the café tables spill over on to the street, and sometimes block one of the ramps.

Tourist Information Office, Archaeological Park, HaBanim Street *Tel:* 06 672-5666 situated outside the Jordan River Hotel. The office is in a stone building in the middle of the park and is reached via −30 steps from the street. If you go down alongside the hotel, there is step-free access round the back. On the near side there are +3 but if you go right round the back it's flat, although there are 2m of rough cobbles. Unfortunately, no information on or understanding of access issues.

Hakishoon Street Archaeological Park (no 28 on LP map p295) just to the east of HaBanim Street, contains some Roman remains. The

Archaeological Park is quite attractive, and there's a small amphitheatre in one corner where they obviously put on performances from time to time. A chair user could see easily enough from the top, and on the right-hand side there's just +1 [5cm]. It is below street level, and there is a step-free route down from the small road leading to the Jordan River Hotel. There is smooth paving round the park with good views of the remains.

The **Post Office** is on HaYarden Street at the junction with HaBanim Street. Pavement in front is sloped, with step-free access at one end and +3 steps at the other. Flat throughout.

Midrahov (see LP p295) is the main pedestrianised street, approached from HaBanim, with a ramp from the south, but −11 steps from the north.

On the promenade at the bottom of Midrahov, there's a small **shopping centre**, mainly selling souvenirs, with +1 [15cm] step to the GF.

The **Galilee Experience** is in this centre. It is a slide show with information about the region, with entrance +15+9. Opposite is the Great Mosque, long disused. Some guidebooks suggest that it is planned to convert it into a museum, but we saw no signs that this was happening.

Boat trips around the lake go from the Lido/Decks just north of the town, and access would be/is a hassle. There's a CP, but −12 steps down to the gangplank and +8 on the boat to the upper deck (the easier option!). The regular service to and from Ein Gev has been discontinued.

The **Greek Orthodox Monastery of the Apostles** is at the southern end of the promenade. Follow the path round in front of the Tiberias Rowing Club to the uneven paving, and it's on your left. You need to ring the bell (H215) to gain admission. Entrance ±1 threshold [+20−10cm], followed by −15 steps and a small threshold into the church which has a number of attractive icons.

St Peter's Church (Terra Sancta) is a Crusader church, just to the north of Midrahov. It is next to the Galei Galil Restaurant with +3 steps and a ±1

[5cm] threshold to the garden and then +2–7 into the church. –1–1 into the back courtyard.

Rambam's (Maimonides) Tombs and those of others, are just to the north of the town centre, at the junction between Hatannim and Yohanan Ben Zakkay (*see* IH map p662). Ben Maimon was a 12thC scholar, and physician to Saladin, who sought to rationalise Jewish Law. Ben Zakkay was an eminent sage at the time of the Roman destruction of the Temple. On-street parking, with a layby about 100m up Yohanan Ben Zakkay. Entrance via steep ramps bypassing +15 steps which are grouped in threes, and then +3 to the open-air synagogue in front of the tombs with both a men's and women's section. There is an alternative entrance from the parking layby mentioned. Come some 20m downhill to a step-free entrance W70, into the women's side of the synagogue. There is unlikely to be any problem with a disabled man using this route, so long as visitors show respect for the sacred site.

Rabbi Akiva's Tomb is also in the north of the town, reached via Trumpeldor (off Yehuda ha-Nasi), up the hill and well signed. He was a 2ndC rabbi who led Jewish resistance to Roman rule, and was executed as a result. Go down Trumpeldor, and follow the road until the CP. From there a 30m long ramp with a gravel surface bypasses –6–5–5–2 steps to the open air synagogue in front of two small caves.

Rabbi Hiyya's Tomb is off Brenner Road to the north of town, and well signed.+146 steps, and 'unremarkable' reported our survey team.

South of Tiberias

The sites are listed heading south from Tiberias.

Hammat Tiberias Hot Springs Spa, *Tel:* 06 672-8500 *Fax:* 06 672-1288. About 2km south of Tiberias. A large health and leisure complex offering hot spring baths, massages and various beauty treatments, and open to people staying locally. There are two outdoor pools, one indoor pool as well as a restaurant and sun terrace. Disabled persons' parking by the main entrance. Flat to reception. To the right is the treatment centre reception where there are toilets with **wheelchair cubicles (D95 ST112)** and wheel-in showers (D95 with plastic bench inside) in both gents' and ladies'.

To the left of main reception there is a platform stairlift to bypass +5 steps to the swimming pool locker room. There is a large (D84 W115 L180) cubicle for changing. Flat access to indoor pool. There is no hoist into the pool, but staff will help. To the right of the changing rooms is a ramp to the restaurant, bypassing +4 steps. Step-free access to outdoor pools and sun terrace through the indoor pool or through doors in the main reception opposite the main entrance.

The **Tomb of Meir Ba'al Ha-nes (the Miracle Worker)** was used as a place of pilgrimage by Jews from Babylon and Persia when Jerusalem was in ruins and unapproachable. Rabbi Meir was an important 2ndC rabbi attributed with the codification of the Mishnah: the oral law. It is off route 90 just south of the hot springs spa. Two synagogues mark the site: the lower, white-domed Sephardi one, and the upper, blue-domed Ashkenazi one, both of which have small CPs in front. The Ashkenazi one is +2 steps from its CP: the Sephardi one is +6+6 from its CP, bypassed by a ramp which zig-zags up the steps to the courtyard. There is then a further 25m to +20+3, bypassed by a "ramp" to the left with 35 [2cm] steps giving access to the rear of the synagogue.

Tiberias-Hammat Hot Springs Archaeological Park contains the remains of the Roman hot springs, with a small museum, the remains of a 4thC synagogue and a well preserved mosaic pavement. Heading south from Tiberias, it is down a small turning on the right just after the Hot Springs Spa Complex. Parking in a layby outside the front. Flat entrance to small museum with rough flagstones. There is then a 200m long, slightly gravelled path, steep in parts, which runs round the site past the mosaic and the hot spring. For a good view of the mosaic follow the path round to the rear of the excavations: a closer view involves +4+1 steps to the left-hand side of the mosaic.

The Sea of Galilee beaches

Because the water level in the Sea of Galilee has dropped considerably during recent years, going swimming in the lake has become much more difficult. Where piers and stepped access were provided some years ago, the water has dropped so far, probably at least 2m, that the facilities have been left high and dry. To reach the water now, at most of the beaches, there is a shingle stretch to cross, or even some rocks. There are a few places with gravelly sand, and we found two which are at Nof Ginossar and Karei Deshe. There may well be others, as we did not visit all the beaches, but at many of the ones we did look at, getting into the water would have been quite difficult. Quite a lot of the beaches are privately owned, and some are attached to hotels.

Sites around the Sea of Galilee

Beit Yigal Allon Museum, Kibbutz Ginosar *Tel:* 06 672-1495. Subtitled the Museum and Education Centre – Man in Galilee, the museum is located behind the Nof Ginosar Hotel. From the CP, follow the road around to the left for about 150m up a slope. The museum is basically a cylindrical shape with a sloped path winding up two levels. On the main upper level near the 'Arab village' is a **unisex wheelchair toilet (D85 ST115)**.

The **Ancient Boat** is about 100m from the museum, down a slope. This is a 2000-year-old wreck, found in 1986. Currently housed in a small building with flat access, there are plans to construct a larger exhibition site – hopefully retaining accessibility.

Church of the Beatitudes *Tel:* 06 679-0978. Situated at the north end of the Sea of Galilee, near Tabgha and off route 90. The turning is just past the Galilee Restaurant (coming from the south), and signed, extraordinarily, only in Hebrew. It's a beautiful church, built on the traditional site of the sermon on the mount, with wonderful views over the Sea of Galilee. CP outside, and a tarmac path leads to the church via –1–16+1 [16cm]. There is an alternative route, which will bypass all the steps apart from +1, by using a path going down alongside the site to a pair of metal gates. These were unfortunately padlocked when we visited, and we did not manage to find someone with the key. If you want to get it unlocked, ring first.

P A ◼ E18 & 80%

The **Church of the Multiplication of the Loaves and Fishes,** Tabgha, is situated off route 87, just past the junction with route 90, and well signed. The church is built on the traditional site of the miracle of the multiplication, and has some magnificent and very old mosaics. Somewhat restricted parking immediately outside. +1 [14cm] step to the cloisters outside, and +1 [14cm] into the church. Although there are a further +2 to the altar area where the famous fish and loaves mosaic is, a chair user can see it perfectly well from the nave.

P ◼ E1+1 & 90%

Church of St Peter's Primacy, Tabgha is just along the road from the Church of the Multiplication. There is a limited CP across the road, and it's quite a dangerous place to cross, as it's on a sharp bend. We are told that the steps at the main gate can be bypassed, and there's a gentle slope down to the church. Ramped entrance. −8 steps down to the shoreline.

 80%

Capernaum is situated at the north end of the Sea of Galilee and off route 87, it is well signed. There are the remains of a Byzantine synagogue, and the traditional site of Peter's house, with a modern church built over it. The main CP is some 200m from the entrance, but it is possible to drive past the barrier, and stop right by the entrance. Just ignore the no entry sign and drive between the red posts on the right. Flat entrance. The site is generally fairly flat. The front entrance to the synagogue remains is via +3 very large [27cm] steps, and then a +1–2 threshold. There is an easier way round at the back, and the smoothest path to get there is alongside the railings to the left, going round under the trees. From the back there is simply a +1–2 threshold, and you avoid the big steps. You can see the ruins of Peter's house from ground level, but the church above has +22, and was closed when we visited.

 E6

Note that none of these sites have adapted toilets, and only Tabgha has any toilets at all. There is an excellent wheelchair toilet at the Karei Deshe YH a short distance away, found by going in at the main door, turning right and going past reception. The toilet is then immediately on your right.

Gamla is up in the hills to the east of the Sea of Galilee off route 808, about 3km north of the junction with route 869 in the Golan Heights. It is described as the "Masada of the North" but is less spectacular. The main site is a set of ruins on a camel-shaped hill which was twice besieged by the Romans in AD 67-70. Access is well nigh impossible, but there are some good viewpoints. Large CP with rough gravel surface. Three trails are marked, and one has recently been made wheelchair accessible. There is an 800m loop from the CP on compacted earth, sloping gently. It leads from the far right corner of the CP to the Birds of Prey observation point with spectacular views of the birds hovering above and the valley below. Then it goes down to a viewpoint of the City. There are −3 large steps to the railing, but the view from the top is spectacular.

A new visitors centre is being built, and it is intended that this will be fully wheelchair accessible and have wheelchair toilets to a good specification.

 30%

Korazim National Park is about 1km along the 8277, near the junction between routes 85 and 90. In the New Testament **Korazim** was one of the cities condemned by Jesus for rejecting his teachings. The excavated remains are visible today, and include those of a 4thC CE synagogue. Good

234 GALILEE, UPPER GALILEE AND THE GOLAN

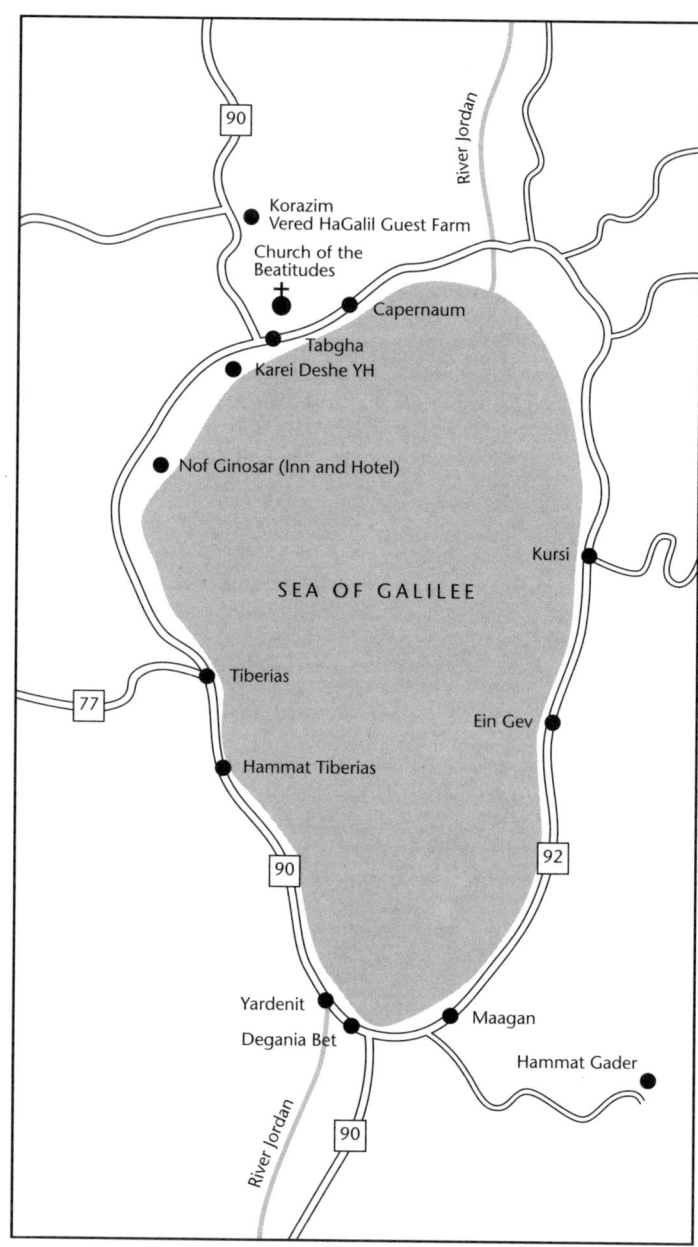

Galilee

diagram in IH p695. Large unsurfaced CP. The whole site is about 200m square. Just before the entrance to the site is the tomb of Sheik Ramadan, one of Saladin's commanders during the crusades. A chair user will have trouble seeing it, as it is behind large boulders.

There is a short, steep, paved ramp up to the shop, café, toilets and ticket office. Inside the park the path consists generally of loose stone chippings, and the ground is quite hilly. There are +9 awkward steps, which vary in depth and height, to the synagogue. A chair user would probably need two able-bodied companions to get there. In the dwellings area, the courtyard has very uneven paving, large rocks that have been smoothed, but are still a rocky ride for chair users. Through the courtyard there are +1–1–1–4, all of which can be bypassed by going down the slippery slope to get to the other side. The path to more houses and the oil press is rather steeper. The toilets near the entrance are unadapted. No on-site seating, except at the café.

Luna Gal Water Park is just by Golan Beach off route 92, and was closed for the season when we surveyed. CP outside. Entrance +7, bypassed by a ramp. Inside are water slides and the like, and possibly a wheelchair toilet (1988 guide). The gravelly/grassy beaches are accessible from the same CP, with about 70m to the waterline and some bars, restaurants and barbeque areas at the back of the beaches. No accessible toilets.

Kursi, near the eastern side of the lake on route 789 about 50m from the junction with route 92 (Samakh Junction), is the presumed site of Jesus's "miracle of the swine" and subsequently the largest Byzantine monastery in the Holy Land was built here. The partially restored remains can be seen today. CP outside. Entrance +5 steps, steeply ramped. Then –1 [12cm] after 50m. From here there is 50m to the Church over a rough cobbled Roman Road. Entrance into it is over a ±1 [5cm] threshold: inside surfaces are better and there are some surviving mosaics. A small chapel on the hill is +38 and 100m steeply uphill, with more mosaics. One bench +4 from the church level and no others. Toilets in CP: D63 cubicleD50.

5km further south, **Ein Gev** is a kibbutz- turned holiday village with a boat link across the lake to Tiberias. Driving in, you can see some of the farm activity. The tourist "train" from the CP is awkward for chair users with a step up and narrow entrances. In the main building is a souvenir shop and the Ein Gev fish restaurant, with a **unisex wheelchair toilet (D90 ST90)** in between the two. The auditorium is behind the fish restaurant: going around on the road, it is 200m away, clearly signposted. It was closed when we visited, but the entrance is +1 [3cm]. Toilets here are –3 (men) and –4 (women), non-adapted. To the beach there are –10 widely spaced steps, then a 30m long gentle ramp into the sea.

Yardenit Baptism Site is about 8km south of Tiberias by the lake and well signposted from route 90. This isn't the traditional site at which Jesus was baptised, which is in a sensitive border area. Yardenit has been developed as a somewhat commercial site where pilgrims can come to be baptised or to reaffirm their faith, in/alongside the River Jordan. CP outside. Flat entrance to foyer and reception. Shop on the left, and a little further on, there's a restaurant on the right with a **unisex wheelchair toilet (D80 ST80: lock may need opening with a coin!)** some 10m inside on the right.

Beyond the foyer are two baptism sites along the path outside to the left. The first you reach is via –24 steps to a multi-level crescent-shaped area in which groups can gather by the water. The second area involves a ramp and –12, and it has a similar arrangement. In the middle is a covered platform stairlift (W80 L100) which will apparently take a chair user and a companion down to the water's edge, and even dunk them in the water for the baptism! A drawback of the arrangement is that a chair user getting baptised will be rather separated from any friends who've come as well, as there is nowhere to gather round at the bottom of the lift, although there is a flight of stairs on either side. We understand that what happens is that a chair user can be helped to float along the few metres to one or other of the crescent shaped areas. More sites are being built, and one with a ramp to the water's edge would be a valuable alternative, even if the ramp is somewhat steep. Platform stairlifts are (in our view) a last resort provision, suitable for old buildings where there is no alternative. Currently there's a maximum of 100/150m from the CP to the baptism sites. Note that handrails are virtually non-existent, and there are no seats, other than on the steps (which would be very low for some).

Hammat Gader Park, Tiberias, POB 15171 *Tel:* 06 665-9999 *Fax:* 06 665-9998. Hammat Gader is right up against the Jordan border, on the Route 98, so the Tiberias postal address is misleading. The drive to it takes you past some fine scenery, and alongside the minefields separating the two countries. It is an extraordinary mixture, with zoo enclosures, hot and cold springs, a swimming pool, restaurants and some Roman remains. *See* the plan in IH p680. You are given a pictogram leaflet at the ticket office, and the numbers in the write-up refer to those used on this.

CP outside with five disabled persons spaces, with space for door opening and getting out – which not many such spaces have in Israel. It is quite large, measuring some 500 by 300m. It is on generally flat ground, but there's a slope down to the swimming pool. A six-seater buggy with open sides is available to take disabled visitors to and from some of the facilities.

The reptile area and aviary (5,6,7,8) are some 150m to the left of the entrance, and going around the 'circuit' involves about 600m. The path is fairly flat, but there's about 100m of rough stone paving and 150m over a wooden-slatted bridge with a slope at one end, and −1 [13cm] step. The aviary is step-free, but a chair user would need to get both doors opened to get in. The amphitheatre where birds are 'displayed' has a few spaces in the front where a chair user can sit, but get there in good time for the performance.

The swimming pools are some 250m to the right of the entrance. Changing rooms, toilets and showers (24) are situated at the top of the 40m slope down to the pools. The only **wheelchair toilet (D70 ST150)** is in this block, it is not signed outside, and is just inside the men's door. It is for use by anyone. The observation point (14) is a real military site, up a 75m long slope. The Machvat Restaurant has +12 steps which can be bypassed by using a 30m ramp. The excavations, with a Roman bath house (11) is about 150m from the entrance, and it is possible to get a good view without any steps.

Zefat/Safed

Zefat is the capital of Galilee and one of the four Jewish holy cities (the others are Jerusalem, Hebron and Tiberias). It is built on a hilltop and although the main street, Jerusalem Street, is fairly flat, most of the town is built on steep slopes with buildings and streets almost literally clinging to the sides, connected to each other by long flights of stairs.

The location provides stunning views of the area: however, access is generally, and inevitably, poor. Most of the hotels are built on the hillside with steps everywhere, and we were unable to find accommodation that we could recommend.

Jerusalem Street makes a complete circle around the hilltop, starting and ending near the bus station. It is full of shops and cafés and is very lively during warm evenings in the summer, when everyone in town seems to be there. The street is entirely one way and there has been an attempt to pedestrianise it where most of the shops are: traffic can still drive through, however, so take care! Near the top of this section is a monument in the form of a bunker covered in bullet holes outside the Regional College. It is dedicated to the forces defending the town in the 1948 war who died, when cut off from other Jewish forces. At the bottom is the Artists' Quarter which has steep cobbled streets. A chair user would need strong helpers with considerable stamina to see all the galleries. A few are down a steep ramp, but tend to have the odd step or two at the entrance.

We recommend that you park your car in the CP in Aliyah Bet Street down the first turning on the left after joining Jerusalem Street from the bus station. Most of the synagogues listed in the guidebooks are grouped around the bottom of the Artists' Quarter, but were closed when we tried to visit them.

There are good maps in LP (p314) and RG (p239).

The **Post Office** is almost opposite City Hall and has +1 [17cm] step.

The **Visitor Information Centre** is in the Wolfson Community Centre at the Junction of Aliyah Bet Street and HaPalmach Street, just below the prominent clock tower. +14 steps.

To get to the **Israel Bible Museum** there is another one-way route turning right off Jerusalem Street soon after the last shops along Hativah Yittah Road. The museum was closed when we visited, but was in an old building, so the first floor is likely to be up some steps.

There is a significant **shopping centre** reached from the lifts (D75 W120 L130) by Bank Hapoalim. It is built into the hillside with several floors underground, down to a bomb shelter at the bottom. Unfortunately, much of the space was not being used when we visited, and it seemed that this commercial development had not been particularly successful.

We did not find any wheelchair toilets, and have to say again that Zefat presents significant access challenges and problems.

Upper Galilee and the Golan

Tel Hazor *Tel:* 06 693-7290. An ancient citadel of some importance. Excavations, which are still continuing, have uncovered twenty-one cities on top of one another. The oldest dates back nearly 5000 years, whilst subsequently one of the cities was rebuilt by Solomon and is mentioned in the Bible. The site is up a steep road off route 90 and only a limited part of the excavations are open to the public; these are on the Tel itself. The ground is inevitably uneven, but **you can drive up and park very close to all the main excavations**, and with a little sense of adventure and determination you can see quite a lot. It is only by getting out of the car that you can get a real feel for the place, and for its history.

The site is divided into lettered areas as designated by the archaeologists who did the excavating. There is an upper city area, and a lower city. In the upper city, the first area you reach (Area A) includes some of the oldest remains. The viewing area is +4 steps, but you can see quite a lot from the ground. To get close to the excavations themselves there are no steps, but some very uneven surfaces.

Area L is the underground water system built for use in sieges. There is a partial view of it from the road, but for a better one you need to go down –4 steps to the viewing area. From here, there is a 50m gentle slope down to the four room house. To get to the bottom there are –46+4–82–53: you get out via +53+87+46!

Area B, also at the top, is occupied by the citadel. There are fantastic views over the area. Again there is +4 to a viewing platform, but visibility is good from the flat.

The **Hazor Museum** *Tel:* 06 693-4855 is across the highway from the excavations, in Kibbutz Ayelet HaShasha. It contains some of the items found in the excavations. There are +2 steps at the entrance and some introductory displays: however, all the main exhibits are +19.

P ◼ E2N19

Hula Valley Nature Reserve, *Tel:* 06 693-7069. A wetlands nature reserve created about forty years ago when the surrounding area was drained for agriculture. A large variety of rare birds and animals can be seen, if you're lucky. From the CP just beyond the entrance barrier there is a surfaced path to the loos, where there is a **unisex wheelchair toilet (D80 ST80)**. Key kept by cashier at the entrance barrier).
   A good path leads to the small visitors centre, which has step-free access throughout, and then around the 1.6km circular trail. There are no steps on the trail, or to viewing points, and there are only moderate slopes. There is a bridge across the lake along part of the walk which is used as a bird-watching hide: in it there are low-level viewing holes in the walls. The viewing tower is +1+39 steps. A lot of thought has clearly gone into the site's accessibility, but bear in mind that it's quite a long walk in the heat!

Dubrovin Farm, *Tel:* 06 693-7371/4495. Down the same side turning off route 90 as Hula reserve. A small farm dating from the time of the first "Aliyah", the Jewish resettlement of the Holy Land in the 1880s. CP partly gravelled. All the buildings are around the main courtyard, which is step-free. +2–1 into the house with a small, fairly uninspiring exhibition about the migration of the 1880s and some period furnishings.

From the courtyard to the kitchen there is +1–2, then +1 [17cm] to the split level in the kitchen, which can be reached by a 7cm threshold from the courtyard. There are similar thresholds to the exhibition room and stables. The restaurant is +1 [15cm] from the courtyard, with movable tables and chairs, whilst the audiovisual show is +1 [5cm] from the courtyard.

There may be farm muck or the occasional cow on the courtyard path, which can be narrow. To bypass this, you may have to go across the centre of the courtyard, which is rough and is bordered by big stones.

Ancient Katzrin Park and Museum, Golan Heights *Tel:* 06 696-2412. Just outside Katzrin (Quasrin) the new Jewish settlement in the Golan on route 9088. It has the remains of an ancient Jewish settlement, including a 3rdC synagogue. Two disabled persons' spaces in the CP. A ramp bypasses +5 steps to the ticket office. **Wheelchair cubicles (D80 ST70)** in both the men's and women's toilets.

Paths are uneven throughout. The suggested route involves +6, which can be bypassed by turning left directly after the ticket office. There is a 100-150m walk over rough ground to the excavations. All can be seen without steps. House A is entered via –4. Entrance to House B (which is fully restored) is step-free but with very uneven floors. To avoid steps, go out through the entrance. At the synagogue there are –2, and it is easiest to leave by this route. The **Museum** is about 1.5km from the Park. Turn right and then third left. CP. Ramped access, and movable seats in the cinema.

[P] [/\] [/\] [A] [&] 80%

Bet Ussishkin Museum *Tel:* 06 694-1704 is about 2km from Tel Dan, and reasonably well signposted. It is named after the director of the Jewish National Fund, and has exhibits covering the flora, fauna, topography and history of the region. The presentation of exhibits has been considerably upgraded and improved. Tarmac CP. There is a new ramped entrance bypassing +3+10 steps, though with a 2cm high grating at the start. Ticket office +1 [15cm] step, then –10 to the main displays and –10 to the basement.

Across the corridor from the ticket office is an audio-visual display and exhibition +2–14 (maximum) to the seated area. There is alternative step-free access to this area on request. **Adapted toilet (D90 ST40)** to the left of the CP, but it was locked when we surveyed, and being used as a store cupboard.

Tel Hai is just north of Kiryat Shmona. It is the Hill of Life, in remembrance of Josef Trumpeldor who established a shepherd's camp there in 1917, and three years later was killed when the settlement was attacked by Arabs. CP, and a 100m path down to the old settlements watchtower and stockade, which is now a museum. There is a collection of agricultural implements, farm house equipment and a display of different cultures living in the area through the ages. Uneven paved path. Inside there are +3–1 steps. It is about 150m all the way round the exhibition. An audio-visual can be screened for groups. The adapted toilet (down a steepish slope) was locked, and full of equipment.

Just up the hill, and 30m up a steep tarmac path is Roaring Lion Statue – the Lion of Judah inscribed with Trumpeldor's last words 'It is good to die for our country'. There are some panoramic views.

Banias Nature Reserve *Tel:* 06 695-1410. A beautiful site with a cave sanctuary dedicated in ancient times to Pan, god of the countryside, flocks and herds. Tarmac CP. Rough paving and gravel for about 30m to the shop, and 100m to the restaurant. There's a good view of the Pan grotto from near the shop. Access to get up to the grotto is quite difficult. Although it's less than 100m, it's via +30 to +50 rough steps (depending on how high you go). Additionally there are several big gaps some 30cm wide in the path, providing a water course during heavy rains. Pleasant shaded areas. The nature reserve is quite extensive, but not adapted in any way and consequently presents access problems. **Adapted cubicles (D80 ST25 men's; D80 ST0 women's)** near the restaurant which has a ramped bypass to +3.

The **Banias Waterfall** is about 1km from the nature reserve. CP with a roughish surface. Small café. 200m to the observation point with a good view over the valley. The falls are only visible from here in the winter. There are 80-100 rough steps down to the bottom of the gorge to see the falls. **Adapted toilets (D75 ST60)** up a ramp, near the café.

The **Tel Dan Nature Reserve** is a beautiful spot just past Kibbutz Dan, and off route 99. There is a CP, and although the reserve is hilly, there is a trail for about 800m which has been made reasonably wheelchair-friendly.

There are some wooden bridges over some of the rough stuff, and near the CP there are good picnic spots with tables and plenty of shade. Café with ramped access.

The drive around Mount Hermon on the route 999, and then southwards on the 98 can provide some spectacular views. You can encounter thick snow (and hence difficult driving conditions in the winter), and it is a militarily sensitive area, so you may see a considerable amount of activity. Similarly the drive up the route 989 past Nimrod Castle affords fine views on a good day.

Be'er Sheva, the Negev and Eilat

This chapter covers:
- **Be'er Sheva** and the area around.
- the **Negev** including **Mitzpa**, **Ramon** and
- **Eilat**

The Negev is not the most popular tourist area. It has an austere but interesting, wind-eroded and stone-strewn landscape. Simplistically labelled a 'desert', the Negev actually has a number of distinct climatic regions. It is generally arid, and can be very hot (up to 45°C) in the summer. In the north is Be'er Sheva, with some nearby sights. In the middle is the Mitzpe Ramon crater, surely one of the wonders of the world, and right in the south is the all-the-year-round resort of Eilat.

Be'er Sheva

Beersheba (its Biblical name) is the capital of the Negev, and is at its northern boundary. The city is fairly flat, and there are maps in RG p273 and LP p359. This consists of a grid of roads most of which are one way only, and it may take a little while to work out where you are going if you are driving. A good street plan was available from the hostel where we stayed. There are a few interesting sites, and it makes a good starting point for exploring the northern Negev. Note the adapted accommodation in the Hi-Beit Yatsiv Guest House.

A **Bedouin Market** takes place on Thursday mornings, but it is becoming increasingly organised and formalised, and hence less interesting. The site is at the junction of two main roads (Hebron and Eilat) just out of town, and when we visited was split into two sections. The more conventional market has been developed with proper sites for the stalls, paved surfaces and a nearby CP. It covers an flat area of perhaps 100 by 100m, but because of the 'modernisation', seems to have lost some of its flavour and hence some of its attraction. The other half of the market which you can get to along the road, is about 400m away. This part was on rough ground, but if you wanted to buy a sheep, a goat or even a camel, this would be the place to go. It was busier, more interesting, smellier, and we have to say, slightly less accessible because of the roughness of the ground. It felt as though it was rather nearer in atmosphere to Bedouin markets that had been held there, probably for centuries.

Abraham's Well is right next to the **Tourist Office**, near the junction between Keren Keyemet Le-Israel Road and the Hebron Road. The CP is reached by going between two petrol stations on the Hebron Road. Access to the Well is either through the Tourist Office via +7 steps, or via a front entrance with a ramp bypassing +3. Unfortunately the gate to use this route was locked, and the key was held in the Tourist Office. I wonder where we have heard that story before ?! The Well is a 12thC reconstruction, at the traditional site where Abraham once swore an oath with a Philistine.

The **Negev Museum** was closed for renovation when we visited.

Bet Yad-Lebanim is in the NE, on the Junction of Ha Nessim and Shazar. It is an imposing modern building which is a memorial centre for those from Be'er Sheva who have been killed in Israel's wars. It shares a CP with the City Hall. 50m to the entrance via +1 [5cm] with a ramp to bypass +4 steps. The memorial room is about 50 by 50m in size, there are plenty of seats, and most of the inscriptions are in Hebrew.

The **Kanyon, Ha-Negev Shopping Mall**, is on the junction between Ha Nessim and Eilat see IH p331. UGCP with disabled persons spaces and lift (D200 W200+ L200+). **Wheelchair cubicles (D70+ ST70+)** in both men's and women's toilets on the top floor near the lift.

Sights/sites around Be'er Sheva

The **Air Force Museum**, Hatzerim Air Base, is 9km west of Beersheva. Take the Derekh Joe Alon, and go past the kibbutz to the edge of the base, from which it is well signed. It has a fascinating collection of planes used (and captured) in various wars, and gives a unique insight into the Israeli struggles in the 1940s and 50s. It also has the plane used to fly the hostages freed at Entebbe in 1976 by Israeli commandos.

> Considerable efforts have been made to make the site accessible, and with the exception of the toilets, access is really good. CP outside with disabled persons' spaces, and a ramped kerb. Access is step-free almost everywhere, and surfaces are flat and paved. To see all the aircraft and exhibits would take you 600-800m. Most of the aircraft are parked outside and are easily seen. The Entebbe plane is provided with lift access, and the Stratocruiser has a platform stair lift. The Heritage Hall has +2 steps at the entrance, but there's a flat way in round to the right, giving access to all but a small section which is –3. **Adapted cubicle (D70 ST40)** in the men's part of the toilets near the entrance. It is intended as unisex, and we were

assured that "it met Israeli standards", although there was inadequate space for ST in a small cubicle. This is what gave us the idea for an extended section in the guide on Design Criteria.

The **Bedouin Heritage Centre**, Rahat *Tel:* 07 991-8263, is in the first Bedouin city in Israel, which is rapidly developing. It is some 18km north of Be'er Sheva. Follow the signs into the town, and go past the new shopping centre and market. A brown sign with a camel points right, opposite a petrol station. It is some 100m up that road. Parking outside. The site is quite small with gently sloping, slightly rough paths. It is only about 100m all the way round. It is step-free to the main tent over slightly rough ground, if you want to take Bedouin tea or coffee. +1 [10cm] step to the other tent.

[P] [&] 90%

The **Museum of Bedouin Culture** is in the **Joe Alon Centre** in the Lahav Forest some 17km north of Be'er Sheva. Take the Lahav Forest turnoff and go past the picnic area up to the top of the hill. CP outside. Steeply ramped kerb and slight slope up to the ticket office and paved courtyard. The Museum has +3 steps at the entrance, bypassed by a ramp which is itself partially blocked by an air conditioning unit so it is only W68. The lower floor is reached via −18, thus half the exhibits can be seen without steps. The Bedouin tents (for tea and coffee) are reached via about 50m of slightly rough, gently sloping ground. The toilets are down some 30m of a steepish ramp. There is a **wheelchair cubicle (D70 ST70)** in the men's, intended for use by either sex, but with no exterior indication of its existence.

Avdat National Park and Nabatean Centre *Tel:* 07 655-0954. The Nabateans were tribal nomads who made a living from the spice trade. Their trading network depended on various permanent encampments to provide services (water, food and camels) for the travelling traders. Some excellent new facilities have been built nearly 50km south of Be'er Sheva, just off route 40 with a CP, restaurant, ticket office and **wheelchair toilet (D75 ST200+)** by the CP. There is +1 [6cm] step to the ticket office, while the restaurant is step-free.

To see the extensive remains, drive up to the upper CP by the skyline camel sculpture. To get to the main walled structure, the city fortress, involves 300-400m of really rough but mainly level ground. There are nearly 20 steps of assorted sizes en route, including two where there is a step up, a small ridge and then a step down which is particularly difficult for a chair user. **An alternative route** is to take the rough track around behind the camels, starting from the CP, where there is a

Halt/Do Not Enter sign. It is possible to drive right round to the edge of the city fortress. Leave your car outside as you might do damage if you try to drive in, but the site is certainly more easily accessible from there, although surfaces are rough.

There are superb views from the top, and on the way down, there's the remains of a Roman Villa and an observation point where it's relatively easy to stop.

Ein Avdat National Park *Tel:* 07 655-5684, is a little way north of the Nabatean Centre, and some 45km south of Be'er Sheva. Various trails have been set up, but the hikes in the park are VERY rough, and are inaccessible by almost any criteria. There are two CPs, and oddly enough in the one approached from the Ben Gurion University, they've provided a **wheelchair toilet (D75 ST90)**, although it was being used as a storecupboard when we visited. The road down from the University gives spectacular views of and in the valley.

Ben Gurion's Tomb is signed from the entrance to Ein Avdat by the University. CP, then 350m along a level paved path to the tomb/s on the edge of a wonderful view over the desert valley. The other path marked 'return' is gravelled, so go back the way you came in.

Mitzpe Ramon

Mitzpe Ramon is a small desert town in the middle of the Negev some 65km south of Be'er Sheva, and founded in 1956. It is right by the Negev's greatest natural wonder, the Makhtesh Ramon crater. At the top of Nahal Gerofit Street (by the junction with Nahal Arod Street) is a viewing point. Parking about 100m up a gentle slope. It juts out over the cliffs into the crater itself. **The best viewing time is in the early evening.**

Mitzpe Ramon Visitors Centre, off Nahal Ela Street, Mitzpe Ramon *Tel:* 07 658-8620 *Fax:* 07 658-8620. Built on the edge of crater, it provides superb views from the observation platforms. **Not to be missed.** There is an audio-visual show explaining various aspects of the crater and of the wild-life around.

CP below the centre, and there's a ramped bypass to +17+6 steps to the entrance. Inside a ramp bypasses +21 to the observatory platform from which the view is fantastic. There's a further ramp to an outside observation point on the roof. **Adapted toilet (D70 ST35)** near the ticket desk. Restaurant in a separate building with a ramped approach (bypassing –6–10), step-free and with movable chairs and tables.

Bio Ramon is at the bottom of the hill leading up to the Visitors Centre. There are –60 steps, or you can go step-free down the road. The displays and environment represent the natural habitat of a range of animals and insects found in the desert. It is quite small, and a complete tour takes you only about 250m. Most of the ground is rough, although it is fairly level.

The **Desert Sculpture Park** runs along the top of the escarpment. You can find it by following signs to 'Tourism Centre' from the big roundabout on route 40. The TC does not seem to exist, but the sculptures certainly do. They are weird formations of desert stones, requiring a lot of imagination to work out what they represent. Note that the Survey of Israel map is incorrect in showing the park and the road leading to it.

Succot in the Desert *Tel:* 07 658-6280, is a place where you can go and stay, and experience something of the lifestyle of the children of Israel during their wanderings in the desert. It's about 7km from Mitzpe Ramon, and to find it you go straight through town from the big roundabout on the main road. Go round the hill with the water tower, and immediately turn right, following the signs to the camels (Alplaca Farm). Go past the turn for Desert Archery, and pick up the signs for Succot about 2km from town. The last 4km are on a rough dirt road.

As you would expect, the ground and terrain are quite rough. However, many of the slopes are not steep. There is a CP and a main communal building, step-free, and people sit at low tables or on the floor. People sleep on mattresses on the floor of an airy tent or a small hut. These vary in accessibility, but some would be possible for a chair user, preferably with one or two strong companions. The toilets cannot be remotely be described as accessible, being sited in a small steeply-sided ravine. Those with hearing impairment have shared the experience of Succot. A chair user, and possibly other disabled visitors would be strongly advised to come with a portable chemical toilet, although anyone doing this would need to accept minimal privacy. We were told that this would not be out of the spirit of the enterprise. Many people in the community go to the toilet *au naturel*, just as people would have done 3000 years ago. If you are interested, talk to those running it.

Timna Park and Solomon's Pillars, Hevel Eilot *Tel:* 07 631-6756 *Fax:* 07-635-6215. Some 25km north of Eilat off route 90, the park contains a number of extraordinary rock formations, and the oldest copper mines in the world. Although the park is extensive, there is a road which enables the visitor to see most things without going too far from the tarmac.

Among the sights are the Mushrooms, and our surveyor's comment was that parts of Star Trek might well have been shot here. There's an excellent view from a CP area of the odd rock formations resulting from erosion. The nearest mushroom is about 300m from the CP down a rough steep slope which is quite slippery because of loose shale. The valley at the bottom consists of soft sand and rock.

One of the main rock formations near the Arches and Chariots is very similar to parts of the Grand Canyon in the USA, and there is a similar impression of grandeur and timelessness. At the Arches you can see some spectacular formations, including one complete ring/arch, from the CP. The path leading to other sites from here is extremely rough and difficult with rock steps covered with sand and steep paths with shale.

Solomon's Pillars are about 100m from the CP over some slightly rough but level ground. A long winding staircase leads up to some rock drawings. At the lake there is the Oasis Restaurant with +1 [15cm] step and 20m of stony ground to cross to reach it, then +1 [5cm]. The toilets attached to the restaurant were closed, but there was a supposed adapted toilet by the lake some 150m away across rough ground. It was unlocked for us by an attendant and we found it to have D70 ST0, of limited value to a chair user!

 60%

Eilat

A modern seaside resort in the far south with a major port facility about 2km to the south. Because of the port activity, there are commonly large tankers or freighters 'parked' a little way offshore. It has a very favourable climate, and consequently a year-long season. It is about a five hour bus journey from Tel Aviv or Jerusalem, although you can also fly to one of its two airports. The one which is right in the town centre is for domestic Arkia flights, and aircraft fly down one of the main streets prior to landing. There are plenty of shops and eating places, although (as is common in Israel) few wheelchair toilets. The Youth Hostel is potentially a cheap and accessible place to stay, and the Four Seasons Eilat Hotel has a number of well adapted rooms (see *Accommodation* chapter). **The Underwater Observatory is a sight not to be missed**, and there's a wide variety of things to do including diving and camel treks. There are lots of ordinary things to do involving pubs and restaurants and swimming pools, but there's also a range of more adventurous activities, some of which are detailed below.

The waterfront has been attractively developed, with generally step-free access. There's still a lot of building and development work going on towards the east. Many of the hotels are grouped around the North Beach with the step-free promenade but in the middle over the marina entrance the bridge is fairly steep (on both sides!). The bollards at either end of the bridge have at least one gap of W70+ to allow a chair user to pass through. The most expensive hotels are either on the seafront, or grouped around the marina, which is currently being extended eastwards. A second 'row' of hotels is on Kamen Street, and then a third 'row' on Kampen Street. In their brochures the hotels all seem to list themselves with the address North Beach which conceals their exact location. There's a map in the IH (p396) showing hotel locations. A number of the slightly cheaper hotels are grouped in the older part of town, around the Red Canyon Centre and are on or near Hativat Hanegev Street.

Most of the hotels have their own swimming pool. If you do swim in the sea, or go diving, you'll find it particularly buoyant, as the salt concentration is about 7%. It also means that it is more painful if you get water in your eyes, and an even nastier taste if you swallow it. 'Normal' seawater has about 3% salt – while in the Dead Sea it's 25%.

Most of the boats operating trips to places like Coral Island, and including the glass-bottomed ones, have stepped access, but you can get quite close to the jetties where they depart, so you can assess the practicality of a trip for yourself. With the glass-bottomed boats, even if you can get on board, there are steps down to the bottom.

There are three parts to the Eilat area. These are:

- the new North Beach hotels already mentioned,
- the main older part of the town on the other side of the airport runway, and
- the coastal road going off to the south from the central roundabout (where the Tourist Office is).

The main part of town has the bus station and post office, shopping areas, restaurants and some of the less expensive hotels and hostels. It is built on a gently but steadily rising hill, and some of the older shopping areas and restaurants have stepped access. One block proudly calling itself 'Shopping Centre' has two disabled persons spaces outside, and then +7–4 steps to get in! The hospital is part way up this hill.

The coastal strip goes south to Taba on the Egyptian border, past various developments of interest to the visitor, such as Dolphin Reef, the

Underwater Observatory and the Coral Beach Nature Reserve.

The main shopping centres are in small malls, because it is easier to provide air conditioning in blocks like this. Most malls have a lift, but are not really designed with access in mind, even the new one on the sea front, although this one has step-free access from the promenade.

Taxis are widely used in Eilat, and are not expensive, as the distances are generally small.

Airports. Eilat has two airports. One is virtually in the town centre, and the other at Ovda, some 20km to the north. Internal Arkia flights come into the town centre airport. International flights would arrive at Ovda.

Wherever you arrive, getting on and off the plane will involve steps. For disabled passengers needing help, the steps will be bypassed by one of three methods. These are:

- using an aisle (ambulance-type) carrying chair;
- using a Scalomobile, which is a motorised version of the carrying chair; or
- on one of the fork lift devices used for loading food supplies on to the plane.

There is a **wheelchair toilet** at the town centre airport, said to be well adapted by a chair user who travels regularly. The one at Ovda is better described as an **adapted toilet**, and we are told that it is not very well adapted.

Israel Government Tourist Office, Arava and Yolam Intersection *Tel:* 07 637-0555 *Fax:* 07 637-0666. Sited by the big roundabout almost at the end of the airport runway, and at the meeting point between the old town area, the North Beach development and the road going south to the Coral Beach.

The step-free route to the tourist office is not at all obvious. Starting from the roundabout, you are confronted with +16 steps. The ramped route goes to the left, up the hill to Burger King. The first ramp is by the sculpture, towards the Avis office, and goes left apparently to the wrong side of the complex. At the top, you have to come all the way round the building to the right. The distance is almost 200m, rather than about 40m if you can get up the steps.

The main **Post Office** is in the Red Canyon Centre in the main town, in the back section, easily reached from the CP outside. Access is step-free.

There are wheelchair toilets at:

- **Howard Johnson's Plaza Hotel**, North Beach. Stepped access from the town side (at the end of Tarshish Street and near the end of the airport runway). Step-free via a ramp in the paving from the main CP entrance. **Wheelchair cubicles (D80 ST70)** in both ladies and gents;

- **Ranch Burger,** Spiral Centre at the Marina entrance, west side, on the main North Beach waterfront. Approached via a ramped bypass to +12 steps. **Adapted toilet (D70+ ST60)**, BUT the door opens inwards, making it of limited value. We were told that this will be changed, and the door hinged to open the other way, and then it will be a good facility. Restaurant with movable chairs;

- also in **Radisson Moriah Plaza, Holiday Inn Patio,** and **Mercure Mirage** hotels (see *Accommodation* chapter).

The coastal strip

The sites are listed going south from Eilat towards Taba.

Coral Beach Nature Reserve (Coral Reserve), Coral Beach, Eilat *Tel:* 07 637-6829. On the coast some 5km south of Eilat with a unique opportunity to snorkel along 150m of coral reef on the shoreline.

Step-free entrance, but a small lip [3cm] to the toilets and changing area. A gently sloping paved walkway about 200m long leads to a jetty, jutting out over the sea. There are –12 steps down to the sea, with the last 3 under water, which is about 6m deep. The swim along the reef is about 150m, with resting poles floating on the water every 50m, and you are going with a gentle current. At the other end there is a similar jetty (with +12) on which to get out of the water. There is 100m of paved path back to the changing rooms. Small kiosk for refreshments with fixed tables and benches – like you find in an English pub. **Wheelchair toilet (D80 ST100+)** via a small [3cm] lip.

Dolphin Reef, POB 104, Southern Beach, Eilat 88100 *e-mail:* reef@netvision.net.il *Tel:* 07 637-5935 *Fax:* 07-637-1824. About 3km south of Eilat on the coast road. CP outside with disabled persons spaces. Steepish ramp with rough irregular paving-stones bypasses –17 steps to the ticket office.

Activities include:

- watching the dolphins train;
- swimming with the dolphins (which needs to be pre-booked)
- snorkelling, and diving, both at an introductory level, and for qualified divers.

They operate to the standards of the International Association of Handicapped Divers (IAHD), but it is essential to contact them by fax or e-mail about a month in advance if you want to dive. You can complete the necessary questionnaires, and they can then organise an appropriate programme. Remember that fitting you up with a suitable wet suit may be a problem. They have a special buggy with very big soft tyres and a retaining frame, for helping chair users into the water.

The site is quite small, with some 250m from the CP to the viewing point for the dolphin training. It is on the side of a hill, so there are some roughish slopes on the way down. Surfaces include hard sand and irregular paving. No steps. If you want to see the dolphin training, get there quite early as the most accessible area tends to get more crowded than the other places that people can watch from.

There is +1 to the changing rooms, toilets and showers. The **adapted toilet (D75 ST40 with an inward opening door)** is totally inadequate, but an improved facility is being considered.

Camel Ranch, Wadi Shlomo, Eilat *Tel:* 07 637-0022 *Fax:* 07 637-8638. Turn right off the coast road going south between the port and Coral Beach. It is about 3.5km south of Eilat. The road quickly becomes a dirt track, and the site itself is on slightly sloped, rough and stony ground. Driving directly into the site avoids the +4 rough steps at the main entrance.

The ranch offers a varied programme, including camel treks, donkey chariot treks, short camel rides for children inside the compound, and "the Bedouin experience" every Wednesday. The staff are well used to having disabled customers, and if you want to join in something, give them a ring.

Aqua Sport, POB 300, Eilat 88102 *e-mail:* info@aqua-sport.com *Tel:* 07 633-4404 *Fax:* 07 633-3771. 1.5km south of Dolphin Reef. Has a sandy beach, but with a rocky edge, about 100m from the CP area. They can offer special scuba diving instruction for people with disabilities, and if you are interested, take it up with them directly. The restaurant area is shaded, but with fixed seats and tables.

Snuba, POB 2, Eilat 88100. *Tel:* 07 637-2722 *Fax:* 07 637-6767. About 7km south of Eilat, and just before Taba. A small facility for snorkelling and snuba. The people running it are friendly and practical. If you want to try something, talk to them, and they'll be helpful. Snuba is a method of diving where the air tank remains on a lightweight raft on the surface.

Maximum depth for diving is therefore restricted to 6m. It's suitable for anyone over 8 years old in good health. Obviously if you have respiratory or other problems, consult your doctor first. They need a day or two's notice of a booking.

The site is quite rough, with the main office and changing rooms some 80m off the road away from the sea. Surfaces are uneven, with some loose gravel. It is 40m from the road to the sea, down a shingle slope with rocks at the sea edge. Chair users would need to be carried into the water.

Underwater Observatory Marine Park, Coral Beach, Eilat 88000 *Tel:* 07 636-4200 *Fax:* 07 637-3193. On the coast road about 6 km south of Eilat. An amazing site where you can see the widest possible variety of extraordinary fish, turtles and coral. It is compact and flat, with less than 150m between the main attractions. Most of the site has ramps, and only the one to the top of the shark tank is steep. The underwater observatory has a lift.

Parking is just across the road. The step-free route involves going to the left from the main entrance, towards the cafeteria. By the gift shop, a ramp bypasses +3 steps, giving step-free access to the observatory, straight ahead, or to the various open pools and across to the Oceanarium, to the right. In the following descriptions, the numbers in brackets are those used on the site map.

The **Underwater Observatory** (9) is some 150m from the entrance. Step-free using the lift (D80 W100 L140) to bypass –52 with HR. Restaurant area on the surface, and two chambers under water with big windows about 1m high looking out on an extraordinary variety of sea creatures. The **Aquarium** (10) has beautifully lit tanks at 110cm height. There's a low step 30cm deep all the way round for small children to stand on. Step-free throughout. A short section to see the luminescent fish is pitch dark and only about 90cm wide. The **Yellow Submarine** is accessible only to the very fit and agile, and we didn't fit down the steep steps and the vertical ladder in the conning tower!

The **Oceanarium** (20) has fixed blocks of seats which are moved around violently during the performance. If you can transfer up +2 and through a 70cm gap, then you can get the full effect. For a chair user to sit in the front, there are –4, or anyone can stay in a step-free space at the side. The **Cafeteria/restaurant** (11) is step-free although it's slightly easier to get in through the exit. There are **wheelchair cubicles (D80 ST110)** in the gents in both toilet blocks, with the better ones by the gift shop (13).

Our top twenty sights

The following is a list of the places that we would put amongst out 'top twenty' places to visit, on the basis of a combination of interest and accessibility. At all of them, access is reasonably easy, and at most, it is good. They illustrate what a wide range of places it is possible to visit, and we hope that the list may encourage you to explore further than you might have done. Ultimately any such list is a matter of personal choice. We have left the Caves of Macpelah at Hebron out of the list because of the combination of access and security problems. There are dozens of unavoidable steps.

1. Haram al-Sharif with the Dome of the Rock and Al-Aqsa – the site of the two great Jewish temples in Jerusalem. Of unique significance to both Jews and Moslems, and with the classic Dome dominating the view of the Old City from the Mount of Olives
2. Eilat underwater observatory – a fantastic and unusual site
3. Masada – stunning geography; representing a turning point in Jewish history
4. Church of the Holy Sepulchre
5. Western Wall of the Temple, and the Western Wall Tunnels
6. Jewish Quarter of the Old City
7. the Arab Souq in the Old City
8. Church of all Nations, Gethsemane
9. Caesarea
10. Basilica of the Annunciation, Nazareth
11. Mitzpe Ramon crater and visitors centre
12. Jericho cable car and associated development
13. Neot Kedumim
14. Acre/Acco the old walled city
15. Gaza, with its refugee camps
16. Shibli Bedouin Centre
17. Church of the Nativity and Manger Square, Bethlehem (this gets a low rating because of its relative inaccessibility)
18. Qumran
19. The Supreme Court, Jerusalem
20. Tel Aviv Museum of Art

As we say, this is a highly personal and subjective list. However, if it makes you rethink your priorities so that you include one or two places you hadn't previously considered seeing, then it will have fulfilled its purpose.

Design advice

> This chapter covers:
> - **advice** relating to the design of disabled persons' toilets; of bathrooms in hotels and hostels;
> - **general guidelines about the provision of access** in buildings and other facilities.

The object of this section is to introduce many people such as hotel managers, and professionals involved in supplying tourist information, an insight into the 'access' requirements of disabled travellers. It is also for builders, specifiers and designers, and is concerned with the built environment. It is not concerned with people's more subtle needs such as diet, and having adequate time to rest between visits, nor with accessible transport.

It covers particularly the design of toilets and bathrooms, where requirements are specific, and there is a section on aspects of the design of buildings and of the provisions at open air facilities. It is very short, and can only provide an introductory overview to the topic.

In Britain the main source of authoritative information on these subjects is the **Centre for Accessible Environments (CAE),** Nutmeg House, 60 Gainsford Street, London SE1 2NY *Tel:* 020 7357-8182 *Fax:* 020 7357-8183. Among their useful publications is one called *Designing for Accessibility* which includes a range of useful sketches and descriptions relating to common design issues. There will be similar organisations in other countries. One of the best publications we have come across is called *Designing to Enable* and it is unusual in that it explains the reasons for different specifications as well as outlining and defining the requirements. It is available from The **Gateshead Access Panel**, John Haswell House, 8/9 Gladstone Terrace, Gateshead, NE8 4DY *Tel:* 0191 443-0058 *Fax:* 0191 443-1947 at a cost of about $50, and a new edition is planned during 2000.

Unfortunately, many architects, designers, construction engineers and builders do not understand the needs of disabled people. It is important that everyone involved, including the building manager, the architect and those involved in construction work actually understand WHY certain design features are there. A classic (and oft repeated) blunder when installing a disabled person's toilet is to provide a large enough cubicle, and then for someone to say "It looks stupid to put the pan in the corner. Put it in the middle of the wall..." thus blocking side transfer on both sides. Another classic is to have the toilet door opening inwards, so that a chair user cannot close it after getting into the cubicle. Yet another is to omit to put proper grab rails in bathrooms with slippery floors. Usually, just one such bar is provided on the far side of the bath, and this is totally inadequate for many users. The result is that many people cannot take a bath/shower as it is simply too difficult and dangerous for them.

In our view, understanding is much more important than ensuring that an installation meets precise specifications (whatever they are).

We are told that the Israeli Standards Institute is currently revising the 'standards' to be applied to new buildings in relation to access. This may help, but standards are not the whole of the answer. A major limitation is that they can stifle thought, and make the aim of the designer to be simply 'to meet the standard'. Another limitation is that standards are commonly only applied in new buildings, and when modifications are made to a building they do not always apply. Architects and builders need to upgrade existing facilities as well as building new ones to a high standard. When designing, the architect needs to know and understand which aspects of the specification are critically important, and which are simply desirable but which (if there were a good reason) can be slightly relaxed if meeting the full standard is impossibly expensive.

Most important, is an understanding of how EXISTING facilities and buildings can be made more 'disability friendly', with the application of a little common sense and ingenuity. Many of the requirements are quite simple, and meeting them will require minimal cost. An example of good practice is the Haganah Museum in Tel Aviv where the steps in the front have been ramped, and there is a handrail at the side. An excellent example of what can be done is at David's Citadel in Jerusalem where a really old and potentially difficult building has been made much more wheelchair and disabled person friendly – albeit, in this case, at considerable cost. An example of the simplicity of change is the planned modification at the Karei Deshe Youth Hostel. This will make it possible for a chair user (and other disabled users) to use the toilet and shower attached to the rooms by the simple expedient of widening a door and removing the internal wall between the toilet and shower area. This should cost very little.

There are some very basic considerations, illustrated in the diagrams on p26/28 as follows:

- a disabled person's preference is to have facilities like door levers, switches and controls at a height broadly between 50 and 100cm;

- the maximum width of a manual wheelchair is just over 70cm;

- disabled walkers and elderly people who may need to lean on someone's arm need wider doors and corridors for getting around comfortably;

- to enable a chair user to turn around a clear circle of 160cm is required.

While chair users are not the only people to be considered, if the facilities are suitable for them, implying step-free access, then they will be suitable for most disabled walkers, and many people with visual impairment as well.

Care needs to be taken with colour contrast where appropriate and with texture changes (a pimpled surface for example) that blind people can sense through their feet to give warning of a hazard. For those with a hearing impairment, most of the built environment will not present problems and the most important provision (in our view) is staff training and disability awareness. In some places the provision of induction loops, Sennheiser infra-red hearing systems and *Minicom/Typetalk* telephones can be an enormous help.

Outline specification for a disabled persons' toilet

There is a range of possible users to design for, and these include:

- people with arthritis who lack strength and dexterity, and require lever fittings that are light and easy to use (such as the flush handle, tap, and door handles);

- people who are paralysed in varying degrees. Many will be able to transfer from their wheelchair to the toilet themselves: others may require assistance. Good design allows sufficient space for someone to help;

- elderly and disabled people who can walk, but who may need support rails for balance;

- visually impaired people who need good colour contrast in the fittings and tiling, and good lighting.

Unisex toilet cubicles are much preferred by most disabled people as a partner or friend of the opposite sex can more easily assist if necessary. **Disabled persons' toilets SHOULD NOT be kept locked, and should be as readily available as those for everyone else**. They should also be well maintained and looked after, and one of the real access problems for disabled people is facilities that are provided, but are not usable after some months or years.

The first architectural step is to provide a large enough cubicle, and the dimensions are shown in the diagram on p26. It is possible to 'get away with' a slightly smaller space, but this will result in some inconvenience to particular users. The reason for the design is to provide space for a chair user to back the chair alongside the toilet OR to transfer from the front, depending on which is easier. There should be grab rails to assist transfer, and also one folding one to help someone with arthritis to get up and down when sitting – provided the rail is properly recessed. **The door MUST**

open outwards, unless a very large cubicle is provided.

An ideal layout is shown in the diagram on p28, which illustrates various design aspects. Note the colour contrast in the tiling, and in the grab rails, to help those with visual impairment. Wherever possible, an alarm cord should be incorporated, so that someone can call for help if they need it.

All kinds of refinements are possible, but in this outline, we have applied the 'keep it simple' principle, and our hope is to increase people's understanding, so that the design of toilets can be greatly improved in the future. Please note that these are not architects drawings, but are diagrams intended to illustrate the principles. An extract from the relevant Israeli standard is shown in the diagram on p263.

Outline specification for a hotel bedroom/bathroom designed for use by disabled persons

The range of disabilities to be catered for is the same as that listed above in the section on toilet design. In the bedroom there should be wheelchair turning space if possible. People may have requirements relating to bed height, and the hotel should keep some small blocks/risers to raise the bed if needed. This is a good example of a low cost facility which depends on an understanding of peoples' needs. Plugs and switches should be located at an easy height for a chair user to reach them, ideally between 50 and 100cm from floor level.

There should be a minimum of four adapted rooms with step-free access, two with a wheel-in shower and two with a low bath, anywhere where there are more than twenty or thirty rooms. This gives a guest the choice, and means that more than one disabled guest can stay at the same time. Even in small establishments with only a few rooms, there is no reason why one room should not have a low bath and another a wheel-in shower. Since the rooms can be used by anyone, there should be no loss of revenue in making such a provision. This is more than the standard required in Israel, and is an example of where the 'we are fulfilling the standard' approach to making provisions is inadequate.

It should be noted that the provision of a bath in an adapted room for disabled guests is often NOT the most practical. Baths are difficult to get into (and out of), and for elderly people they are slippery and dangerous, particularly when one tries to take a shower while standing in the bath. Accidents can very easily happen – and often the disabled guest is unwilling to use the facility because of the risk. Providing a 'sticky' mat for baths can help, but **a much better approach is to provide a board across the bath** (see diagram opposite). This is pinned in place by supports inside the bath, and enables someone to sit on it with their feet outside the bath and then lift both legs over the side. It would be possible to use the shower head while sitting on the board, and as the guest is sitting down the risk of slipping is minimal.

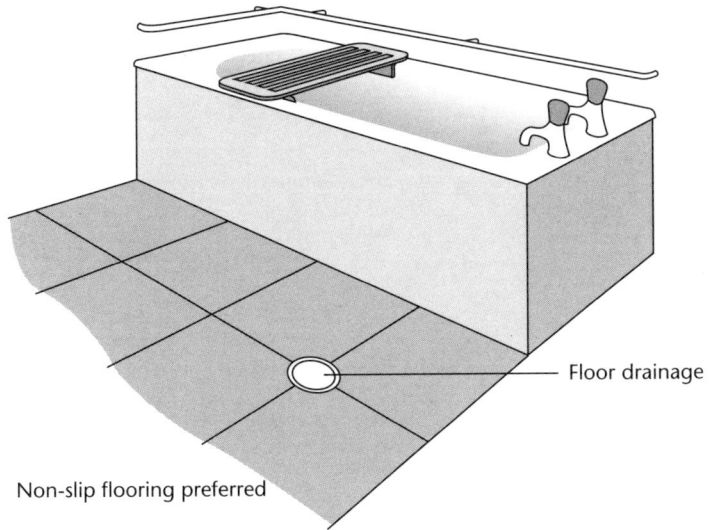

Providing a bath board

IF one design is adopted, the low cost design which meets the needs of many if not most disabled people is the provision of a wheel-in shower with grab rails and a fold-down seat, and with adequate space (see p26). A key consideration is to provide a sensible and useful facility at minimum cost, and the approach here is to outline first the provision of a basic and functional design which would meet the needs of many disabled people.

The necessary provision is of a bathroom with:

- an outward opening (or sliding) door of 75cm width;
- a washbasin with space underneath for someones' feet and knees to fit, if they are sitting in a chair;
- a toilet with side transfer space of over 75cm; and,
- a wheel-in shower with a fold-down seat, movable shower head, easy lever based controls, and some grab rails, both horizontal and vertical, for a disabled walker.

Shower heads should have a flexible hose attached, and it is worth spending a few extra dollars on good shower controls and on grab rails. Curtains can provide some segmentation in the bathroom, so that a chair user can take a shower without soaking their wheelchair. Drainage must direct the water into a corner, so that it does not flow/spill back into the bedroom.

The advantage of such a design is that provision can be made both for a wheel-in shower and for side/lateral transfer on to the toilet in quite a small space, thus minimising the cost involved. It would be possible to provide this arrangement in many existing bathrooms which currently have a bath.

A possible design for a room for disabled guests is shown in the diagram opposite. It shows the provision of both a bath and wheel-in shower. It would be possible to provide a smaller bathroom which has only a wheel-in shower with a basin and toilet.

General notes

For all kinds of buildings and facilities, the broad guidelines are that there should be nearby parking with a step-free route to the entrance. The parking spaces should allow for a chair user to get in and out, with clearly marked bands alongside to prevent other cars parking too close (see diagram). This enables a disabled person to get out easily, and transfer into a chair alongside the car.

The step-free route may require ramping the kerb (something which is often overlooked). There should be a step-free way in which is normally open and available, signed if necessary. If there are steps at the entrance which can be ramped, with a slope of no more than 1 in 12 (or even better 1 in 20), then they should be ramped.

Avoid the use of rough stones or gravel (outside) and of thick carpets (indoors). All these are difficult for chair users.

Inside the building or facility, there should be easy step-free routes to as much of it as possible. In large public places, signposting is important. This is because the effort involved for some disabled people who go the wrong way is disproportionate. Split levels should be avoided, unless ramped as well. Proper shaft lifts are greatly preferred to small open lifts or to platform stairlifts. This is because the smaller lifts are (overall) much less reliable, and may not be properly maintained.

Different considerations apply, depending on whether you are building something completely new (in which case the provisions should generally be the best possible) or whether an existing facility is being adapted and improved. There will then be certain limitations of space and practicality.

Other key aspects include:

- **both management and staff training should include all aspects of disability awareness, and such courses should generally be run by**

Bedroom design 261

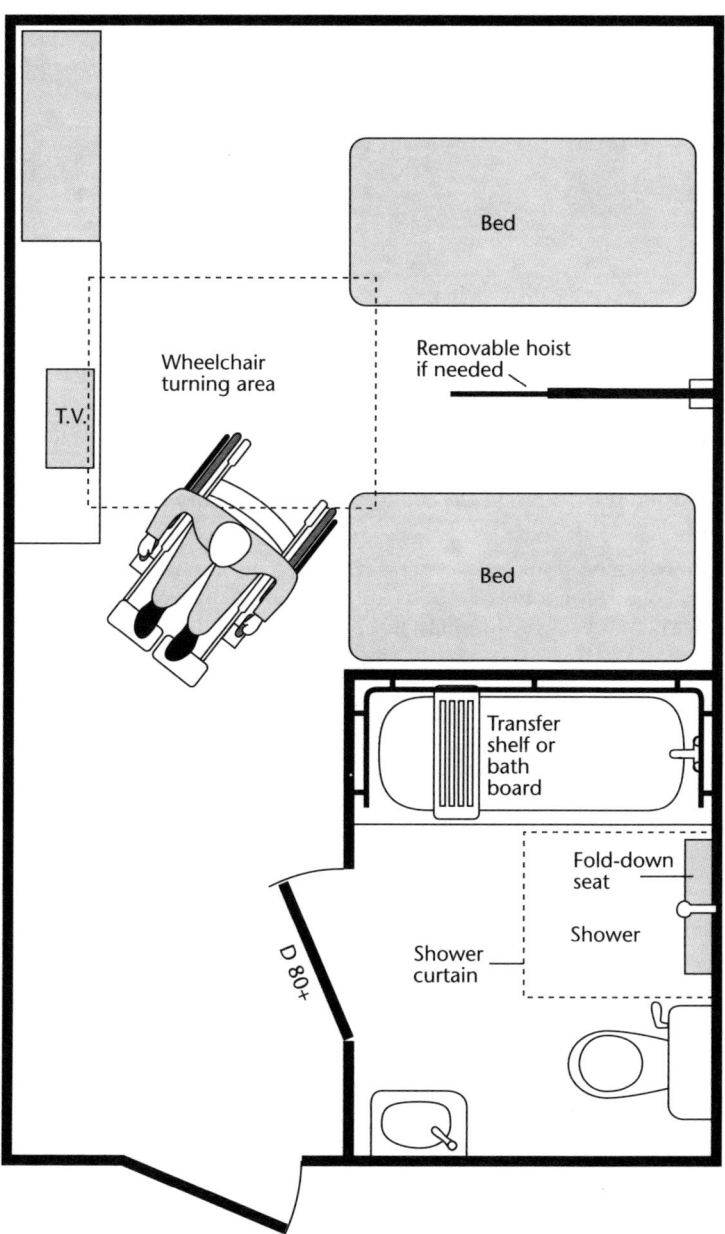

Room design for disabled guests

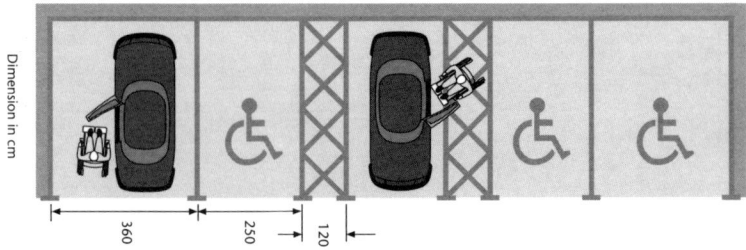

Parking facility

disabled people. On the basis of our experiences during the past year, we think that this would be a fairly revolutionary suggestion! It is, however, very important;

- **the information available at the reception desk and/or by the telephone operator as well as from the site manager, should include a brief description of the building or facility from an 'access' point of view;**

- **there is a need for good organisation/systems and management. It is no good if the toilets are normally locked; if ramped bypass routes are closed or if facilities are not properly maintained.**

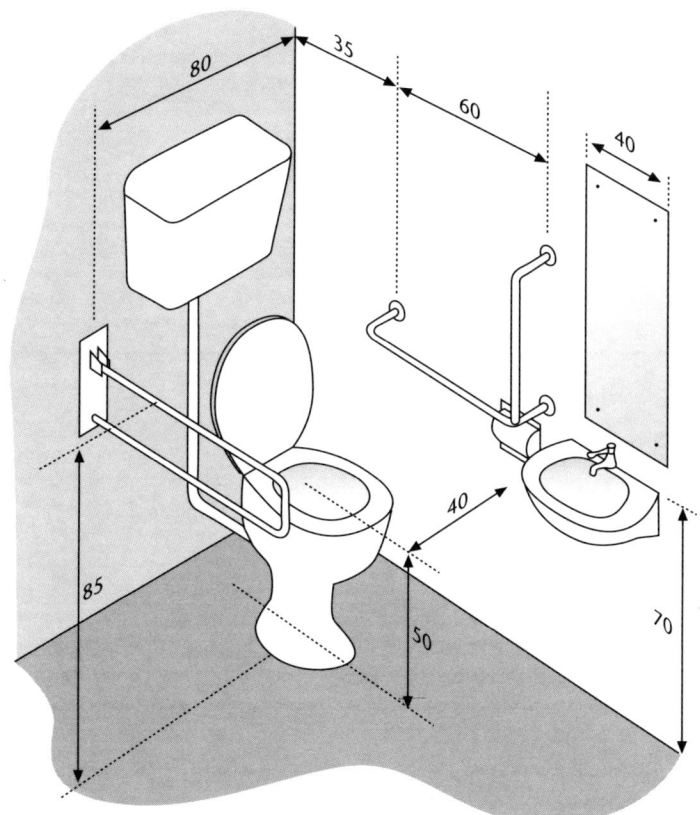

Israeli specification for a disabled person's toilet

Symbols

Parking with flat, lift or ramped access, normally attached to the building or site.

Parking avec accès plat, par rampe ou par acenseur, attaché à l'immeuble ou au site.

Parken mit ebenem Zugang. Lift oder Rampe, normalerweise angrenzend an das Gebäude oder Areal.

Parking normally possible within 200m.

En principe, parking à proximité (moins de 200m).

Parken normalerweise innerhalb von 200m möglich

Parking may well be difficult.

Parking pouvant être difficile.

Parken könnte schwierig sein.

Hilly area.

Zone fortes pentes.

Hügeliges Gebiet.

Flat area.

Surface plate.

Flaches Gebiet.

Long distances may be involved.

Longues distances probables.

Möglicherweise müssen größere Entfernungen zurückgelegt werden.

Bumpy surfaces.

Revêtement accidenté/inégal.

Unebenes Gelände.

Main entrance without steps

Entrée principale plate.

Haupteingang ohne Stufen.

There is a step-free way in. Normally open

Accès plat possible, en principe ouvert.

Es gibt einen stufenlosen Zugang. Normalerweise offen.

SYMBOLS 265

P	موقف بمدخل منبسط أو منحدر أو بمصعد متحرك قريب جداً من المبنى أو الموقع. **חניה עם גישה מישורית, באמצעות מעלית או כבש, בדרך כלל צמוד למבנה או לאתר.**
P (dashed)	وقف [صف السيارة (المركبة)] ممكن ضمن مائتي متر. **בדרך כלל ניתן לחנות בתחום של 200 מ'.**
P (triangle)	وقف السيارة صعب. **ייתכן שהחניה תהיה קשה.**
H (triangle)	منطقة كثيرة التلال **אזור הררי.**
F	منطقة منبسطة **אזור מישורי.**
D (triangle)	قطع مسافات طويلة قد تكون إضطرارية للوصول للهدف. **ייתכנו מרחקים גדולים.**
(bumps)	منطقة مطبات. **משטחים גבשושיים.**
M	المدخل الرئيسي مُنبسط. **כניסה ראשית ללא מדרגות.**
A	هناك مدخل آخر مُنبسط – عادةً مفتوح. **קיימת דרך ללא מדרגות, הפתוחה בדרך כלל.**

There is a step-free entrance on request. May require portable ramps

Accès plat disponible sur demande, peut être par rampe amovible.

Es gibt einen stufenlosen Eingang auf Anfrage. Tragbare Rampen könnten erforderlich sein.

 Steps.

Escalier/ marches.

Stufen.

E   Entrance E3 or E1+1 etc indicate the steps at the main entrance. Alternatives are indicated thus: E12/2.

Entreé E3 ou E1+1 etc indique le nombre de marches à l'entrée principale. Les alternatives disponibles sont indiquées de la façon suivante: E12/2.

Eingang E3 oder E1+1 weist auf stufen am Haupteingang hin. Alternativen werden wie folgt angezeigt: E12/2.

N   Inside. Where numbers are added, they indicate the steps up or down from the GF. If you can go either way it is indicated thus: N+25/14 (25 steps up or 14 steps down).

À l'intérieur. Lorsque suivi d'un nombre, indique le nombre de marches pour accéder au rez-de-chaussée. S'il possible de soit monter, soit descendre, cela est indiqué de la façon suivante: N+25/_14 (25 marches en monter, 14 marches en descendant.

Innen. Etwaige Zahlen beziehen sich auf Stufen, die hinauf ins Erdgeschoß bzw. hinunter vom Erdgeschoß führen. Wo beide Richtungen benutzbar sind, ist dies wie folgt angegeben: N+25/_14, d.h. 25 Stufen hinauf oder hinunter.

 Lift, larger than D70 W90 L110. Flat from foyer or equivalent.

Ascenseur dont les mesures sont au minimum: largeur porte 70cm, largeur ascenseur 90cm, profondeur ascenseur 110cm. Accès plat à partir du foyer ou équivalent.

Lift, größer als Tür 70cm Breite 90cm Länge 110cm. Flach vom Foyer o.ä.

 Lift, but it is of small size. May be a platform stairlift or open lift.

Petit ascenseur. Peut être un ascenseur d'escalier avec plate-forme ou ascenseur ouverte.

Lift, jedoch in kleiner Ausführung. Kann Treppenlift oder Hebeplattform sein.

Symbols 267

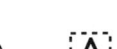
هناك مدخل آخر منبسط مع الرجاء.
قد يستخدم مصعد متحرك.

קיימת אפשרות כניסה ללא מדרגות, לפי דרישה. ייתכן שיידרשו כבשים ניידים.

،رجات

מדרגות.

E

المدخل ج ۳ أو ج ۱ + ۱ يعني عدد الدرجات عند المدخل الرئيسي.
البدائل مشار إليها بـ ۲/۱۲ على النحو التالي ج ۲/۱۲ يعني هناك ۱۲ درجة عند أحد مداخل المبنى ودرجتان عند مدخل آخر.

כניסה E3 או E1+1 וכו' מציינות את המדרגות בכניסה הראשית. החלופות מצוינות כך: E12/2.

N

في داخل المبنى وعندما يضاف للأرقام الرموز التالية أ(+) يعني درجات للأعلى بـ(-) يعني درجات للأسفل مثال ن+/۲٥- ۱٤ يعني أحد المداخل بـ ۲٥ درجة للأعلى والآخر بـ ۱٤ درجة للأسفل.

בפנים. אם צמודים לכך מספרים, הם מציינים את מספר המדרגות שיש לעלות או לרדת מקומת הקרקע. אם ניתן ללכת בשני הכיוונים, הדבר יצוין כך: 14-/25+N (לעלות 25 מדרגות או לרדת 14 מדרגות).

مصعد أكبر من عرض ۹۰ سم وطول ۱۱۰ سم منبسط المدخل.

מעלית הגדולה מ-70 (עומק), 90 (רוחב), 110 (אורך), בגישה מישורית מקומת הכניסה.

مصعد ولكن حجم صغير، قد يكون مع درجات أو مفتوح.

מעלית קטנה. ייתכן שזו מעלית שירות או מעלית פתוחה.

Flat/ramped/lift access everywhere, after any steps at the entrance.

Accès plat, par rampe ou par ascenseur dans l'ensemble du bâtiment, une fois les marches de l'entrée gravies.

Überall flacher Zugang/Rampe/Lift, nach etwaigen Stufen am Eingang.

 Flat/ramped/lift access to part of the building, after any steps at the entrance. The percentage figure (%) is the proportion which is accessible step-free.

Accès plat, par rampe ou par ascenseur dans ceraines parties du bâtiment, une fois les marches de l'entrée gravies. Le pourcentage indiqué correspond à la proportion du bâtiment accessible sans escaliers.

Teilweise flacher Zugang/Rampe/Lift, nach etwaigen Stufen am Eingang. Die Prozentzahl (%) gibt an, weicher Anteil ohne Stufen zugänglich ist.

 Narrow doors or gaps less than 70cm. Cannot be bypassed.

Portes ou espaces étroits inférieurs à 70cm ne pouvant être contournés.

Unumgehbare schmale Türen oder Zwischenräume unter 70cm.

 Toilet facility for a wheelchair user, with side transfer and door width over 70cm and flat access.

Toilettes pour utilisateurs de fauteil roulant avec porte et transfert latéral, dont la largeur est plus de 70cm, avec accès plat.

Toiletteneinrichtung für Rollstuhlfahrer mit flachem Zugang. Eingangstür und Platz an der Seite von jeweils mehr als 70cm.

 Adapted toilet/s not meeting the specification of D70+ ST70+ but with flat access.

Toilettes par utilisateurs de fauteuil roulant avec porte et transfert latéral, dont la largeur est moins de 70cm, avec accès plat.

Umgebaute Toilette(n) mit flachem Zugang. Eingangstür/Platz an der Seite betragen jedoch weniger als 70cm.

 Café/restaurant facilities accessible to a wheelchair user.

Café/ restaurant accessible aux utilisateurs de fauteuil roulant.

Café/Restaurant für Rollstuhlfahrer züganglich.

المدخل مُنبسط أو مُنحدر أو بمصعد مُتحرك في كل مكان (بعد أي درجات عند مدخل المبنى).

גישה מישורית או באמצעות מעלית או כבש לכל מקום. ממוקמת אחרי מספר כלשהו של מדרגות בכניסה.

 المدخل مُنبسط أو منحدر أو بمصعد متحرك لبعض أجزاء المبنى (بعد أي درجات عند المدخل). هنا الرقم النسبي يشير إلى درجة الإنبساط أو الإنحدار أو التعرج عند المدخل.

גישה מישורית לחלק מהמבנה או באמצעות מעלית או כבש, הממוקמת אחרי מספר כלשהו של מדרגות בכניסה. המספר באחוזים (%) מציין את החלק היחסי הנגיש, ללא מדרגות.

 باب صغير بمدخل أقل من ٧٠ سم. يتعذر اجتيازه.

דלת צרה או מרווחים של פחות מ-70 ס"מ. לא ניתן למעבר.

 حمامات خاصة للمقعدين بمدخل أكبر من ٧٠ سم ودخول منبسط.

שירותים עבור המשתמשים בכיסא גלגלים. עם אפשרות מעבר מן הצד, דלת רחבה מ-70 ס"מ וגישה מישורית.

 حمامات قد تستخدم للمقعدين مع مدخل منبسط ولكن أقل من ٧٠ سم دخول.

שירותים מותאמים שאינם עומדים בתקן +ST70 +D70 (עומק גדול מ-70 ואפשרות של יותר מ-70 למעבר מן הצד), אך יש בהם גישה מישורית.

 مطعم أو مقهى بمدخل مُنبسط.

בית קפה או מסעדה נגישים עבור משתמשים בכיסא גלגלים.

Accommodation with flat/ramped/lift access to the main facilities (reception, bedrooms and restaurant) and with adapted rooms for disabled visitors.

Logement avec accès plat ou par rampe ou par ascenseur à l'acceuil, au restaurant et aux chambres. Chambre(s) disponible(s) pour personnes handicapées.

Unterkunft, deren Haupteinrichtungen (Rezeption, Schlafzimmer und Restaurant) über Rampen, einen Lift oder einen ebenen Zugang erreichbar sind und mit Zimmern, die für Besucher mit Behinderung umgebaut sind.

 Accommodation with flat/lift access to some of the main facilities and with adapted rooms.

Logement avec accès plat ou par rampe à certaines parties communes. Chambres disponibles pour personne(s) handicapée(s).

Unterkunft, deren Haupteinrichtungen teilweise über einen Lift oder einen ebenen Zugang erreichbar sind und mit umgebauten Zimmern.

R Number of adapted rooms (where at least one has been seen).

Nombre de chambre(s) pour personnes handicapées (une chambre vue).

Anzahl der umgebauten Zimmer (wovon mindestens eins besichtigt wurde).

 Number of adapted rooms (but none has been seen).

Nombre de chambre(s) pour personnes handicapées (aucune chambre vue).

Anzahl der umgebauten Zimmer (wovon jedoch keins besichtigt wurde).

 A friend or escort is advised eg. because of the size or surface.

Personne ou ami conseillé à cause de al longeur ou de la surface de l'ensemble.

Rollstuhlfahrern wird empfohlen, einen Bekannten bzw. Begleiter mitzubringen, z.B. aufgrund der Größe oder aufgrund von Unebenheiten.

 Access is particularly difficult.

Accès particulièrement difficile.

Der Zugang ist besonders schwierig.

مكان استقامة مع مدخل منبسط إلى غرف القعدة والنيامة والمطعم. الغرف ممكن استعمالها للمقعدين.

מגורים שיש בהם גישה מישורית או באמצעות כבש או מעלית למתקנים העיקריים (קבלה, חדרי שינה ומסעדה) וחדרים מותאמים לאורחים נכים.

مكان استقامة مع مدخل منبسط أو مصعد متحرك لبعض الغرف. ممكن استعمال المكان للمقعدين.

מגורים שיש בהם גישה מישורית/במעלית לחלק מהמתקנים העיקריים וחדרים מותאמים לאורחים נכים.

عدد الغرف الممكن استخدامها للمقعدين (على الأقل غرفة واحدة كانت مزاره)

מספר החדרים המותאמים (לפחות אחד מהם נבדק).

عدد الغرف الممكن استخدامها للمقعدين (لكن لم تُرى أي الغرف)

מספר החדרים המותאמים (לא נבדקו).

يُنصح وجود رفيق مع الزائر المُقعد وذلك بسبب مساحة الموقع الكبيرة ووعورة الموقع ككُل.

מומלץ לבוא עם חבר או מלווה, למשל בגלל הגודל או המשטח.

إختراق المدخل صعب للغاية.

הגישה קשה במיוחד.

Index

Abraham's Well 244
Access-Able Travel Source 29
Acre 210
Air Force Museum 244
Akhziv 214
Akiva, Tomb of Rabbi 230
Akko 210
Al-Aqsa Mosque 118
Al-Jazzar Mosque 211
Alternative Tours 157
Alternative Tourism Group 157
Annunciation, Basilica of the 221
Aqua Sport 252
Armenian Museum, Jerusalem 125
Armenian Quarter 125
Ascension, Church/ Mosque of the 131
Atlit Immigration Camp 209
Avdat National Park 245

Bahai Shrine, Acre 213
Bahai Shrine, Haifa 203
Banias Nature Reserve 241
Beatitudes, Church of the 232
Bedouin Culture Museum 245
Bedouin Heritage Centre, Rahat 245
Bedouin Heritage Centre, Shibli 225
Bedouin Market 243
Beit Chagall 204
Beit Jala 165
Beit Sahur 164
Beit Yigal Allon Museum 232
Belvoir Castle 227
Ben Gurion Airport 62
Ben Gurion Exhibition Centre 188
Ben Gurion's Tomb 246
Bet She'an 227
Bet She'arim National Park 210
Bethany 133
Bethlehem 159
Be'er Sheva 243
Bialik House 181
Bible Lands Museum 138
Biblical Zoo 144
Botanical Gardens 140
Burnt House 123

Caesarea 196
Cana 223
Capernaum 233
Car Hire 35
Carmelite Monastery 208
Carmel Market 183
Carmel Winery 192
Chagall Windows 145
Christ Church, Jerusalem 126
Christian Information Centre 113
Christian Quarter 124
Church of All Nations 132
Church of the Ascension
 (Lutheran) 134
Church of the Holy Sepulchure 124
Church of the Nativity 163
Citadel and Subterranean
 Crusader City 211
Clandestine Immigration and Naval
 Museum 207
Coral Beach 251

David's Citadel 125
Dead Sea 147
Diaspora Museum 188
Disability Net 20
Dizengoff Square 184
Dolphin Reef 251
Dome of the Rock 116
Dominus Flevit Church 132
Dorval Airport 62
Dubrovin Farm 239

Eilat 248
Ein Avdat National Park 246
Ein Gedi 153
Ein Zukim 151
Elijah's Cave 207
Emmaus Monastery 194
En Feshka 151
Eretz Israel Museum 189
Etzel Museum 189

Franciscan Pilgrim's Office 113

Galilee 238
Gamla 233
Garden Tomb 130
Gatwick Airport 64
Gaza 173
Gaza Airport 177
Gaza City 174
Genesis Land 149
Gethsemane 132
Givat Ram 137

Habima Square 184
Habima Theatre 184
Haganah Museum 183
Haifa Zoo 205
Haifa 201
Haifa beaches 208
Hammat Gader 236
Hammat Tiberias Hot Springs Spa 230
Haram al-Sharif 116
Hass Promenade 112
Hazor 238
Heathrow Airport 63
Hebron 165
Heichal Shlomo Complex 141
Helena Rubinstein Pavilion 186
Herodion 167
Hisham's Palace 169
Hiyya, Tomb of Rabbi 230
Holy Sepulchre, Church of the 124
Hula Valley Nature Reserve 234
Hurva Square 122

IGTO offices 18
Independence Hall 183
INDIE 29
Inn of the Good Samaritan 149
Insurance 45
Irgun Museum 189
Israel Museum 137
Israel National Museum of Science 204

Jacob's Well 171
Jaffa 190
Jericho 167
Jerusalem 111
Jerusalem International Conference Centre 140

Jewish Quarter 119
John F Kennedy Airport 65
Judin Fortress 215

Katzrin 240
Keli Tours 32
Khan Yunis 177
Khirbet al-Mafjar 169
Knesset 138
Kochav Hayarden National Park 227
Korazim 233
Kursi 235

Lester B Pearson Airport 62
Lohamei Hageta'ot 212
Los Angeles Airport 66
Luna Gal 235
Lutheran Church of the Ascension 134

Magister Tours 32
Maimonides, Tomb of 230
Manchester Airport 65
Mané-Katz Museum 205
Manger Square 163
Mann Auditorium 186
Mar Saba Monastery 167
Mary's Tomb 132
Mary's Well 222
Masada 154
Mea She'arim 135
Megiddo 224
Meir Ba'al Ha-nes, Tomb of 231
Meiron 223
Metzoke Dragot 151
MILBAT 30
Milk Grotto Church 164
Mitzpe Ramon 246
Model of Ancient Jerusalem 146
Montefiore's Windmill 141
Moslem Quarter 115
Mount Gerizim 173
Mount Herzl 142
Mount of Olives 131
Mount Scopus 133
Mount Tabor 224
Mount Zion 128

Index

Nabatean Centre 245
Nabi Shu'eib, Grave of 225
Nablus 170
Nahariya 213
National Maritime Museum 207
National Parks Authority 19
Nativity, Church of the 163
Nazareth 219
Neot Kedumim 193
Netanya 194
Netanya Diamond Centre 196
Newark Airport 66

Old City of Jerusalem 114
Ovda Airport 250
O'Hare Airport 65

Package Tours 55
Pater Noster Church 131
PNA Areas 157
PNA Ministry of Tourism 175

Qumran 150

Rabin Square 187
Rachel's Tomb 160
RADAR 20
Rafah 177
Ramallah 170
Rambam, Tomb of 230
Rockefeller Museum 127
Rosh Hanikra 215
Rubin Museum 181

Safed 237
Samaria/Sebaste 172
Sepphoris 226
Shalom Tower 183
Shekem 170
Shibli 225
Shrine of the Book 137
Snuba 252
Solomon's Pools 165
Solomon's Pillars 248
Solomon's Quarries 127
St Anne's Church 118
St James's Armenian Cathedral 126
St Berferjos' Church 175
St Catherine's Church 164
St George's Cathedral 130
St George's Church, Lod 193
St Mary Magdalene Orthodox Church 132
St Peter in Galicantu Church 129
St Porphyrios' Church 175
Stansted Airport 64
Succot in the desert 247
Sultan Cable Car 168
Supreme Court 138
Sycamore Tree 168

Tabgha 232
Tel Aviv 179
Tel Aviv Museum of Art 186
Tel Hai 241
Tel Jericho 168
Temple Mount 116
Tiberias 228
Ticho House 136
Tikotin Museum of Japanese Art 206
Time Elevator 137
Timna Park 248
Tomb of the Prophets 131
Tripscope 20
Turkish Baths 171

Umbrella Organisation of Associations for Disabled People 30
Underwater Observatory 253
UNRWA 174
Ussishkin Auditorium 140

Weizmann Institute of Science 192
Western Wall 119
Western Wall Tunnels 120
Wolfson Museum 141

Yad Sarah 31
Yad Vashem Holocaust Memorial 143
Yardenit Baptism Site 236
Yehi'am National Park 215

Zefat 237
Zippori 226

Jerusalem Old City Step Map